Praise for

BEFORE
PEARL HARBOR

"World War II is arguably the most researched, documented, and published period of time in history. As a graduate of the US Air Force Air Command and Staff College, I can attest the doctrines of modern warfare are deeply rooted in this well-documented past. So in light of the overwhelming information available to us, one can easily conclude that we know all there is about World War II. Our future is firmly rooted in the knowledge of the past. There is nothing left to not know.

As author and historian Michael Lemish reveals, nothing could be further from the truth. Lemish takes us on a journey of remarkable discovery tinged with intrigue and cloaked in secrecy... Four paragraphs in Lemish had me completely hooked learning a past I never knew existed yet had been in front of me the whole time.

Lemish carefully, piece by piece, shares with his readers the results of years of superbly documented and painstaking research in a manner that erases any doubt the reader might have about the accuracy of the facts he's uncovered. Unlike many historical books that are tedious reads with a never ending litany of facts, Lemish brings heretofore unknown events to light in a style that is both engaging and compelling. In fact, and I say this quite honestly, this is the first book on history I couldn't put down.

A definitive work of impressive detail and analysis, *Before Pearl Harbor – China, FDR and the Plot to Bomb Japan* is a must read."

– Lt. Col. James Huggins,
Producer, *The Robert Hartsock Story*

© 2019 Michael Lemish. All rights reserved. No part of this book may be scanned, copied, uploaded or reproduced in any form or by any means, photographically, electronically or mechanically, without written permission from the copyright holder.

ISBN: 978-1-943492-63-3 (Hardcover)

ISBN: 978-1-943492-64-0 (Paperback)

Cover design by design**panache**
Author photo by Jill Hayward

Elm Grove Publishing | San Antonio, Texas | www.elmgrovepublishing.com
Elm Grove Publishing is a legally registered trade name of Panache Communication Arts, Inc.

BEFORE PEARL HARBOR
China, FDR and the Plot to Bomb Japan

Michael Lemish

Contents

Foreword by Ron Werneth 7

Author's Preface 9

Prologue: Pearl Harbor Hawaii 13

Part One: 1929 – 1936 China Embraces an Air Force – Or Tries To 25

Part Two: Chennault and the Soviets 75

Part Three: The End Game – And Time Runs Out 125

Afterword 217

Post Script: The Key Players 221

Index 226

Foreword by Ron Werneth

Author, *Beyond Pearl Harbor*
and *Fall of the Japanese Empire*

WORLD WAR II IS ONE OF the most significant events to be recorded in human history. It changed how future wars would be fought, from the emergence of carrier-borne naval aviation to the new, grim realities of combat - the use of atomic weapons. As a result of World War II, an estimated 70-85 million people (both military and civilian) died during the war and once the fighting ended; our world would never be the same.

Given the importance of WW II and just the amazing scope of potential topics to be written about – from military combat to technological developments in warfare; there are literally thousands of books and related publications about it. In a recent visit to my local bookstore I found WW II-focused books ranging from the D-Day invasion to a work solely about Hitler's personal automobiles. Furthermore, in many cases, much of the same material can be found rehashed albeit sometimes in a slightly different way in numerous literary works. With that said, when I was given the opportunity to read historian Michael Lemish's *Before Pearl Harbor – China, FDR and the Plot to Bomb Japan*, I was amazed. This book is something totally new being told about WW II. Have you ever read about the potential joint American and Chinese bombing attack on the Japanese mainland before Pearl Harbor? What about the birth of the modern-day Chinese Air Force and its sad condition during the early days of WW II? He also covers the unfathomable bureaucracy in the United States and Chinese governments that most certainly played a large role in the failure of potential joint military action leading up to Pearl Harbor. For example, why didn't the United States military heed the warning of the reports coming out of China about Japan's new and powerful Mitsubishi Type 0 carrier fighter? What if things were different?

In order to really understand how the United States and her allies joined together to fight Japan along her axis counterparts, Germany and Italy, you must look well before what occurred at Pearl Harbor on 7 December 1941. Nevertheless, it is safe to say that during the 1930s, the United States completely misunderstood and were dismissive of what was happening in Asia, including Japan flexing her military might. Instead, America was more concerned with what was occurring in Europe and the rise of Adolf Hitler on the continent. This misunderstanding and isolationist thinking undoubtedly led to the tragedy that played out at Pearl Harbor.

Veteran historian and author Michael Lemish has spent most of his life perfecting his trade and it shows in the quality of this book. Before Pearl Harbor is gift for anyone interested in learning more about the Pacific War. He chose to write about an important but often overlooked time period just prior to the official outbreak of war between the United States and Japan. What if a successful joint Sino-American aerial bombing mission of Japan had occurred prior to Pearl Harbor? Everything that followed this mission would have been different.

Lest We Forget,
Ron Werneth

Author's Preface

LIKE MOST PEOPLE I have many interests as life progresses and the years move on. Besides family, perhaps dogs and aviation interested me the most and I like writing about both these subjects. I can remember the day when I was at my local library reading a book about the Vietnam War. I came across a photograph of a Marine dog handler and a German Shepherd. The book referred to them as "police dogs." I did not know at this time that the dogs were used by the military outside of sentry dogs - this was 1995. It intrigued me and I went looking for further information.

I started searching for more books I could read about the subject and couldn't find any. The latest book I could track down about military working dogs was *Dogs for Defense* published in 1955. Wow! Now here is a story that has not been beaten to death over the years. With a lot of effort and travelling across our great country, I wrote two books, *War Dogs – A History of Loyalty and Heroism* and *Forever Forward – K-9 Operations in Vietnam* and learned a lot about writing and research in the process. I not only learned a lot about these amazing dogs and their handlers but also how to research material that you need to build a book around a specific topic. The information was scattered across the country and it was not one-stop shopping to cultivate material. At the time most research was conducted in-person, or via telephone and the typewritten letter that was placed in an envelope and a stamp attached. Times have certainly changed since I began this endeavor, in particular with the internet, but one still needs to pound a lot of shoe leather to find every repository of information.

As an "aviator" I am not a well-to-do like the late John Kennedy Jr. or others with deep pockets. I worked as an avionics radio repair guy and I lived at home as I took flying lessons. My first airplane was a 1946 Piper J-5C Cub that I purchased for a whopping $3,000 – big money for me in 1973 and my dad had to cosign the note. Besides the love of flying I also believed this would lead to more dates with the opposite sex – and it did so to a certain degree. Things did not always go as planned as my date would show up at the airport and I would ask her to get situated in the rear seat of a 30 year-old fabric airplane and ask her to hold the heel brakes while I hand-propped the plane to get it started. Things do not always work out the way you expect them to when you are young.

For several years I wrote aviation stories for an American east-coast tabloid publication called The *Atlantic Flyer*, submitting over 100 pieces for them and a few articles for several national magazines. After writing two books about war dogs I wanted to pen one with an aviation slant. I pondered this for several months and then years on what would be an interesting subject that hasn't been worked over and where I might provide a fresh perspective. I believed the world doesn't need another book about the fabulous single-engine fighter, the North American P-51 Mustang nor another volume relating to the "untold story" about the Flying Tigers. There had to be another narrative out there that needed to be nurtured and developed that people would be interested in reading and learning about.

Then I remember a story I did for the *Atlantic Flyer* after watching an episode of ABC News 20/20 in 1991. Correspondent Stone Phillips interviewed an assistant for President Franklin D. Roosevelt named Lauchlin Currie, who resided in the South American country of Columbia at the time. Currie related an incredible story about a plan hatched before the Japanese attack on Pearl Harbor where the United States intended to bomb Japan. I then realized this is a story worth retelling.

The clandestine bombing is mentioned briefly in several paragraphs in various books about the Flying Tigers over the years. Author Alan Armstrong laid out this plan in his 2006 book, *Preemptive Strike: The Secret Plan That Would Have Prevented the Attack on Pearl Harbor.* But I thought there was still a lot missing information and a lot of voids that needed to be filled, especially about those involved. I decided to dig deeper.

I wanted to find out more about the characters involved and what their motivations were ahead of time before they hatched a plot that danced the fine line of what was legal and the activities that were essentially deemed criminal. I also learned the people caught up in this enterprise did after the war answered many questions why they participated in such a nefarious operation. I have learned from experience that certain events in history are developed over a period of years and decades. It is for this reason I stepped back years before the Pearl Harbor attack to understand the relationship between the United States and China regarding both their military and aviation interests. Chains of history are forged over time and do not develop overnight.

It was also fascinating to explore the folks embedded around this operation of questionable legality. Until I began research for this book, I did not realize how many potential communist agents or those with a soft spot for the Soviet regime operated within the Roosevelt administration. Nor did I know that author Earnest Hemingway spied for the United States and may have also been a spy for the Soviet Union (code name Argo) as well. Unfortunately, as a writer, I can only rely on written documents since all the participants involved have shed their mortal coils. I just wish I could eavesdrop at the locations when so many of these conversations took place that have never been documented on paper. History would have certainly been recorded differently. Alas, the best one can do is to work with the material that has been presented to me and what can be retrieved. I hope this version of the events meets your expectations.

ML

Michael Lemish

Prologue:
Pearl Harbor, Hawaii

PEARL HARBOR LAY QUIET and serene as the sun began to rise at 6:39AM (local time) on another beautiful Sunday morning. Ships were stacked up at berth or in dry dock around Ford Island and the few sailors on duty aboard them were relaxed and not vigilant at their posts. There was little reason to be attentive – the United States was not at war. Most men were fast asleep in their bunks aboard ship or perhaps passed out in some gutter in Honolulu after a night of drinking and whoring. Others may have started cutting into their bacon and eggs as families prepared for church. Just a typical Sunday morning in a Hawaiian paradise. Then the planes came.

As the early morning sun rose in the sky, 152 planes appeared from nowhere and began bombing and strafing American naval vessels at will and with no opposition. Mayhem ensued as sailors scrambled to their battle stations. But it was too late. Ships were either sunk or severely damaged from the aerial onslaught. Once they expended their payload of machine gun ammunition and bombs the attacking planes abruptly withdrew and returned to the safety of their two carriers poised many miles out to sea.

On the bridge of the lead attack aircraft carrier the commander beamed as his aerial fists of fury returned from their assault on the United States Pacific naval military port. Success! But this was not Admiral Isoroku Yamamoto of the Japanese Imperial Navy smiling. The date was February 2, 1932 and it would be none other than Admiral Harry Ervin Yarnell aboard the United States Navy aircraft carrier USS *Saratoga* (CV-3).

Admiral Yarnell entered the U.S. Naval Academy in 1893 and served during the Battle of Santiago de Cuba in 1898, during the Spanish-American War, and the Chinese Boxer Rebellion in 1900. Yarnell faced a court-martial trial in 1907 for the grounding of the battleship USS *Connecticut* (BB-18) near Culebra, Puerto Rico. Eventually acquitted of the

USS *Saratoga* (CV-3) off San Francisco, California, circa 1930. (U.S. Navy)

Admiral Harold Yarnell, circa 1935, would continue to have a brilliant career, but Navy brass insisted he "cheated" when he launched his surprise attack against Pearl Harbor during 1932 maneuvers. (U.S. Navy) charge, he managed to surge forward and advance in his naval career. In 1928, as Chief of the Bureau of Steam Engineering for the development of fleet submarines, he pushed for larger vessels stating "...our prospective opponent [Japan] has always started operations by attacking before a declaration of war." Years before their rise to power, Yarnell could foresee the influence of Japanese military operations in the Pacific.

This "surprise" attack orchestrated by Admiral Yarnell was part of the annual combined Navy Pacific war games. At this time United States Naval command was maintained at San Diego, California. What would usually happen during these annual exercises is that a large contingent of ships would depart San Diego and engage the battleships (then considered the backbone of the Navy) and their support ships that were either based at Pearl Harbor or cruising the open seas around Hawaii.

But Yarnell would turn everything upside down this time around. First up was his decision to attack on a Sunday morning. He knew that it was a time that the military backed off from its usual routine and relaxed like most civilians. Secondly, with so many ships at his disposal, Yarnell could have easily have gathered many more vessels than what were present at Pearl. Yet he decided on a different strategy – no naval engagement at sea this time but let the carrier aircraft do the heavy work. Yarnell, although an old-school naval officer he was a man ahead of his time and believed that future offensive at sea laid with carrier-based aircraft. At this period in history most top commanders within the United States Navy considered airplanes (along with submarines) a sideshow to the true warrior in naval battles – the battleship. Inside the United States Navy hierarchy, the premise that coursed like blood through an artery pumped from the heart to the brain was the false belief that bigger was always better.

Yarnell's plan was not only ingenious, but devious. He had departed San Diego with just two carriers, the *Saratoga* and *Lexington* (CV-2) along with three escort destroyers. He ordered that all ships maintain radio silence and that the fleet stay off the well-travelled merchant shipping lanes to prevent any civilian radio traffic. The cover of a Pacific winter storm also enhanced his stealthy approach towards the Hawaiian Islands prior to the assault.

An after-action assessment described the attack, known as "Fleet Problem 13," determined that every ship at Pearl was either sunk or severely damaged and that every land-based aircraft on Oahu could be considered destroyed. Yarnell's fleet was not even located until 24 hours later and the military exercise umpires declared the attack a total success. Incredulously in their follow up written report the umpires stated, "It is

Aircraft on the flight deck of the USS *Saratoga*, preparing for launching, circa 1929-30. Planes in the foreground are Boeing F3B-1 fighters. In the background are fifteen Martin T4M-1 torpedo planes of Torpedo Squadron Two (VT-2B). (Naval Historical Foundation)

doubtful if air attacks can be launched against Oahu in the face of strong defensive aviation without subjecting the attacking carriers to the danger of material damage and consequent great losses in the attack air force." Fortunately, this attack only involved flour bombs, flares, and blank ammunition. It would not be the same nine years later. [1]

On the surface this war game exercise illuminated both the weaknesses and strengths of the United States military, but few ranking commanders saw the light. And just as quickly as the results were tallied they were dismissed by the elder battleship Admirals that countered that if this was indeed an actual attack the enemy force would be destroyed. Even as a casual observer with no military experience knows that this could only be viewed as nonsense and a protectionist measure for the United States Admiral's fiefdoms. Yet it shaped how the United States would conduct itself in the preceding nine years leading up to the surprise Japanese attack on Pearl Harbor. It would also display how the United States viewed the potential Japanese aggression in the Pacific compared with that of Germany in Europe. [2]

The *New York Times* reported on the exercise and United States intelligence also knew that Japanese writers took note of the operation publicly known as Fleet Problem 13. Although the attack scenario was dismissed by the Navy elite, the Japanese military paid attention to Yarnell's success and sent a detailed account of it to Tokyo. Just four years later in 1936 the Japanese Navy War College, located at Kamiōsaki (a district of Shinagawa, Tokyo) studied the attack and formulated the following judgment: "In case the enemy's main fleet is berthed at Pearl Harbor, the idea should be to open hostilities by surprise attack from the air."

President Roosevelt, as the former Secretary of the Navy, loved this branch of the military and he believed what his Admirals told him. Yarnell's surprise attack and success were dismissed for ambiguous reasons. Roosevelt, with all the information provided to him still ordered the building of twelve more battleships and just four aircraft carriers. Only one of those carriers, the USS *Enterprise* (CV-6) would be assigned to the Pacific Fleet. This appears to reinforce the assertion that the Roosevelt administration did not take Japan's military aspirations seriously. [2]

Washington, D.C.

IT WAS NOT YOUR typical Monday on December 8, 1941 at our nation's capital even as the sun rose in a clear blue sky. A slight breeze passed through the trees now bereft of leaves. That would soon change with a passing front leaving a chill in the air and gray skies. The weather complemented the nation's mood at this time. At 12:30PM President Franklin Delano Roosevelt was scheduled to address a joint session of Congress. Across the United States, families gathered around their radios to hear what their President had to say. More than 80 percent of the American people would hear the President's speech live on radio. It would be a galvanizing moment for the citizens of the United States.

The current situation for most Americans during this time remained bleak as Europe was engulfed in war. The U.S. unemployment rate came in at ten percent, although much lower than the twenty-five percent the country suffered in 1933 during the height of the Depression. Yet the country was still reeling from the long-drawn-out economic downturn. Meanwhile the drums of war continued to beat around the globe. Roosevelt stood at the lectern to address the Joint Session of Congress, his strong arms helping to support his frame along with the aid of iron straps that kept his withered legs from collapsing. His haggard face made him look much older than his 59 years, but his voice remained strong and firm as he stated:

> *"Mr. Vice President, and Mr. Speaker, and Members of the Senate and House of Representatives:*
>
> *Yesterday, December 7, 1941—a date which will live in infamy—the United States of America was suddenly and deliberately attacked by naval and air forces of the Empire of Japan.*
>
> *The United States was at peace with that Nation and, at the solicitation of Japan, was still in conversation with its Government and its Emperor looking toward the maintenance of peace in the Pacific. Indeed, one hour after Japanese air squadrons had commenced bombing in the American Island of Oahu, the Japanese Ambassador to the United States and his colleague delivered to our Secretary of State a formal reply to a recent American message. And while this reply stated that it seemed useless to continue the existing diplomatic negotiations, it contained no threat or hint of war or of armed attack.*
>
> *It will be recorded that the distance of Hawaii from Japan makes it obvious that the attack was deliberately planned many days or even weeks ago. During the intervening time the Japanese Government has deliberately sought to deceive the United States by false statements and expressions of hope for continued peace.*

The attack yesterday on the Hawaiian Islands has caused severe damage to American naval and military forces. I regret to tell you that very many American lives have been lost. In addition, American ships have been reported torpedoed on the high seas between San Francisco and Honolulu.
Yesterday the Japanese Government also launched an attack against Malaya.

Last night Japanese forces attacked Hong Kong.
Last night Japanese forces attacked Guam.
Last night Japanese forces attacked the Philippine Islands.
Last night the Japanese attacked Wake Island.
And this morning the Japanese attacked Midway Island.

Japan has, therefore, undertaken a surprise offensive extending throughout the Pacific area. The facts of yesterday and today speak for themselves. The people of the United States have already formed their opinions and well understand the implications to the very life and safety of our Nation.

As Commander in Chief of the Army and Navy I have directed that all measures be taken for our defense.

But always will our whole Nation remember the character of the onslaught against us.

No matter how long it may take us to overcome this premeditated invasion, the American people in their righteous might will win through to absolute victory. I believe that I interpret the will of the Congress and of the people when I assert that we will not only defend ourselves to the uttermost but will make it very certain that this form of treachery shall never again endanger us.

Hostilities exist. There is no blinking at the fact that our people, our territory, and our interests are in grave danger.

With confidence in our armed forces—with the unbounding determination of our people—we will gain the inevitable triumph- so help us God.

I ask that the Congress declare that since the unprovoked and dastardly attack by Japan on Sunday, December 7, 1941, a state of war has existed between the United States and the Japanese Empire."

The speech was short, lasting about seven minutes. This was against the advice of his close associates including Cordell Hull, the Secretary of State, who argued for an extensive explanation for this declaration of war against Japan. Many Americans at this time were non-interventionists and opposed any conflict that took place beyond our shores. Yet Roosevelt believed the shorter the better – it would be more dramatic that way. And he was right. (3)

Just thirty-three minutes later Congress declared war on Japan. The Senate vote was unanimous, 82-0. Congress voted 388-1 in favor of war. The lone dissenting vote in the House was Montana Republican Jeanette Rankin, a pacifist and suffragist and the first woman elected to Congress. Booed and hissed by her colleagues and afraid of being assaulted, she took refuge in a phone booth after the vote until she was rescued and escorted away by the Capitol Police. Two days later Congress voted to declare war against Germany and Rankin abstained. Above all it provided credence to her convictions although she would never run for office again.

Everything that President Roosevelt had said in his speech was true. It was what he didn't say in his short discourse is what this book is all about. The United States was already in a de facto state of war with Japan and part of this planning involved the surreptitious bombing of mainland Japan.

President Roosevelt signs the declaration of war against Japan just four hours after delivering his famous "Infamy" speech to both houses of Congress. (LOC)

The characters in this opus would play out well in a Hollywood film of international intrigue. They included alleged Soviet spies, retired military men, conspiring entrepreneurs, corrupt Chinese officials, war merchant profiteers and those with an unknown motive. A few of these individuals would later partake of efforts to overthrow governments in Central America and even support CIA operations during the Vietnam War. Ultimately President Roosevelt endorsed the concept of covert guerilla air operations and would push the switch illuminating the green light to move forward on this action.

Ironically, the only thing that prevented United States manufactured bombers from being adorned with Chinese markings and flown by American pilots intent on pounding Japan, would be the glacial pace that the wheels of government turned and the speed of the secret Japanese attack on Pearl Harbor. It just so happened that Japan landed the first punch - and what a hell of a devastating blow it was. In the space of less than two hours, the Japanese warplanes flew unmolested over Pearl Harbor, killing more than 2,400 Americans and wounding over 1,000. Twenty naval vessels were either sunk or damaged along with the destruction of three

A Japanese pilot's view of the attack on Pearl Harbor during the second wave. (Hirata Matsumura Collection via Ron Werneth)

hundred aircraft.

Like a boxer taking a hard upper cut followed by a gut punch, the United States staggered a bit and stumbled back a few steps but never dropped to her knees. The other attacks elsewhere in the Pacific by the Japanese were hard body blows and caused serious damage, but over a period of months and years America would hit back hard, viciously delivering the knockout blow at Hiroshima and Nagasaki to end the war.

The United States never intended to attack Japan directly. The bombing of mainland Japan was simply an extension of the on-going Sino-Japanese War as China would provide the bombing force and the United States the material and men to accomplish such a mission. The intent being to blunt Japanese expansion in the Pacific and it would be the same lend-lease arrangement that the United States had with the British in dampening the onslaught from Adolf Hitler and Germany. The wild card in this secret endeavor was that most of these "Chinese" aircraft were to be flown by American volunteers.

Unfortunately, many Americans had little understanding of what was happening in the Far East. There was also the racial component to be considered. Many citizens, immigrants themselves, could relate to what Great Britain and Europe were experiencing as German troops gobbled up huge expanses of real estate. The same did not hold true for those Asians threatened by Japan.

And more significantly as a democratic and capitalist society, it is difficult to make military decisions while obstinately declaring neutrality and this led to a labyrinth of bureaucratic squabbling and hand wringing. Throw in back room deals, inter-service rivalry, profiteers, and the United States moved ever so slowly to support a China that was in dire straits. The Japanese had no such impediment for their military goals.

From conception to "mission accomplished" the air attack on Pearl Harbor took Japan less than ten months. The United States could not even deliver a single bomber for China to attack Japan in the 18 months preceding the Pearl Harbor attack. One wonders what course of history might have taken had the Chinese been provided with the aircraft and materials they requested – and indeed if Tokyo was bombed in 1941 before Pearl Harbor.

These actions, highlighted by the Pacific naval war games of 1932, and subsequent naval expansion plans would also set the tone for the military support that the United States was willing to provide to China in the upcoming years with their war against Japan. This detritus, lost in the records of history, would prove to be a misplaced opportunity for the United

States. It also provides a baseline premise of why it was so difficult to get fighter and bomber planes to China and ultimately to possibly prevent the amazing attack that the Japanese wreaked on Pearl Harbor.

Another factor that prejudiced our global military doctrine is that the citizenry of the United States remained isolationist and solidly anti-interventionist. Americans for the most part believed that the Atlantic and Pacific oceans would insulate the United States from any potential foreign attack. This was based on the warfare technology available at the time. Surprisingly, the interventionist position would gain momentum and strengthen in the years leading up to World War II. The perception of American isolationism began to change as Germany launched attacks in Europe that included our old allies France and Great Britain. Yet Americans, overall, still considered the Japanese an inferior race and not an immediate threat. Our indifference to Japan and what they could accomplish militarily deeply influenced not only how our country would defend Pearl Harbor but also how America would support the establishment of a Chinese air force and their potential to strike the Japanese homeland.

The historical trail to be followed is both a chain and a river. Solid like a chain in the sense that each link is forged by the people and events at a particular time and something that eventually terminates with a solid fitting. Yet it is also like a river, with still waters and rapids, and separating tributaries that may reconnect into a single path to empty into common water. And that is the challenge of recounting history, to merge both the chain and river of history.

For the most part, historians record the activities of the participants of the time they are writing about and fail to mention what they achieved earlier or later in life. If they do, it is often a footnote in the back pages of their book in a section that is seldom read. For those of us who look at the Americans who wished to bomb Japan before Pearl Harbor it is wise to review their activities as a whole. When you do that you can see where their roots were developed and nourished. It is a perspective seldom explored in history books and one that should be looked at, especially if these activities are possibly illegal or unethical. The secret attempt to bomb Japan will be explored completely and will balance those with a high ethical standard and virtues and others who simply play the game and strive to win at any cost.

---

1. *Yarnell's surprise attack was repeated in 1938 by Admiral Ernest King with the aircraft carrier Saratoga once again leading the way. The attack yielded the same devastating results achieved in 1932. And like before no plan was developed to protect Pearl Harbor against a covert aerial attack.*

2. After World War I the United States developed war plans for various scenarios, including a two-front war. Based on colors assigned to different countries potentially involved these were called the Rainbow War Plans. For the most part it was an "Atlantic first" policy and this held true in World War II.

3. After Roosevelt delivered his famous "Infamy speech" he returned to the Whitehouse and asked his son James, acting as an aide, "Where is the speech?" His son replied, I don't know." The missing speech would not turn up until 1984 during a routine examination of the Senate Papers of the United States at the National Archives.

Part One: 1929 – 1936
China Embraces an Air Force – Or Tries To

"Cannot tell where path lead until reach end of road."
Charlie Chan, *Charlie Chan at the Circus* (1936)

DURING THE 1930s, few people in the United States knew it at the time (or some simply chose to ignore it) that the 4,000-mile distance between Japan and Hawaii was razor thin – made so by aggressive Japanese military intentions. That gap would be reduced in the forthcoming years but not through political or military clout but with the ongoing advancement of aviation and naval aircraft carriers. This chasm would be closed by raw American capitalism and by our aviation industry's quest to obtain capital, sales, and expand their businesses, and the advancement of high performance aircraft. In the months leading up to the attack on Pearl Harbor there would be a decisive shift in our relationship with China and an abrupt turn from the private sector providing foreign support to direct involvement by the United States government at the highest levels within the bureaucracy possible.

The plan to have China bomb the homeland of Japan would be years in the making and it would begin with the American exportation of commercial aircraft. Agreements would be made, aircraft sales contracts signed, connections established, handshakes to consummate deals, and questionable legal maneuvers by many of those involved. A bevy of characters would be on stage during this period that included arms merchants, mercenaries, politicians, spies, businessmen, con men, and civilians with altruistic aspirations. They would all have the same general starting point in either commercial aviation or political interests in China, but the definitive ending would be on December 7, 1941.

Early American Interest

DURING THE SPRING and summer of 1929, the United States unemployment rate was just 3.14%. With the stock market crash on 24 October (Black Thursday) the American economy began to spiral downward and out-of-control in what would later be described as the "Great Depression." The economic decline in the United States rippled across the globe affecting many countries and global economies. [1] Japan's economy was able to blunt most of the effects of this worldwide depression as they continued their militarism and their imperial ambitions in the Pacific.

As business began to sour at home, American aviation companies began earnestly to expand their operations overseas looking for new sources of revenue. While some transportation companies like Pan-Am focused on South America, others involved in the manufacture of aircraft, principally Boeing, Douglas, and Curtiss-Wright, focused their attention on China as the premier foreign market to peddle their wares. Both American aviation industries and China were inexplicably intertwined and dependent on each other. However, this new Asian frontier presented many obstacles and hurdles to be bypassed and overcomed in stark contrast to South America and other parts of the world.

The China of 1929 is not what we have today - It was not a unified country. After the Chinese Revolution of 1911 the opportunity of a democratic republic fell apart and the country splintered into various power struggles between warlords all vying for the power seat of a central government in Peking (Beijing). Years later after the revolution, China remained fractured and in turmoil as various factions vied for additional power but with no real intent to unify the country. Entire books have been written about this period of Chinese history, and rightfully so, as it was a turbulent time. The one person who would eventually emerge to unify the country, at least temporarily, would be Chiang Kai-shek. Born in 1887 Chiang was both a political and military leader and a powerful member of the Kuomintang (KMT), the Chinese Nationalist Party.

Chiang was a close ally of Sun Yat-sen's. Sun was a Chinese physician and writer, and more importantly a revolutionary. Born in 1866 he is considered the "Father of a Nation" in the Republic of China (ROC). He later co-founded the Kuomintang and served as its first leader.

Chiang became the Commandant of the Kuomintang's Whampoa Military Academy and headed the KMT following the Canton Coup in early 1926. Eliminating the communist left wing of the party, Chiang then led the Northern Expedition, a military campaign to conquer or reach agreements with China's many warlords.

An early photo of Chiang Kai-shek. (Wikimedia commons)

International Intervention

AFTER WORLD WAR 1 several countries, principally Great Britain, France, and the Soviet Union provided a handful of arms to any Chinese entity that could pay for them. However, things changed in the latter part of 1919 when the China Arms Embargo Agreement was enacted. Besides the United States the signatories to the agreement included Russia, Japan, Great Britain, France, Spain, Portugal, and Brazil. This was an attempt to help stabilize the splintered country and reduce the in-fighting between the various warlords by reducing the easy acquisition of the weapons of war.

Although the agreement was intended to reduce the materials of war from being exported to China, the United States also believed it should include commercial aircraft as well. The embargo was not legally binding in the United States until January 31, 1922 when Congress signed a joint resolution entitled, "To Prohibit the Exportation of Arms or Munitions of War from the United States to Certain Countries and for Other Purposes." Two months later President Warren G. Harding reinforced the joint resolution with Proclamation No. 1621 and added "…all airplanes and aeronautical equipment and parts…" [2]

President Warren Harding (right) alongside General John J. Pershing. President Harding would stop aircraft sales to China in 1922 allowing foreign enterprises to fill the void. (LOC)

As President Harding handcuffed commercial American aviation interests, businesses and governments in Great Britain and France did not share this view and remained unshackled to continue the exportation of civilian aircraft to China. Undoubtedly many of these planes were converted to military use. And as with most laws and proclamations emanating from Washington, D.C. there always seemed to be the proverbial "loophole." In this situation, the State Department could issue an export license on a case-by-case basis.

Knowing that other countries were exporting airplanes to China, James Slevin, representing the Curtiss Aeroplane Company, believed he could use this information to his advantage as he approached the Department of State. Slevin had a contract in hand from a Chinese businessman to deliver twelve war surplus J.N.4 planes, nicknamed Jenny, and powered by OX-5 engines to the Great China Air-Way Company. [3] Stating they were being sold to establish commercial airways, the State Department issued a permit authorizing their export.

Six aircraft were already shipped when the American Legation in China got wind of the deal and protested on the grounds it violated

Proclamation No. 1621. The State Department caved in immediately and abruptly reversed course cancelling the sale and informing the Curtiss Company not to ship any more aircraft to China. Slevin complained loudly to those who would listen but to no avail.

It was the Model T of its day. More than 6,000 Curtiss JN-4 "Jenny" aircraft or variants were built. (Army Signal Corps)

Even with the State Department reversal, six Jenny aircraft along with hundreds of boxes of aviation equipment and parts arrived in Shanghai and was then sent north. An aircraft shop was established in Canton in the Kwangton Province with the help of two Curtiss Company representatives. Using a spare engine, the Americans also designed an airplane that would turn out to be the first plane to be truly manufactured in China.

The embargo against China was slightly reconfigured after a meeting of foreign diplomats in Peking in October 1922. American, British, and Japanese representatives agreed to include all aircraft in the embargo, but the French insisted that commercial aircraft be exempt. The best anyone could agree on was a small addition to the China Arms Embargo Agreement stating, "This is understood to include aircraft other than commercial aircraft." This ambiguous statement simple opened a door you could drive a truck (or airplane) through.

The following year Slevin, embracing another sales opportunity, looked to sell 24 Curtiss planes to China. Peking's American minister Jacob Schurman protested, and Secretary of State Charles Hughes agreed. Once again Slevin was stymied as would be every American aircraft manufacturer for at least for the next few years. Every Washington bureaucrat knew that it was always easier and less work to say "no" than "yes." The State Department held the high ground and denied every request it received regarding sales of aircraft to China. That lofty position would eventually give way under pressure from foreign governments and their abundant sales of aircraft to China. American manufacturers continued to pound this narrative amid the turf battles in and around Washington, D.C. as the embargo slowly unraveled.

China was a vast territory with primitive roads and a poor and limited railroad infrastructure. The Nationalist government believed commercial airways were needed in the immediate future to conquer the immense distances efficiently. There was also the military requirement in that fighters and bombers could tamp down the various warlord factions. If necessary, that would include the modification of commercial aircraft imports to military use as required. This would help consolidate power in Nanking under Chiang Kai-Shek and eventually unify the country. China would pull out all stops possible to acquire any aircraft that she desperately needed.

Towards the end of 1927 the British De Havilland Aircraft Company shipped several Gypsy Moth training aircraft to Canton and in the spring of 1928 France shipped about fifteen aircraft in defiance of the ban. American aircraft representatives continued to complain vehemently to the State Department. The Aeronautical Chamber of Commerce of America stated in the Aircraft Yearbook of 1928:

> *However, due to the unfortunate policy of the State Department, the exportation of American aircraft and parts has been hindered by embargoes on two foreign markets [Mexico and China].*
>
> *The American embargo is severe enough to practically close the market to American aircraft industry. Selling our aviation products in foreign markets is a costly process, involving the development of prospects which can eventuate only in conditional sales, depending in the case of Mexico and China upon the consent of the State Department in each individual case. Under these conditions American manufacturers are severely handicapped in competition with European constructors whose governments place no such restrictions*

upon their activities but go far towards facilitating successful negotiations through direct aviation missions with aircraft and demonstrating personnel paid for by their governments.

A De Havilland DH.60 Moth after a forced landing on a farm in Australia in 1932. (John Oxley Library)

An American minister in China, John Van Antwerp MacMurray, contacted the Secretary of State, Frank B. Kellogg, to exempt commercial aircraft shipments to China. Several days later, Kellogg on his own volition decided that the Department of State would allow the export of planes to China. It is not clear if Kellogg could lawfully change the requirements of the embargo set forth by Congress and President Harding, but no one stood up to challenge his directive. Therefore, just about any aircraft designated as "commercial" would be allowed to be exported from the United States to China and a blind eye by government officials given to their ultimate use.

Incredibly it would be another six years since those handful of Jenny aircraft arrived in Shanghai before another American airplane would be delivered to China. This would be a single-engine Ryan Brougham that was delivered on October 9, 1928 to the government in Canton and not the Nationalist government headquartered in Nanjing.

Stepping seamlessly into this sales opportunity was Lloyd E. Gayle whose first exposure to the intricacies of the Chinese market was in 1914 while employed by Standard Oil Company as a civil engineer. Several years later he would acquire the defunct American Trading Company in

Secretary of State, Frank B. Kellogg, allowed the exportation of commercial aircraft to China in 1928 but it is unclear if he had the legal authority to do this. (LOC)

A Ryan B-1 Brougham. This was the initial production version with the Wright J-5 and about 150 were built. (SDASM)

Hankou and specialize in the sale of automobiles. Changing the name of the enterprise to the Lloyd E. Gayle Company, operatives of Mahoney-Ryan aircraft interests enlisted him to sell their airplanes. Gayle would later expand his loyalties and represent Boeing aircraft interests as well.

Gayle delivered quickly by having the Wuhan Civil Aviation Company, Ltd., in Hankou, sign a contract to purchase five Ryan aircraft that were eventually given to the local military when delivered in February 1929. Other aircraft were also acquired during this time from Mahoney-Ryan and delivered to South China and military officers in the Yunnan province. The door for American-made aircraft was slowly opening to the Chinese market through intrepid entrepreneurs in-country and often with subtle and sometimes overt action by the United States government.

During this period while the State Department wrangled and massaged the aircraft embargo requirements to China the Commerce Department took a different tact and tried to support American aircraft manufacturers fully. The two government departments were destined to clash in the upcoming years.

The Brougham served as the personal aircraft for General Zhang Weizhang who had received aviation flying instruction in the United States and was director of the Canton Aviation Bureau. The Ryan Brougham design was based on the Spirit of St. Louis, the plane flown by Charles Lindbergh just two years earlier to cross the Atlantic Ocean.

Manufactured by Mahoney-Ryan, the Brougham could accommodate four passengers and the pilot and with a range of 700 miles and served as viable airline transport plane during this time. It was powered by the venerable Wright J-5 Whirlwind engine providing 225 horsepower and could cruise at 124 miles-per-hour. At its peak Ryan produced about twenty Brougham model aircraft per month and ceased production after 228 of various configurations were shipped. [4]

One can easily see the similarities of the Ryan Brougham and the Spirit of St. Louis flown by Charles Lindbergh. (LOC)

Zhang, with the help of another officer assembled his personal plane and promptly renamed it the Spirit of Canton, in deference to Lindbergh's transatlantic trip. A few weeks later another Ryan-Brougham arrived. In November, Zhang took the Spirit of Canton on a far-reaching publicity tour departing Canton for Hankou to the north and onto Nanjing, Peking, Shenyang, and then south to Tientsin and Shanghai, before returning to Canton on 20 November. The exciting tour earned him the nickname the "Lindbergh of China" and subsequently he became director of the Central Government Aviation Bureau in Nanjing. Zhang's tour continued to open the door to American aviation interests and broadened the general appeal of aviation among the Chinese populace many of whom have never seen an airplane in flight before. American Consul General Douglas Jenkins enjoyed seeing American made aircraft plying the skies over China and helped lubricate the path of purchase and importation of these airplanes.

This was one of the reasons the Canton Aviation Bureau subsequently ordered ten Waco-10 biplanes from the Advanced Aircraft Aviation Company of Troy, Ohio in November 1928. Powered by the OX-5 engine and although outdated by this time, the biplane could accommodate two passengers side-by-side with the pilot in the rear bay. Waco manufacturing would build 1,623 aircraft over a seven-year period from 1927 to 1933. China received the GXE export version, powered by the Wright J-5 Whirlwind engine producing 220 horsepower. The straight wing biplane fighter/bomber had twin 30-caliber Browning machine guns and additional racks that could hold five 25-pound or two 100-pound bombs. Gun and bomb racks were installed in the front cockpit and could be removed if it was desired to reconfigure the plane as a trainer for students.

Over 1,600 Waco 10 aircraft were built with the model GXE designation as the export version. (SDASM)

Canton opened their arms and purses to the purchase of American aircraft for a couple of reasons. Several Cantonese pilots were trained in the United States including General Zhang and it was naturally expected that these pilots would gravitate to American manufactured aircraft that they were familiar with and not those of European origin.

Once again, the L.E. Gayle Company consummated another aircraft sale to the Cantonese in March 1929. Representing the Gayle Company was Earl F. Baskey who was enabled by the United States government in a concerted effort that would be repeated many times in the years leading up to World War II. Baskey was a consummate airman earning his wings at Elington, Texas in 1918 and became an airmail pilot after the Great War from July 1920 to March 1921. Along with Baskey's flying acumen this sale would be assisted by the consul general at Hankow (Wuhan) at the time, Walter A. Adams.

Adams provided the letter of introduction for Baskey and Consul Douglas Jenkins forwarded a Baskey document in a gray consular code through the Navy Department to facilitate the sale. The sale for five Waco planes was consummated on 2 April by the Canton Aviation Bureau and the note was guaranteed by the City Bank of New York. American diplomats greased the rails for the deal and it was not an aberration but a pattern of assistance that would continue for several years to come. China would seek out other foreign entities for aircraft purchases and assistance but would continue to rely on the United States for aircraft, materials, instruction, and eventually pilots.

Commercial and military aviation interests have always gone together as advancements in each arena would be reflected in the other. This was quite evident as China began to modernize and expand their airborne assets. As testament to this fact one only must look at the American aircraft manufacturer Curtiss-Wright and the foothold they established in China in 1929.

Industrial magnate Curtiss Melville Keys acquired the financially strapped Curtiss Aeroplane and Motor Company in 1920 and later merged it with Wright Aeronautical in 1929 to form Curtiss-Wright and become its new company President. Keys would eventually head 26 other aviation companies including Pitcairn Aviation that he purchased that same year and flipped it two weeks later creating a company that eventually became known as Eastern Airlines.

In December 1928, Keys sent Curtiss representative R.O. Hayward to meet with Sun Fo, the Chinese Minister of Railways and President of the China National Aviation Corporation to establish exclusive mail and passenger routes in China. The well-educated Fo was the son of Sun Yat-sen, the founder of the Republic of China. The Nanjing government promised an exclusive contract with Curtiss if negotiations could close before April 1, 1929. To reinforce his position Keys sent Major William B. Robertson and several aviation experts to Shanghai in February 1929.

An accomplished pilot, Major Robertson became the first commanding officer of the Missouri National Guard Air Unit 35th Division in 1924. He later formed the Robertson Aircraft Company at Lambert-St. Louis Flying Field in Missouri. The company was absorbed by the Curtiss-

In 1932 Keys withdrew from the aviation business citing health reasons, but the directors of North American Aviation had discovered that he had embezzled funds at this time. (SDASM)

Wright conglomerate in 1928 and another subsidiary was formed. A cartel of American aviation interests with Robinson as the nucleus was formed and became known as the Aviation Exploration Corporation. [5]

Offices in Shanghai were quickly established to accommodate the Curtiss-Wright representatives and their arrival did not go unnoticed by the local media. In an interview with the *China Weekly Review* Robertson stated "We shall probably be here for several weeks. During this time, we expect to visit as many Chinese as possible who are interested in aeronautical industry and to determine how American airplanes can best satisfy China's need in this respect."

History has shown repeatedly that parallel events occur at the same time and sometimes intersect. This would happen in February 1929 as Curtiss-Wright attempted to carve out a piece of the Chinese market for their airplanes. The Nanjing government reorganized the Aviation Department of the Ministry of War that was established just four months earlier and renamed it the National Aviation Administration and would place its control directly under the Nationalist government and under direct authority of General Zhang Weizhang. And in April 1929 the Nanjing government began to use "Air Force" to describe their military aviation assets.

While Nanjing made their administrative changes in March, Robertson ordered three aircraft be shipped from San Francisco to Shanghai ostensibly as "demonstration" aircraft and as such he didn't feel obligated to notify the State Department at the time. The shipment was comprised of Curtiss aircraft that included the Challenger Robin, an early version powered by a 165HP radial engine and a Model B Ryan powered by an OX-5 engine along with a Teal two-seat flying boat.

However, the fourth aircraft may be the real reason that Robertson didn't want to notify the State Department of this intended shipment. This was the OC-2 Falcon biplane and was part of the Curtiss family of military aircraft. The Falcon could be used as an observer or an attack aircraft and even though only 338 were built they were clearly never intended for commercial purposes. Circumventing the arms embargo is clear with this transaction although it was purportedly for exposition and potential future sales purposes – and recorded on paper as such.

Around this same time an American advisor for Chinese railroad development, Robert Stanley Morgan, reached out to Robertson to set up a meeting that included Sun Fo and the head of the Aeronautical Bureau of the Chinese Army, Colonel Zhang Qingyu. Colonel Zhang was willing to pay $51,000 (USD) for the Curtiss shipment on the contingency that Sun Fo take delivery of them. Everyone present knew about the arms embargo and everyone took the necessary steps to bypass it at least from the stand-

A U.S. Marine Corps Curtiss OC-2 Falcon assigned to the Marine Observation Squadron, VO-7M, pictured on the ground evacuating troops, possibly during service in Nicaragua. (US Navy)

point of a paper trail. These were smart men with their eyes to the future. Why Morgan set up this meeting is not known. With Sun Fo as the minister of railways and Morgan as an advisor for railroad development the two must have surely had a working relationship. But what is known is that Morgan was a lawyer and enabled Sun Yet-san to enter the United States in 1904 and that would allow him to solicit funds for his future revolution. At the time, there was a ban on Chinese immigrants entering the United States and Morgan was instrumental in opening the door for at least one Chinese national, Sun Yet-san. With just about every aircraft commercial endeavor conducted in China and in the future, the military deals that would develop as the United States became more involved, there would be scant degrees of separation between civilian and politicians involved in these transactions. And one can only guess at the content of the conversations that took place among these individuals that has never been recorded on paper.

Prior to the sale agreement Robertson sent a telegram to the American Department of State administrator currently stationed in China, John MacMurray. MacMurray informed Robertson that he had no objections of the sale of aircraft to Sun Fo. President Chiang Kai-shek then instructed his finance Minister T.V. Soong to pay Robertson $25,000 in gold as a down payment once the transaction was completed. Robertson said once he got the green light from his boss, Clement Keys, the transaction could be completed. Robertson did not get the okay from Keys until two days later and on his own accord decided to "loan" two aircraft to the Chinese. That same day E.L. "Slonnie" Sloniger flew the Falcon while a Chinese pilot and Colonel Zhang flew the Robin alongside each other as both aircraft landed in Nanjing.

Curtiss did formally ask MacMurray permission to sell or rent planes to the Chinese military, and personally McMurray favored the lifting of the arms embargo. Other countries were openly or secretly selling arms and aircraft to the Chinese so why shouldn't the United States have a piece of the action? A couple of days later, the secretary of the Department of State, Henry L. Stimson, who had just succeeded Frank Kellogg the previous month, telegraphed MacMurray a terse response stating "... the Department of State can give no approval and cannot allow itself to be associated with this particular proposed transaction." Once the Chinese took possession of the two aircraft there was little recourse or enthusiasm to retrieve them. It was a trivial issue as the 10-year arms embargo was soon fading out as a noble but ineffectual measure to reduce civil war and strife in China. In retrospect, it may have emboldened the Japanese to pursue their military endeavors that would ultimately lead to the attack on Pearl Harbor.

A Curtiss subsidiary, Aviation Exploration, signed two agreements with Sun Fo on April 17, 1929. Within a few months' contracts were established to carry mail between Shanghai and Hankow, Nanking, and Canton. A separate agreement called for Robertson to provide flight training for prospective Chinese aviators and to establish flight facilities at several locations in China. Sun Fo also allowed Aviation Exploration to pursue passenger flights and carry freight.

Just a week later the arms embargo against China was officially lifted as Great Britain had pulled out unilaterally earlier in the year and other prominent countries like Germany never signed on to it. Russia originally signed on but quickly decided it wanted no part as it was not in her best interests both economically and politically. Japan for a multitude of reasons, always favored the embargo but in the end under political pressure capitulated as well. The flood gates of free trade to China for munitions, arms, and aircraft were officially cast opened. It was just a short period of time to see what country would take the lead and suck up the potential profits to be made.

In America, business for Curtiss-Wright in China began to take off and with it the lines between politics, commercial interests, and the Chinese military began to blur. The Unites States consular in Nanjing, Ernest Batson Price, left his cushy government job to form the China Aircraft Company with the sole responsibility of supporting the interests of Curtiss-Wright.

Price had spent over 15 years in China, was fluent in Mandarin and good friends with Sun Yat-sen, when he was the President of the Republic of China. Price and his wife were invited to the inauguration of Sun Yat-sen as President, but the offer was rejected by the State Department since the United States only recognized the rival government in Peking at the time. Only Price's wife could attend since she was not a government official. The couple did attend the official burial of Sun on June 1, 1929 that took place on the outskirts of Nanjing.

With the embargo gone, aircraft sales representatives from America and Europe flocked to China. The L.E. Gayle Company was the exclusive distributor for Chance-Vought Corsair biplanes or that is what his sales chief Earl Baskey believed. Then Weston Birch "Bert" Hall arrived in China sometime in May and things got a bit messy for Chance-Vought.

Bert Hall was an aviator and one of the original seven pilots in the Lafayette Escadrille during World War 1 before America entered the war.

He was also a writer and authored two books about his exploits. Above everything else he was a liar, con man, bigamist, card cheater, deserter, mercenary, and carried many more labels over the years which made him into a very interesting person to say the least.

Bert Hall flew with Lafayette Escadrille in France before the U.S. entered World War I and was certainly one of the more colorful characters to be found in China during this time. (LOC)

Like just about every aspect of his life, Hall's dealings in China were shady, and that is being generous about his affairs. The Missourian from Higginsville at some point was commissioned a general by some warlord and later obtained the dubious title of "advisor" of aeronautical interests to the Nationalist government. Nanjing accepted Hall on face value and with no surprise Hall's quote for the Vought Corsairs was substantially lower than what Baskey offered. Yet there was never any record that Hall was authorized to represent the Chance-Vought Company of Long Island, New York.

Chinese purchasing agents may have believed something was

afoot and looked to deal with the Chance-Vought Corporation directly. Once again, the lines between government and commercial interests was erased as the Chinese asked American consul Walter Adams to get a direct quotation from the manufacturer. Adams even approached Baskey saying that he would be willing to help. So, on the 5 October, Adams, in a sleight of hand way, sent a telegram asking the State Department to forward the request to Chance-Vought officials. The United States government was not directly selling aircraft to the Chinese, but they sure did grease the skids to enable the sale.

During this same time Baskey was able to sign a contract with the Chinese to purchase twelve 02U-12 Corsairs valued at $1,000,000 (USD). These biplane Corsairs were powered by a Pratt and Whitney 450HP Wasp engine and had a maximum speed of 151MPH – which was state-of-art at the time. It featured a single forward mounted 7.62mm machine gun and two machine guns on a rear cockpit trainable mount. The first shipments were expected to begin in November.

As a side note, Bert Hall departed the aircraft business and entered the black market for smuggling small arms into China and scammed the Nanjing government out of $20,000 in silver. He was arrested at the American embassy in Tientsin, China and prosecuted by the American government for arms smuggling. He was found guilty and spent two and one-half years at McNeil Island Federal Penitentiary in the State of Washington. Upon his release from prison in 1936, he started a manufacturing facility that made children's toys.

Even with the arms embargo to China lifted the United States State Department was still hesitant at times to release overseas weapon shipments. The Chinese Legation in Washington, D.C. notified the State Department that they would like approval to have the 02U-12 Corsairs equipped with machine guns and bomb racks. The State Department took the easy route and permitted the sale of the Corsairs without armament. In Washington, what represented the least amount of work had the minimal amount of potential repercussions hailed supreme. Little has changed in 80 years.

Nanjing was not happy with the response from the State Department that the Corsairs would be shipped unarmed and threatened to cancel the order and indicated that they would pursue the aircraft sale with Great Britain. The State Department blinked and the United States, Consul Edwin Cunningham, sent a telegram to his superiors in Washington, D.C. stating "I venture to express that no difficulties will be placed in the way of this contract, I cannot but view with great concern the very serious effect the cancellation of this contract may have upon the future trade in American airplanes." (6)

The State Department then threw the proverbial ball to the War Department on 5 November even though they did not have definitive authorization to okay the deal. For economic reasons the War Department favored the sale of surplus equipment to foreign powers. Everyone was hampered by decisions made by President Harding in 1919 and 1923 that prohibited the sales of arms that may be used in foreign civil wars. Bureaucrats in Washington discussed the situation intensely but could not come to a resolution and Secretary of War Patrick J. Hurley decided to pass the buck to the recently elected President Herbert Hoover. Hurley stated:

> *American aircraft manufacturers cannot compete with foreign manufacturers in the sale of military aircraft to foreign governments unless the former can deliver their products fully equipped with military equipment...American aircraft manufacturers' needs must, therefore, depend upon the government for such equipment or arrange for the development and manufacture by commercial concerns.* (7)

President Hoover dragged his heels but eventually permitted the sale of Chance-Vought Corsairs to China in a memorandum to the War Department on January 30, 1930 stating:

> *In view of the special situation referred to, and to the end that the American aircraft industry may not be adversely affected in the development of American trade relations with foreign countries, authority is hereby granted to make exception to the policy established by the President's letter of April 23, 1923, in so far as pertains to the selling of surplus military aircraft, that is not an article of common commercial production, to foreign governments or their agents when the sales of such aircraft equipment have been approved by the Department of State and when such sales will not disclose any military secret.* (8)

Since America was in the beginning of the Great Depression, the economic climate within the country may have influenced his position. Three days after the War Department received this drawn-out one-sentence judgement and digested it, approval was granted for the shipment

President Herbert Hoover acquiesced to American commercial interests and allowed the export of some military planes to China in 1930. (LOC)

of armed Chance-Vought Corsairs to China.

Although the United States acquiesced to the Chance-Vought shipment, Nanjing was not pleased with the delays in acquiring American military planes and hoped things would improve. The Chinese were not only dissatisfied with procurement from the Americans but other countries as well. They had ordered twenty German Junker pursuit planes earlier in the year and were not pleased with their construction or performance. A few British planes also arrived on the scene and the Chinese were disappointed with their capabilities. It was very evident from various U.S. consul dispatches in China that Chinese pilots liked what the American planes had to offer in performance as well as their easy flying capabilities compared to their European counterparts.

American's Hot Pursuit of Aircraft Sales

THE DOOR DID NOT creak open to American aviation interests in 1930 but flew open with a bang. One person on hand to step in was Floyd Newman Shumaker, a native of Fullerton, Nebraska, who established a multi-faceted role as a representative for Douglas Aircraft of Santa Monica, California. Shumaker was vice-president of the Aviation Corporation of America and a quasi-advisor to the Chinese Air Force.

When World War I broke out Shumaker was an electrical contractor in Shanghai shifting the gas lighting infrastructure in the city to electrification. He joined the U.S. Army Air Service in 1917 and remained in the United States military until 1929 eventually attaining the rank of Major. Shortly after his military service ended he returned to China and looked to advance the development of aviation civil transportation lines, aerodromes, and wide-scale radio net encompassing hundreds of miles around Nanking. He also recommended that civil aviation activities be under the direction of the Ministry of Aviation and not the Ministry of Communication.

The Nanjing government agreed and there was no dissent from Minister of Communication Wang Pei-chun. Shumaker continued suggesting that the air mail service be managed by the military and advocated a strong air force with Nanking as both the geographic and political center. Of course, Douglas Aircraft would be more than willing to help the Generalissimo to achieve these lofty goals.

In May 1930, the Nationalists placed an order for twenty Douglas Type 02MC military biplanes. Several variants of this robust Hornet radial engine-powered biplane would appear in the skies over China over the next couple of years and was a favorite of Chinese pilots. About 80 of this series of conventional biplanes with the designation "MC" were manufactured and destined for export to either the Chinese or Mexican governments. The 02MC fitted a multi-faceted role and could be utilized for observation, light bombing, or ground strafing when a pair of machine guns that were mounted and twin bomb racks installed.

In the following month, a report to the War Department from a

Douglas BT-2 (near camera) and BT-1 at training field in Waco, Texas. (SDASM)

United States military attaché in China, Lieutenant Colonel Nelson E. Margetts, related how Shumaker went above and beyond the scope of your typical airplane salesperson and participated in aerial bombings by the Nanking government against the communists. On 14 July 1930, Shumaker piloted a plane on a bombing raid to try and take out a railroad bridge spanning the Yellow River at Chengzhou. The State Department was not impressed and informed him that he risked losing his United States citizenship. Purportedly the sketchy con man Bert Hall participated in these bombing raids as a ground coordinator shortly before he was arrested by American officials on gun smuggling and fraud charges.

Several internal and external forces would shape the future of Chinese military aviation going forward. Many countries would be involved in the years ramping up to World War II and in the end, America would emerge as the predominate power. Yet the United States did not vault to this position on its own accord but was pressured there by Japan, a country that considered itself an equal if not a superior presence in the Pacific. It would take quite a few years as each country jockeyed for a better military position. Ultimately a showdown would take place that would have devastating consequences for all involved.

An American Hero in China

HIS NAME WAS ROBERT MCCAWLEY SHORT and he served in the United States Army Air Corps reserve as a second lieutenant. He would have a profound effect on the future of Chinese military aviation. He was born just outside of Tacoma, Washington in 1904, only a year after the Wright brothers' first flight at Kitty Hawk. Short was the eldest of two sons and had a sibling sister who died at the age of eight. The father abandoned the family when Robert was eight and he grew up tall and handsome, a devoted son to his mother, Elizabeth. From a young age he remained fascinated with everything surrounding aeronautics.

Within two years of his high school graduation in 1925 he became an airframe and engine mechanic. But Short yearned to be an aviator and was accepted as a recruit with U.S. Army Air Corps. He underwent basic flight school at March Field, California and purportedly his boisterous demeanor led to his temporary downfall as he washed out from training after dropping watermelons from his plane onto a civilian truck. Even in 1928 the United States Army had no sense of humor.

Short would continue flying as a part time flight instructor, earned a commercial transport license, and flew sporadic mail runs between Spo-

In a twist of fate, Tacoma, Washington resident Robert Short would be the first aviator to die in the Sino-Chinese conflict, and the first American, years before the Flying Tigers arrived on the scene. (Robert Short Collection/Museum of Flight)

kane and Seattle. He was even invited back into the Army Air Corps and flew for a brief time to pick up some easy dollars and became a second lieutenant during this stint. With over 2400 hours of flight time accumulated he was a hot aviation prospect and sought after by several interests. According to Lee Corbin, a Tacoma, Washington resident and biographical expert on Short, he believes Short learned of his being commissioned in the Army Air Corps and assigned to a bomber squadron at Sand Point, just days before sailing to China. The possibility of a "lucrative" deal flying mail in China, a deal too good to be true, came from no other than Bert Hall.

Short arrived in Shanghai in February 1931 and soon realized that flying mail in crappy, poorly maintained airplanes would shorten his time on earth. Lloyd Gayle then approached Short and asked if we would be willing to work for his company and demonstrate Boeing aircraft for prospective sales to the Chinese. Short accepted and around the same time he was approached by the Nanjing government if he would be interested in becoming an instructor and advisor for the Nationalist government. On June 24, 1931, T.V. Soong sent a telegram to Dr. Arthur N. Young, an American financial advisor to the Nationalist government inquiring about Short's military record and qualifications. After receiving the information Short was considered a valuable asset and he was hired later in the month as an expert in the Military Aviation Bureau at Nanjing. A pursuit squadron was formed in August to attack Communists and warlords with flight instruction to be given by Short.

Short continued with his instruction activities when on 18 September, Japan staged an event engineered by the Japanese military called the "Mukden Incident." At a railway line owned by Japan's South Manchuria Railway near Mukden (now Shenyang) Japanese officer Lt. Suemori Kawamoto detonated a small amount of dynamite that was so anemic it failed to even damage the rail bed.

Blaming the explosion on Chinese dissidents, the Imperial Japanese Army responded with a full-blown invasion of Manchuria. Japan not only invaded Manchuria securing the territory easily, they also threatened to expand even further. Japan not only wanted to extend her territorial influence, but also needed raw materials to further advance their war machine. L.E. Gale and Company had been courting the Chinese for the past several months and shortly after the Mukden Incident a Boeing Model 218 arrived at Shanghai's Hongqiao aerodrome for assembly. Short, as Gayle's demonstration pilot, periodically checked on the assembly progress of the stubby fighter. For unknown reasons the fuselage was painted green while the wings and tail remained bright yellow. An "X" was also painted on the upper right wing for reasons that remain unknown.

Only one example of the Boeing 218 was built. It was evaluated by the Army and Navy before being shipped to China. From this prototype evolved the P-12E/F4B variant and powered by the 500 horsepower Pratt & Whitney R-1340-17 radial engine. With a pair of 7.62mm Browning machine guns, 1200 rounds of ammunition, and a maximum speed of 189 miles-per-hour it was on par with most top line Japanese fighters of the day.

Sino-Japanese hostilities erupted again on January 12, 1932 as the Japanese Air Force bombed several points in around Shanghai. The Nationalist Air Force did not engage the Japanese for fear that the situation would escalate hostilities and the Japanese would attempt to bomb Nanjing. Things changed dramatically on the first of February when Japanese advanced military aggression and their gunboats shelled Nanjing. Over the course of the next several weeks Chinese aircraft engaged Japanese bombers and fighters over the skies of Shanghai.

With the ongoing aerial fights the Nationalist Air Force decided to purchase the Boeing prototype outright and on 19 February, T.V. Soong asked Short to deliver the plane from the Hongqiao aerodrome to Nanjing. While flying near the town of Nanxiangzhen, Short encountered and observed Japanese bombers dropping their payload on a railway head. And just as quickly three Japanese Nakajima A1N2S from the carrier Hoshou pounced upon Short.

Short, knowing his machine guns were fully armed decided to engage the fighters. In the next 20 minutes he was able to damage each of the fighters before they decided to quit the fight and depart the area. Short soon landed at Nanjing with no damage to him or his airplane. He would be the first foreign aviator to engage the Japanese in the air and it would also cement many relationships between the Chinese and American aviation interests in the upcoming years.

And just a few days later Short would engage the Japanese again in aerial combat. But it should be noted that both engagements have only been published based on anectodical reports of the two dog fights. In a span of 80 years no two stories match up exactly and the reports published of Short's activities have been embellished and massaged over the years and what did occur is still subject to debate.

Certain facts remain consistent and this much is known. On 22 February three Mitsubishi Type 13 biplanes assigned to the Imperial Japanese Navy (IJN) aircraft carrier Kaga, took off from a land base outside Shanghai for a raid on the train station at Soochow (modern Suzhou). The bombers were escorted by three Nakajima A1N2 biplane fighters, and as they approached their target a single defending aircraft rose to meet them. It was Short in the Boeing Model 218 and for reasons we will never know—a desire to defend innocent civilians on the ground perhaps or because he was a fighter pilot to his core, or because he simply wanted to show what the Boeing 218 could accomplish in combat and propel sales —he bored straight ahead at the three bombers and opened fire.

Short engaged the lead bomber and killed the navigator and in a matter of seconds was engaged by the Nakajima escort fighters and was ultimately strafed by two enemy airplanes, one from above and one from below. Short died during the encounter and the kill was attributed Lt. Ikuta Nogiji. It was an action the Japanese pilot regretted for the remainder of his life. [8] Short and his Boeing 218 flamed and entered a death spiral before crashing into a canal near the village of Gaudian. It became the first aerial success for Japan but more notably the first American to enter Chinese aviation history lore.

The death of a single aviator over the skies of China would be just a blip on the screen of world events but needs to be seen in the context around the time it occurred. Upwards of 2,000 Chinese civilians witnessed the dogfight between Short and Nogiji that lasted from two to ten minutes depending on what account can be believed. Word soon spread throughout the populace of the young American fighter pilot who sacrificed himself for the Chinese people. Toss in a healthy dose of Chinese propaganda and Robert Short was venerated as a National hero. The Chinese soon telegrammed Short's mother as to the loss of her son.

Mrs. Elizabeth Short
809 South 39 St.
Tacoma, Washington

Dear Mrs. Short:

With the greatest respect and deepest regret we beg to inform you that, when on February 23 at about 3 PM, six piratic airplanes from the invading Japanese Navy were circling over Soochow, dropping bombs on an entirely unarmed and innocent civilian population, destroying lives and property alike in a wanton fashion unheard of before, your heroic son, Robert Short, flying a Boeing plane, engaged in a fight with the above planes, and after a 10 minute machine gun fire, he was shot and nose-dived to death.

It is true that Robert Short failed to bring down any of the invading planes, but he did kill the Japanese flyer who headed the raid, thereby preventing the Japanese attackers from carrying out their bombing raid to the extent that they originally intended. The best words of condolence are insufficient to express to you our sorrow and sympathy in this bereavement of yours. But we can at least assure you this: No parents could have a more heroic son than Robert who gave up his own life that others might live. He dared Might and died to defend Right for humanity and civilization. To say that he was fighting for China alone would be belittling his gallant and humanitarian deed, because it is for humanity and justice that he died. The name of Robert Short will live long in the scroll of honor of great men, and his meritorious service will ever be in the memory of all Chinese.

Yours sincerely, (signed)
Chiang Kwang-nai
(Nominal Commander-in Chief of the Chinese 19th Army)
Tsai Ting-kai (Commander of the 19th)
Tai Chi (Chinese Shanghai Chief of Police)

Once the telegram was dispatched the Chinese military posthumously awarded Short the rank of Colonel in the Chinese Army and the honors did not stop there. The Chinese invited Short's mother and brother to attend a state sponsored ceremony for him and offered to pay for all their travel expenses. One can only guess how the two of them responded to the request, yet they did accept the invitation and journeyed to China in April 1932.

The loss of Short and his subsequent funeral garnered little attention in the United States. But a brief piece by John Powell, a reporter for the *Chicago Tribune*, was buried on page 18 alongside a piece about a Danish meat workers lockout. Published on Monday, 25 April, Powell reported in part:

More than 50,000 Chinese and foreigners, one of Shanghai's largest crowds, lined the ten-mile route of the funeral cortege yesterday of the American aviator Robert McCawley Short.

Forty-five motor cars bore the floral tributes. Many were elaborate replicas of Chinese and American flags, while one consisted of an airplane fashioned entirely of red, white, and blue corn flowers. About 309 cars carrying high Chinese officials were in the procession.

Judge John C. H. Wu, formerly exchange lecturer at Harvard university and now an attorney in Shanghai, declared that Short's death was an event that sealed closer the union of China and America.

Acting on the instructions of the state department, local American and consular and other officials did not participate in the funeral services, but a company of the American 31st Infantry marched for a few blocks in the procession. [9]

The Chinese regarded Robert Short with such respect that they erected a monument to honor him at the entrance of Hungjao aerodrome in Shanghai. It was destroyed later by Japanese bomber attacks on the field and was rebuilt years later and stands today.

More than 80 years later and after decades of Communist rule, American pilot Robert Short is still revered in China. (Lee Corbin)

Curtiss-Wright in China

EARLY IN 1929 China Airways Federal was incorporated, as a wholly owned government company. with Minister of Railways Sun Fo as president. Two weeks later the Nationalists contracted with Aviation Exploration, Inc., an American firm, to establish air routes between several treaty ports. Aviation Exploration was a personal holding company owned by industrial magnate Clement Melville Keys who at the same time was president of Curtiss-Wright and several other companies. A month later contracts were signed for China Airways Federal to carry mail between Shanghai and Hankow, Nanking and Peking, Hankow and Canton. Operations began six months later but obstacles arose on every side.

Then it became apparent that China Airways Federal had been dealing with the wrong men. Their difficulties were taken before the Chinese Supreme Court which ruled that jurisdiction over airmail lay not with Sun Fo but with the Ministry of Communications, headed by the silent, able, progressive Wang Pei-chun. Mr. Wang, meanwhile, had quietly gone ahead and imported Stinson airplanes and started his own company, named Shanghai-Chengtu Airways, under auspices of his own department, and it competed for the Shanghai-Hankow line. Sun Fo retired in confusion and was replaced by Minister Wang as president of China National Airways. With their position more delicate than ever, China Airways Federal approached the task of making peace with Minister Wang, sending as emissaries two new directors, Americans Max S. Polin and Minard Hamilton. The result was a new company and, a partnership between the Curtiss interests (i.e. China Airways) and the Chinese Government (with the latter in control) embracing all three of the existing organizations. Under Minister Wang service had progressed and expanded nominally. China Airways, originally established in 1929 by Curtiss-Wright, was near bankruptcy early in 1930 before being rescued by Polin and Minard. After merging the three entities the name was changed to China National Aviation Corporation (CNAC). [10]

Another early proponent of American aviation in China was George Conrad Westervelt, president of Intercontinent Aviation. Westervelt was a U.S. Naval Academy graduate with 30 years of Navy service acquiring a vast aviation experience before retiring with the rank of Captain. Westervelt had become friends with William Boeing and worked with him on seaplanes and help co-found Pacific Aero Products leaving the company after 1916 when transferred to the east coast by the USN. [11] Following his retirement from the Navy, Westervelt joined the Curtiss Aeroplane and Motor Company to work on the Curtiss NC float plane and later became vice-president at Curtiss-Wright.

Westervelt went to Shanghai in December 1930 to help the China National Aviation Corporation establish air mail routes. Westervelt had seen much of the Japanese bombing of Shanghai in the early months of 1932 which had distressed him greatly. On January 28, 1932 the Chinese Air Force amassed a large enough group to finally take the fight to the Japanese in the skies over Shanghai. The Chinese flew a mixed bag of fighters that included American Waco 240As, German Junkers K-47s, and English Blackburn-Lincocks. This "war" ended before the Chinese pilots had any chance to engage any Japanese planes. On 5 May China and Japan signed the Shanghai Ceasefire Agreement making the city off limits for Chinese troops yet allowing some Japanese units to remain intact.

Viewing the destruction first hand, Westervelt was incensed with the audacious attacks by Japan upon Shanghai. Although he was never involved in Chinese military operations he went well beyond the boundaries that Curtiss-Wright afforded him and made several recommendations to the Chinese. He then placed these in a letter that was to be sent to an influential administrator in the Kuomintang-controlled government and forwarded directly to T.V. Soong on 10 March, stating:

"The United States is the proper aviation contact and source of supply for China, until China is able to supply its own requirements. This belief is due to my knowledge of the fact that in practically every class of military airplanes and in most classes of commercial airplanes, more efficient and up-to-date planes are manufactured in the United States than in any other country. In addition, due to a similarity in geographical characteristics, and in territorial extent, these planes are more suited for Chinese conditions than planes manufactured elsewhere would be." (12)

T.V. Soong, an up and coming influential bureaucrat in the Nationalist government was born into a powerful Chinese family in 1891. He left China at a young age to earn a B.A. in economics from Harvard University. Soong spoke flawless English and surprised many people with his Boston accent. Returning home, he ascended the corporate and political ladder and in 1932 was the governor of the Central Bank of China and the country's minister of finance. It is also noteworthy that one of his sisters was Soong Mei-ling, better known as Madame Chiang Kai-shek, the wife of the Nationalist Chinese leader and the fourth and last wife of the Chinese leader.

T.V. Soong would yield considerable influence in the upcoming years representing China in his Washington, D.C. lobbying efforts. (Wikimedia commons)

Five days after the Shanghai Ceasefire Agreement was signed, Westervelt dispatched another letter to Soong. In his letter, the corporate troubleshooter and retired United States Navy officer related to Soong how Chinese bombers could light up the cities of Japan and the damage that could be inflicted. "Such planes could easily carry sufficient inflammable bombs of small weight to burn down the major portions of most Japanese cities," stated Westervelt. He also recommended that China hire an American military aviator to set up a school with the goal of training Chinese pilots. Westervelt was no fortune reader, yet his insights into the future of Chinese aviation were right on target. This may have well been the catalyst for Soong to take significant action in engaging a military aviation advisor and as aircraft advancement took hold to try and acquire long range bombers.

Obviously, China couldn't possible launch an air attack at this time against the Japanese homeland - It simply did not possess an air force of any consequence to blunt the aggression of Japanese military forces. Besides no bomber currently existed that could make a trip to Japan, drop its payload of incendiary bombs and return to the mainland safely given the long distances involved. It would be an objective that would have to wait. Soong did like the idea of starting a training academy and so did the American air attaché Colonel Walter Scott Drysdale. In a memo to the State Department Drysdale stated, "The presence of such a mission in China will be invaluable to increasing the use here of American planes and equipment."

Once again it appears the American interests in China appeared to be based on economic gain for the homeland and not so much in helping the Chinese stem the advances of superior Japanese military forces. It becomes more apparent when Nanking government officials reached out to the United States government for assistance in establishing a flight training school and expansion and reform of the Chinese Air Force. This was not intended as a short duration mission but something that would take several years if there was to be any chance of success. The State Department okayed the deal but stayed clear of the plan's details and punted China's request to the Commerce Department.

The Jouett Air Mission

SINCE THE AMERICAN military was not to be involved the entire operation was to be composed of civilians only. This would also help fend off any diplomatic complaints from the Japanese government. Commerce was well acquainted with America's growing aviation industry and looked to help in any way possible. The department turned its sights to an employee of the Standard Oil Company and the head of its aviation department – Colonel John Hamilton "Jack" Jouett (ret.).

Colonel John H. "Jack" Jouett would become a pivotal figure in the early development of the Chinese Air Force. (Author's collection)

In 1932 Colonel Jouett appeared to be the perfect aviation advisor for a foreign flying school. The 39-year-old veteran of the First World War, then a Major, commanded a balloon wing of the Second Army in the battle of the Argonne Forest. Jouett had served as the commander of the U.S. Army Air Corps Training Command during the 1920s and retired in 1930 to run the Aviation Department for the Standard Oil Company in Louisiana.

When the Nanjing government of Chinese warlord Chiang Kai-Shek approached the U.S. government in April 1932 and requested an American training group, the Commerce Department recommended Jouett. Jouett was reluctant to sign on to such an unusual task but relented when Assistant Secretary of Commerce Clarence Young insisted that Jouett's participation would be of great service to the United States. Despite being a recently retired colonel in the U.S. Army, the American government considered Jouett a civilian and the State Department agreed to authorize travel for Jouett and the additional fourteen former military instructors selected for this mission. By May, Jouett and the Commerce Department had crafted a training plan for the proposed Nationalist air force.

One would think that the War Department would be keenly interested, but Army Chief of Staff, General Douglas MacArthur, dismissed the idea of supporting an air mission to China. MacArthur said the War Department was simply not interested and left it at that.

Some objections did arise from the United States government about the Jouett mission. Acting Secretary of State Williams Richards Castle, Jr. in June stated, "If we had known about the project at an earlier date, we should have raised objections, but since the present project had gone so far, there did not appear to be anything that the Department could do about it." As with so many before him, Castle was just another bureaucrat with no backbone and simply wanted to cover his butt if things turned sour.

Colonel Jouett and his group departed San Francisco aboard the S.S. *President Hoover* and arrived at Hangzhou on 8 July. Besides Jouett, the air mission included nine instructors, a flight surgeon, four mechanics, and a secretary. The Jouett training mission represented the first formal attempt by Chiang Kai-shek's government to establish the foundations of a modern, Western-style air force that could eventually compete with the Imperial Japanese Army and Navy for control of Chinese airspace. The training syllabus Jouett extended to the Chinese was based on flying instruction principles developed at Kelly Field in San Antonio, Texas and Randolph Field in Universal City, Texas.

With Jouett in command the Central Aviation School was established at Hangzhou and an initial class of 50 Chinese students began their training on 15 September. Jouett then established a five-year program that included the promotion and salary increases for Chinese aviation personnel like their counterparts in the United States Army.

The estimated planned expenditure for the five-year program totaled about $32,000,000 (USD). Money would need to be drawn from other government agencies to finance the endeavor and a propaganda campaign was conducted to raise funds from its citizens and Chinese commercial interests, many of which resided overseas. Pilots, or potential pilots, were easy to come by. Money to purchase the required aircraft was not so easy. In July of 1933 a Chinese state lottery was introduced to raise money for the development of the country's military aviation and was deemed a successful venture.

1933 – Pawley Arrives in China

IN JANUARY 1933, 37-year-old William Douglas Pawley boarded the SS *President Taft* and arrived in Shanghai, China arriving in early February. Born in Florence, South Carolina, Pawley was an adventurer and entrepreneur whose father was a wealthy businessman in Cuba. As a young man Pawley attended private schools in Santiago and Havana and later studied at the Gordon Military Academy in Georgia. A smooth operator and ambitious (and some would say cutthroat) salesman he would replace Captain George Westervelt as President of CNAC if only for short period of time.

After his arrival in China, Pawley struck up a friendship with the new Chinese finance minister, Dr. H.H. Kung. Like T.V. Soong, Kung would be connected to Chiang Kai-Shek by blood, namely his wife, who was Soong's eldest sister Ai-ling. And like all family politics, things would fracture into winners and losers – if only in the short run. In the intervening years Pawley would exploit any opportunity to sell aircraft to China. He became integral component in the formation of the Flying Tigers and the attempt to secure bombers for China that could be deployed against the Japanese mainland.

But the biggest contributor to the Chinese aviation program and American aircraft interests to come on the scene, at least in the short term, would be Major James Harold Doolittle. Born on December 14, 1896 in Alameda, California, Doolittle enlisted with the Signal Corps Reserve in

Chinese Minister of Finance Dr. H.H. Kung (right) on a Washington D.C. visit jousted with T.V. Soong for the attention of Chiang Kai-shek and had a cozy relationship with Curtiss-Wright aircraft salesman William Pawley. (LOC)

Jimmy Doolittle standing in front of a Curtiss Hawk. (NASM)

October 1917 as a flying cadet. In the subsequent years he became an American aviation pioneer, serving as a test pilot, aeronautical engineer, and military bomber pilot. Recruited by Curtiss-Wright, Doolittle travelled to Santiago, Chile in April 1926 to perform demonstration flights for the military establishment. He did not realize it until after he arrived that he would be competing against the British, Italians, and Germans for a possible sale.

Jimmy Doolittle, racer and stunt pilot who would later lead the first United States bombing run against Japan. (USAF)

Before his first demo flight in Chile, Doolittle managed to break both his ankles – not from a flying mishap but falling from a window ledge while attempting a stunt once made for the cameras by the actor Douglas Fairbanks. Even with both ankles in casts and Doolittle in extreme pain, he was still able to fly the Curtiss P-1 Hawk through a terrific aerial demonstration that was well received by the Chilean military. He earned even more respect considering that a couple of attendants needed to position

The Curtiss P-1 Hawk was the first US Army aircraft to be assigned the P (Pursuit) designation. The first production P-1, serial number 25-410, was delivered on August 17, 1925. (USAF)

him in the cockpit and then lift him out after completing the flight. At this time Doolittle could barely walk with the aid of crutches.

And in 1927, after convalescing at the Walter Reed Army Hospital for those injuries incurred while in Chile, he was the first aviator to perform the outside loop. [13] At the time this was considered an impossible maneuver with fatal consequences. The basic premise remained that the G forces were so great that it would rip the wings from the airplane. Doolittle performed the maneuver at Wright Field, Ohio with a Curtiss P-1B Hawk fighter from a dive at 10,000 feet and a top airspeed of 280

A Curtiss Hawk II destined for the Chinese Air Force. (Wikimedia commons)

miles-per-hour. That performance and record making event cemented not only himself as an extraordinary aviator but Curtiss-Wright as the premier manufacturer of well-built and strong American fighter planes. [14] In time, China would welcome them both.

Doolittle would enter the arena of racing aircraft on a closed course and continued to set more records. In 1932, he set the world's high-speed record for land planes attaining 296 MPH during the Shell Speed Dash in Cleveland, Ohio. Later, he took the Thompson Trophy race flying the infamous Gee Bee R-1 racer with an average speed of 252 MPH. The Gee Bee R-1 was built by Granville Brothers Aircraft of Springfield, Massachusetts. Powered by a Pratt & Whitney R-1340 Wasp rated at 800HP, it was perhaps the most dangerous airplane to fly in the world at the time.

Doolittle left air racing after taking the top three contests and upon retiring he stated, "I have yet to hear anyone engaged in this work dying of old age." It is assumed that this made his wife Josephine, "Jo," quite happy.

Doolittle arrived in Shanghai in April 1933 and demonstrated the Curtiss Hawk for the next two months. His flying exploits enthralled both military and civilian spectators. In his autobiography, "I Could Never Be So Lucky Again," the ace stunt pilot said little of his time there. He did relate that on two occasions his plane was "sabotaged" that resulted in two forced landings but no damage to the Hawk. He also had the opportunity to meet with Colonel Jouett and the two flew along the coastline to view the construction of Chinese airfields and defenses. It is not known what the two talked about or if the subject of Japanese aggression surfaced.

The aerobatic flights Doolittle engaged in were very successful and resulted in the Nationalist government ordering 50 Curtiss Hawk biplanes, including Doolittle's demonstration plane – the single largest airplane order by the Chinese government to date. Doolittle was accompanied by Lt. Colonel Frank M. Hawks, representing Texaco and Curtiss Wright and a respected air race pilot in his own right demonstrating the T-32 Condor II. The Condor, powered by two Wright R-1820 Cyclone engines featured retractable landing gear and could function as a 15-passenger plane or a bomber. [15] Yet in his autobiography, Doolittle does not mention Frank Hawks at all.

Pawley, representing Curtiss Wright, but not exclusively, pushed both the Hawk and the large BT-32 Condor biplane plane upon the Chinese while fending off the aggressive Europeans aircraft sales reps. The Chinese ordered eight examples of the T-32 bomber version.

The Curtiss Wright BT-12 Condor II. The Colombian Air Force operated three BT-32 Condors (the bomber variant) equipped with floats in the Colombia-Peru War of 1933. This one had caught fire on the ground for unknown reasons and will never greet the sky again. (NARA).

Originally fitted as a 12-passenger night sleeper, the Condor was the most comfortable American airliner at the time. (NASM).

According to the newspaper *Marysville Journal-Tribune* that appeared June 16, 1934 an interesting article a reporter based in Shanghai states:

Moreover, Soviet Russia whom diplomatic relations are daily becoming more irritating [to Japan] is reported to outnumber Nippon in aircraft itself, stored in secret hangars near Vladivostok. Both Chinese and Red bomb-laden craft can reach Yokohama in five hours from the mainland.

You can brush off this report of secret bombers in Vladivostok from the author, but he must have been knowledgeable about Chinese aviation as he did relate the exploits of Robert Short a few years earlier and was aware of the strategic position of Vladivostok to the Japanese mainland.

While Pawley pushed aircraft sales for Curtiss-Wright, enhanced by the flying abilities of Doolittle, Jouett, being well connected in China, still had the ear of many government and military officials. American businessmen knew Jouett was the go to guy to reach influential people as American State Department officials took a hands-off approach while every other country relied on diplomatic missions.

And Jouett also laid out a five-year plan for the Chinese to acquire military aircraft, the bulk of which were of American in origin. In the first year Jouett proposed the purchase of:

15 Fleet primary trainers
10 Douglas transports
15 Boeing P12 pursuits
20 Italian B.R. 3 bombers

In 1933 China purchased a total of 105 aircraft from the United States at a cost of a little more than $5 million. Yet China was still not a unified country under Chiang Kai-Shek and Canton operated independently including the purchase of aircraft and the establishment of manufacturing and training facilities.

The Canton Aviation School was founded in 1924 and reorganized in 1928 by General Zhang Weizhang. The American commercial attaché in Shanghai, Edward Howard, turned his attention from the Jouett Mission to promoting an air mission in Canton. He sought out a green light for the project by reaching out to U.S. Department of Commerce. Howard contacted Leighton W. Rogers, Chief of the Aeronautical Trade Division, who agreed with the concept. In December 1932 Howard travelled to Canton and promptly selected Captain Edward Deeds who possessed a vast experience in aviation training to lead the mission. Deeds would be further supported by Lieutenant Stuart D. Baird and Lieutenant Clarence Terrill. Once the State Department caught wind they told Howard to keep the mission as quiet as possible so as not to aggravate the Japanese as the Jouett mission had done earlier.

Before departing for China, Captain Deeds visited the Boeing manufacturing plant. This along with Pawley working the scene resulted in another big sale of aircraft. Deeds was an excellent, albeit a cautious instructor. He refused to let most of the Chinese students fly the newer and faster American planes. In a twist of irony, Deeds himself was killed after crashing a Curtiss Hawk on July 1, 1933. Deeds was replaced two months later by Captain John Claiborne and by July 1936 the Canton Aviation School graduated 150 pilots.

A Curtiss Hawk scheduled to be delivered to Japan. (NASM)

The Italians Come to Town

IN 1933 THE AMERICANS courted T.V. Soong and certainly reaped the rewards. At the same time the Italians aligned themselves with Minister H.H. Kung. Kung visited Italy early in 1933 and met with Benito Mussolini. The fascist dictator was interested in spreading his influence beyond Africa and into Asia. Mussolini offered 12,000,000 taels [16] of silver from the remitted Boxer Indemnity Fund to accept an aviation mission, a delivery of Italian aircraft, and payment for the Italian instructors. And those salaries charged were a fraction of what the Americans were asking.

The Italian consul in Shanghai, Galeazzo Ciano, worked his contacts and smoothed the path for the Italians to establish an air mission at Hankow. Colonel Roberto Lordi headed the mission and was soon embraced by Chiang Kai-Shek and the Shanghai community. Lordi served in World Wat I and was a Gold Medal of Military Valour recipient, equivalent to the United States Medal of Valor. Lordi brought along engineer Nicola Galante and spent three months in Hankow but their tenure would be cut short.

Lordi arrived in China and provided some Fiat B.R.3 bombers [17] for training purposes. The B.R.3 was developed from the IA 9 reconnaissance aircraft designed 15 years earlier. When brought to China the plane was a piece of crap and obsolete by American standards of the time. The Chinese were hoodwinked by the Italians that better aircraft were in the pipeline and that they would soon be delivered. It was the basic "bait and switch" routine that would be honed to a fine edge by American car salesmen over the years.

Lordi was recalled by Benito Mussolini under shadowy circumstances. It appears that Lordi "rocked the boat" by either questioning the commissions received by Italy from China or the quality of the aircraft being delivered. Upon his return to Italy he was committed to a psychiatric hospital and then forced into exile. [18]

Colonel Silvio Scaroni replaced Lordi but would not be well accepted by the Chinese. Chinese officials believed Lordi had been betrayed by his own government and even before Scaroni arrived in China there was talk about dropping the Italian mission forcing H.H. Kung to call the Italian Ambassador Vincenzo Lojacono and telling him so. Mussolini quickly dispatched Captain Enrico Cigerza to pilot a Savoia-Marchetti S.72 to China as a personal gift for the Generalissimo to soften the situation.

The Savoia-Marchetti S.72 was an Italian three-engine transport monoplane and powered three 550hp Alfa Romeo license-built Bristol Pegasus radial engines. Like most commercial aircraft it could be retofitted as a bomber Eventually the Chinese ordered six more aircraft and assembled them in China. These aircraft appeared to have been destroyed during Japanese air raids sometime in1937.

The Savoia-Marchetti S.72 was an Italian three-engine transport monoplane. Designed as a heavy bomber, the prototype was first flown in 1934. (LOC)

China also imported 16 examples of the aerobatic Fiat CR.32 biplane in 1933. The nimble fighter was powered by a water-cooled Fiat A.30 R.A. V-12 designed in 1930 and producing 600HP at 2,600 RPM. A logistical supply weakness was the odd fuel mixture of gasoline (55%), alcohol (23%), and benzole (22%). Chinese pilots believed it was superior to the Curtiss Hawk in flight. The Chinese export version featured twin mounted Vickers 7.7mm machine guns and all aircraft were based at the Nangachang airport near Shanghai. With the difficulty of importing the special fuel no others were ordered. By late 1937 all Fiat CR.32 aircraft were destroyed through accidents or aerial encounters.

With the initial influx of Italian aircraft into China, Scaroni would soon ingratiate himself to Chiang Kai-Shek to the point that the Generalissimo swiftly excepted him and sent him on a tour of China. The flamboyant Colonel often travelled in an open touring car dressed in full Italian military regalia. Scaroni also presented the Generalissimo with a "gift" – his Loyang training facility was able to graduate 100 percent of the enrolled students. This meant that there was no feedback from influential Chinese parents who sent their sons off for pilot training. In his first class, Jouett washed out 50 percent of his initial student population considered as incompetent pilots or medically unfit. Jouett didn't realize it at the time but holding Chinese pilots to high American standards would be just another nail in the American air mission's coffin.

Jouett's mission would ultimately collapse but not from any fault by him or the service his instructors and mechanics provided. The American instructors turned out very competent Chinese fliers, but the Italians knew the art of the deal or better yet the art of the con. They cozied up to Chiang Kai-shek and pushed all the right buttons. Also, the Nanjing government was disillusioned with Jouett as the Americans would not direct any aerial attacks against the communists. Add in the fact that the Japanese government continued to pound the State Department on American "aggression" in Chinese matters although it is interesting to note that the Italian mission received absolutely no vitriolic statements from the Japanese press or government during this period.

In time the Italian mission would prove to be a disastrous adventure, but the Chinese would never admit it. Another issue would be that the Chinese would accept any air assistance whether it be from the French, Germans, Italians, British, Americans, or Russians. Ultimately this would induce a lack of continuity between aircraft and training, maintenance and repair. Regardless of what country was selected, a permanency of product and services from a single source would have provided the Chinese with a better overall and efficient product for the Chinese Air Force than a hodgepodge of aircraft and instruction from all over the world.

In July 1934, Jouett received word that his contract with the Nanjing government would not be renewed when it expired in June 1935. Jouett wrote directly to President Roosevelt imploring a contract renewal for most of his team based on the success that they achieved. The White

House passed the letter along to the Secretary of State, Cordell Hull, who never respected the Jouett air mission from the start and offered no assistance to the air mission. His concern was that any United States support would antagonize the Japanese government and Hull had no stomach for a hardball confrontation with Japan at this time.

Born in 1871 and in a log cabin in rural Olympus, Tennessee, Hull was considered "gifted" as an adolescent. Pursuing a career in law and politics, he graduated from Wilmington College, Ohio in1890 and was admitted to the bar the following year. With a break from politics, he served in Cuba as a captain in the Fourth Regiment of the Tennessee Volunteer Infantry during the Spanish-American War. Hull would go on to serve 22 years in the House of Representatives and was elected to the Senate in 1930. Three years later Roosevelt tapped the highly influential Democrat for his administration.

As Secretary of State, Cordell Hull would be an integral part to any potential war material aid to China in the future and that included aircraft. Beginning in 1933 and lasting for another 11 years, he would become the longest serving Secretary of State in history, although Roosevelt, during World War II, shunned him and relied more on his undersecretary Sumner D. Welles.

Although never endorsed by Hull, Jouett did not leave China empty handed – the National Government presented him with the Order of the Commander of the Jade medal. Instructors were given a beautiful incense burner. And on the night prior to their departure they participated in a lavish banquet hosted by none other than Dr. H.H. Kung. On June 7, 1935

Cordell Hull, Secretary of State, who was against supporting the Chinese, and then supported the Chinese, and then was against supporting the Chinese. (LOC)

personnel assigned to the air mission sailed back to the United States. The training academy was moved to Luoyang, where the Italians took control and the training facility was renamed the Central Aviation School.

The Japanese continued to pressure the United States to stop all war material aid to China and would continue to do so right up to their attack on Pearl Harbor in December 1941. Unfortunately, the United States administration (and most Americans) expected foreign political results to be resolved in days, weeks, or perhaps a few months. The Japanese could accept this and assessed their future ambitions and the subsequent fruit of their endeavors by developing it over a period of years. The United States spoke softly but did not wield the big stick and the Japanese took advantage of this and ultimately the United States and China would pay the price.

A New Bomber Emerges

UNBEKNOWNST TO THE Japanese and China, on August 8, 1934, The United States Army Air Corps (USAAC) released a contract proposal for a bomber that could carry a "useful bombload" at an altitude of 10,000 feet, have a minimum top speed of 200 mph and remain aloft for ten hours. The USAAC desired, but did not mandate a range of 2,000 miles and a speed of 250 mph. These were quite impressive numbers giving that aviation was still in its infancy.

The contract intended to replace the Martin B-10 bomber already in service for the United States Army Air Corps and provide a plane with a greater speed and bombload. The matchup would be between Boeing and Lockheed and the faceoff of the two aviation titans would take place at Wright Field in Dayton, Ohio. It would be another year before the bomber prototypes would take to the air.

Boeing's prototype bomber, based on the U.S. Army Air Corps desired specifications from a year earlier, was designated the Model 299. It first flew on July 28, 1935 with Boeing chief test pilot Leslie Tower at the controls. Bristling with five machine guns, *Seattle Times* reporter, Richard Williams, commented, "Why it's a flying fortress!" The name struck a resounding chord with the manufacturer and public and Boeing trademarked the name "Flying Fortress" for their own use. In a couple of years Chiang Kai-Shek and Chennault would make a great attempt to acquire this superlative long-range bomber for the Chinese Air Force.

The Model 299 four-engine bomber flew from Seattle to Wright Field in Dayton, Ohio on August 20, for the fly off competition. With just a flying time of nine hours, the 299 averaged a cruising speed of 252 miles per hour, eclipsing the top speed of its rival.

Improvements continued with the 299-prototype bomber and on 30 October, a second evaluation flight commenced with Army Air Corps test pilot Major Ployer, Peter Hill, and Les Tower at the controls. Inexplicably, these experienced pilots took off with the "gust locks" still in place although eyewitness accounts state both left wing engines failed before the bomber rolled into the ground. These gust locks secure the control surfaces in place while on the ground preventing possible damage from strong winds. The aircraft climbed, stalled, and then rolled over before crashing, killing both Hill and Tower.

The Board of Officers convened at Wright Field and on 15 October stated in part:

> "...accident was not due to structural failure, or to the malfunctioning or failure of any of the four engines, the airplane control surfaces or the automatic pilot, but to the locked condition of the rudder and elevator surface controls (primarily the latter), which made it impossible for the pilot to control the airplane."

With an estimated development cost of $500,000, the Boeing 299 couldn't finish the competition. This unfortunate incident suited General Malin Craig, who recently replaced General Douglas MacArthur as Army Chief of Staff, just fine. Craig actively opposed a separate

Aftermath of the Boeing protoype Model 299 from the crash and fire in Dayton, Ohio. (USAF)

air force and believed the only mission of the Air Corps was to support ground troops. Craig cancelled an open order for 65 YB-17s and awarded Douglas an order for 133 bombers designated the B-18 Bolo. At $58,000 per plane for the B-18 twin-engine bomber, it was about half the price of the Boeing 299. (19)

Chief of Staff General Malin Craig did not embrace the Flying Fortress but is more than happy to show Cuban dictator Colonel Fulgencio Batista ordnance manufactured in the United States. (LOC)

General Malin's parochial view is not surprising and dates to decisions made in December 1925. A report from a House of Representatives committee chaired by Congressman Florian Lampert recommended an independent Air Force be formed. President Calvin Coolidge appointed Dwight W. Morrow to a review board and their conclusion was that a separate air service was not required. This was accepted and Congress passed the Air Corps Act of 1926, establishing an Assistant Secretary of War for Air Affairs, renaming the Air Service the Air Corps, with a representative on the General Staff.

The new position did provide a stronger voice for those who favored strategic aerial bombing, but like the Navy staying committed to the battleship, the Army stayed devoted to the infantry and aerial tactical resources in a supporting role. That thinking would eventual be shot down as the events in Europe unfolded during World War II.

Boeing may have thought that their fortunes were dashed, but fortunately they had a strong supporter in Major General Frank Maxwell Andrews. The previous March Andrews was appointed by the Army Chief of Staff Douglas MacArthur to command the newly formed General Headquarters (GHQ) Air Force. It was a powerful position that consolidated all the Army Air Corps tactical units under the umbrella of one commander. Andrews believed in the future of long-range bombers and really liked the performance offered by the Model 299 (YB-17). In January 1936 Andrews found a "legal loophole" that would enable Boeing and their four-engine bomber, to be designated the B-17, to get back into the game. His decision was derisively nicknamed at the time as "Andrew's Folly."

Major General Frank Maxwell Andrews supported development of the B-17 but was ridiculed for his comments at the time. (USAF)

Years later, writer Jeff Ethell in a *Popular Mechanics* article would say, "Though the crash of the prototype 299 in 1935 had almost wiped out Boeing, now it was seen as a boon. Instead of building models based on experimental engineering, Boeing had been hard at work developing their bomber and now had versions ready for production far better than would have been possible otherwise. One of the most significant weapons of World War II would be ready, but only by a hair." [19]

Politics as Usual

IN JANUARY 1935 Chiang Kai-shek questioned the American military attaché about providing a high-ranking officer to replace Jouett when his contract expires in July. The attaché stated that the American government would probably not allow this, even if Jouett sought out a replacement for himself. This was subsequently backed up by the American chargé d'affaires in China, Clarence Edward Gauss, and Secretary Hull.

Gauss is a bit of a mystery figure as little is known about him. Born in Washington, D.C. in 1887. he entered the Foreign Service in 1912 and spent many of his formulative years in China. In his correspondence with the State Department it was always as "C.E. Gauss." He would become the first minister to Australia in 1940 and become the Ambassador to China in 1941 until his resignation in 1944.

T.V. Soong looked to travel to the United States early in 1936. This trip was not an attempt to acquire more aircraft for China but to discuss the new proposal by the United States regarding the exchange of silver between various countries. This trade mission would set the tone for the next six years on Chinese relations with the United States and the relationship between Secretary of State Cordell Hull and Treasury Secretary Henry Morgenthau, Jr. In an eye-popping entry in his diary, dated Saturday, January 11, 1936, Morgenthau writes:

> *Secretary Hull called me at home this morning. He told me that thinking it over, that he is afraid to have T.V. Soong come to this country. This is because he is such a well-known anti-Japanese. This may be the cause of a serious flare-up; that the Japanese resent the United States or England taking either a financial or commercial interest in China and that he, Hull, would rather postpone our doing anything at this time. However, he said, if I felt that this is a matter of major importance, he does not object to our suggestion that T.V. Soong come. He wanted me to repeat his objections to the President and if the President still feels that he wants Soong to come, he, Hull, will not object.*
>
> *This, of course, is typical State Department philosophy – "don't do anything that might offend anyone!" Hull has also put himself on record that if this mission fails, I will be the goat. However, I consider it so important to take the risk*

involved. My policy in the Treasury is "Nothing ventured, nothing gained." (20)

This tune played out for the next six years with Morgenthau showing American backbone and Hull vacillating on how to deal with the Japanese. It's incredible that Roosevelt did not recognize this situation early on and make some changes in his administration. The Chinese did and staked their claim on Morgenthau to support China in their resistance against Japanese aggression and bypassing Hull and the State Department altogether whenever possible. It was a good move and they reaped the rewards but still came up a bit short and so did the United States when facing the military aspirations of Japan.

T.V. Soong and Secretary of the Treasury Henry Morgenthau, Jr. (U.S. Army)

As T.V. Soong courted the Americans directly, Pawley continued to sell airplanes to the Chinese, but by the spring of 1936 only four Curtiss Hawk II fighters of the 50 he sold in 1933 were still flying. All of them were lost, not in combat but rather through flight accidents. Pawley knew it was time to sell the Chinese more planes and peddle the newer Curtiss Hawk III fighter. The first delivery took place on March 19, 1936 and another 71 would be assembled and delivered in the next several months. Like the he Hawk II predecessor, most Hawk IIIs would be lost in training accidents. But for Pawley that only meant an opportunity to sell more replacement planes.

In November 1936, the Chinese Air Force consisted of three bombardment squadrons, three pursuit squadrons, four transportation squadrons, and two observation squadrons with a total inventory of approximately 645 aircraft. Chiang Kai-shek had politically unified most of China and the Nationalist government held control of all the provincial air forces. In a couple of months, the Chinese Air Force would change dramatically as the Soviet Union joined forces against the Japanese and a maverick American fighter pilot would alter the course of history.

1. In 1931 with President Herbert Hoover at the helm the unemployment rate soared to 15.82%. At the peak of the depression the United States unemployment rate skyrocketed to 25% while other countries would face a staggering 33% unemployment rate. Between 1929 and 1932 the GDP (gross domestic product fell by 15% compared to the "Great Recession" of 2008 where the GDP dropped by 1%.

2. The Secretary of State to the Secretary of the Treasury (Mellon), May 19, 1922, Department of State, FRUS, 1922, 1: 728-29.

3. Curtiss JN-4 "Jenny" was one of a series of "JN" biplanes built by the Curtiss Aeroplane Company of Hammondsport, New York. Thousands of surplus Jennys were sold cheap to civilians after World War I and were a staple of barnstormers during the 1920s.

4. Three Ryan Broughams were modified to look like the Spirit of St. Louis for the 1957 movie starring Jimmy Stewart as Charles Lindbergh. One of the movie Ryans is at the Cradle of Aviation Museum in East Garden City, New York.

5. Aviation Exploration Inc was a personal holding company of Clement Melville Keys.

6. Cunningham to the Secretary of State, November 11, 1929, File Number 893.113 Chance Vought Corp./14, RG 59, National Archives.

7. Hurley to Hoover, December 26, 1930, File Number 893.248/30, RG 59, National Archives.

8. www.aviationofjapan.com

9. Powell, John. "China Gives U.S. Aviator Burial as Nation's Hero." Chicago Tribune (Chicago, Illinois) Monday, April 25, 1932.

10. In 1933, after a series of disastrous accidents and disagreements with Chinese leader Chiang Kai-shek, Keys sold the company to Pan American Airways, under the control of Keys' arch-rival Juan Trippe. Pan Am placed the company under the control of banker and aviator Harold Bixby.

11. William Boeing then changed the named to the Boeing Company.

12. Westervelt to Soong, March 10, 1932, Young Papers.

13. Jimmy Doolittle attempted to repeat the outside loop at the 1929 Cleveland National Air Races, with a Curtiss P-1C Hawk, serial number 29-227. The airplane's wings came off, but Doolittle parachuted to safety. The Curtiss P-1C used wing radiators instead of the large radiator under the nose of the P-1B. This positioning substantially reduced the aerodynamic drag and wing stress which allowed the airplane to accelerate to a high airspeed and absorb tremendous G-forces during his initial attempt at the outside loop.

14. In the 1975 movie, The Great Waldo Pepper, The fictional World War I German fighter ace, Ernst Kessler, is credited with performing the first outside loop.

15. The Curtiss T-32 Condor II, in American Airlines (and Air Mail) livery, designated "Condor 151", appeared in several prominent scenes in the Shirley Temple film Bright Eyes (1934). The plane also appears in "Traveling Saleslady" (1935) starring Joan Blondell.

16. A weight used in China and East Asia, of varying amount but fixed in China at 50 grams (1-3/4 oz.).

17. Unfortunately, the Italians did not have nicknames for their aircraft which would have provided writers an easier way to refer to them.

18. In October 1943 Lordi fought in the Italian Resistance Movement. Early in 1944 he was captured by the Nazis, imprisoned, and tortured in Rome before being executed.

19.. Ethell, Jeff. "Our Still-Flying Fortress." Popular Mechanics, Volume 162, Issue 1, January 1985, Pg. 124–129.

20. Morgenthau Diaries.

Part Two:
Chennault and the Soviets

"Never write if you can speak; never speak if you can nod; never nod if you can wink."

Martin Michael Lomasney, Massachusetts politician
Political boss of Boston's Ward Eight [1]

Chennault Enters the Fray

HE COUGHED AND BELCHED out a cloud of blue smoke as he flicked the stub of the unfiltered cigarette over the rail of the ship and into the ocean. At just 44 years of age, former Army Air Corps officer Claire Lee Chennault was not the desired physical specimen envisioned by the American public of a United States military aviator. Thousands of hours of flying in open cockpit airplanes damaged his hearing and smoking three packs of unfiltered cigarettes a day destroyed his lungs. Still he would persevere and achieve his greatest fame soon, although that would be several years out with the launching of the legendary Flying Tigers on behalf of the Chinese against the Japanese. Their exploits earned Chennault a place on the cover of *Time* magazine and cemented his position in history as the premier architect of modern aerial warfare.

It was Saturday, May 1, 1937 as Claire Chennault departed San Francisco, California bound for China aboard the freighter and passenger ship SS *President Garfield* that parted the waters beneath the soon to be dedicated Golden Gate Bridge. The 78 passengers on board the ship, owned by the Dollar Line, were attended to by the ship's crew. Not so the hundred or so steerage passengers housed in a lower deck well below Chennault's feet. It would be a long journey for this maverick aviator – at

Captain Claire Chennault, leader of "The Three Men on the Flying Trapeze," poses in front of a Boeing P-12E on October 29, 1934. (SDASM)

least a week to get to Honolulu, then a layover for a day or so before continuing to China.

The same day he boarded the *President Garfield* Chennault was officially retired from the U.S. Army Air Corp and officially described as "…incapacitated for active service on account of disability." Knowing he had no future as an American Army officer he wasn't about to retire to his forty-nine-acre farm in Waterproof, Louisiana and live out life as a farmer. The aerial warrior was admitted to the hospital the previous September in Hot Springs, Arkansas, for exhaustion and pleurisy, a painful inflammation of the inner lung tissue. He would be hospitalized on numerous occasions throughout the winter of 1936. The Army had seen enough, and the retirement board met on February 25, 1937 and suggested it was time for him to retire. Chennault wrote to his brother William: "…both the Army and Air Corps have unmistakably indicated that they each, jointly and severally, could muddle along without my advice and services. While I sincerely believe that the time may come when they regret our separation, I feel that both pride and honor urge me to cooperate fully in assuring that separation at present." [2]

The Army Air Corps would never officially "regret" their decision to sever ties with Chennault. That would become evident in the upcoming years as the Air Corps did not adopt Chennault's, at the time, unorthodox aerial tactics and remained mired in a aerial strategy developed years ago during World War I. There was still a lot of work for him, as both a soldier, airman, and adventurer. Curtiss-Wright offered him a position as a demonstration pilot and Chennault considered that a rather boring employment alternative.

China and Japan were fighting intermittently for six years and Chennault already knew that the Chinese needed a strong air arm. So, when the Chinese government bumped their offer of a three-month advisory position to a two-year contract worth $24,000, it was considered a done deal. Who cared if the United States was officially neutral? He was employed by the Bank of China and it even stated so on his passport which listed his occupation as "farmer." Two powerful figures in the form of the petite Madame Chiang Kai-shek and her brother T.V. Soong made it happen. They would make a lot more happen and be influential in the scheme to assault mainland Japan from the air.

Chennault recently moved his wife Nell and their children to a house on Lake St. John in Louisiana. She was dead set against his employment with China, as she would be saddled with caring for four children at home and another three that were older and moved out. She soon acquiesced to the deal and that would involve having Chennault's retirement pay forwarded to Nell along with part of his salary received from the Chinese embassy. Under the circumstances that presented themselves it was little wonder their marriage collapsed just a few years later.

Chennault had plenty of time to dwell not only on his past but the work that lay before him. And his tactical mind was working overtime on the job at hand. By today's standard travel in 1937 was extremely slow. Air transport was still in its infancy and only for short distances and principally over land. Overseas travel was mostly accomplished across oceans by ship. Chennault would not disembark the SS *President Garfield* for another thirty days except for the layover in Honolulu. And he would not be setting foot on mainland China first, but Kobe, Japan on the main island of Honshu. A little spying mission needed to be accomplished for his fu-

View from land looking at the Dollar Line ship SS *President Garfield* in the Hunters' Point Dry Dock. This was the best travel option at the time for long distances. (NARA)

ture employers and this small affair would be enabled by an old friend and flying companion who awaited his arrival.

The *President Garfield* arrived Thursday, 27 May, late at night at Kobe around 10:00PM. Chennault was expecting to see William "Billy" McDonald the following day although that obviously changed as he spotted him waving from the dock. McDonald flew with Chennault as part of an aerobatic team dubbed the "Three Men on the Flying Trapeze" that also included aviator Luke Williamson. McDonald himself was teaching Chinese airman the art of flight and like Chennault, he was in Japan under a false passport. Whether it was a touch of irony or whimsical mischief McDonald indicated his occupation on the passport as "manager of an aerobatic troupe." Chennault later wrote:

> *"We hired an open touring car and, with cameras concealed under our topcoats, set off to see the country through the eyes of experienced airmen gauging targets.... We filled notebooks full of data on building construction, industrial districts, shipping route and areas where industry seemed to be expanding with the suspicious speed of a military enterprise... We toured the flimsy ant heaps of Kyoto, Osaka, and Kobe and sailed down the Inland Sea, noting well the isolated and heavily industrialized islands that housed many of the new war industries."* (3)

For the next few days, Chennault and McDonald toured Kobe, Kyoto, and Osaka taking photographs and making notes about local manufacturing and war industries, construction of residential homes, railroads, and inland river shipping. Both men agreed that with the cities constructed from wood and paper would burn fiercely with just modest incendiary bombing.

At the same time Chennault and McDonald explored Japan, Japanese "tourists" were also photographing themselves at military locations that stretched from Pearl Harbor to Washington, D.C. and making their own notes on a much grander scale than the two American aviators. There is no mention in the FBI files under the auspices of J. Edgar Hoover at the time of any Japanese spying.

Although the two amateur spies gathered a paltry amount of intelligence information while in Japan it was more than what the United States military possessed at the time of the Pearl Harbor attack. And as Jimmy Doolittle prepared for his secret B-25 bombing raid against Tokyo in 1942 from the USS *Hornet* (CV-8) he could not locate any solid strategic bombing targets in the files of the United States government. (4)

After a couple of days of touring the area, Chennault and McDonald once again boarded the *President Garfield* and then steamed into the East China Sea docking at China's largest city, Shanghai. Shanghai was on par with a city like New York, teeming with people and ships in the harbor and sprouting flags from dozens of different countries. Walled neighborhoods within the city housed legations from many countries that all had nationalistic self-interests with their greatest desire to exploit China for as much money and materials they could acquire.

It seemed appropriate that Chennault would arrive in Shanghai during the Chinese Year of the Ox. Occupying the 2nd position on the Chinese Zodiac, oxen possess such character traits as dependability, strength, and determination. Oxen are tolerant individuals who believe that the road to success involves hard work and scrupulous behavior; they don't believe in taking shortcuts. They characterize those who don't work hard as lazy individuals not worthy of respect. Chennault certainly enveloped all of these traits within his personal character and demeanor and would strive to instill them to the citizens of his host country.

As Chennault departed the freighter he was warmly greeted by Luke Williamson, Colonel Eddie Yen of the Chinese Air Force, and Sterling S. Tatum. Tatum was another aviator held in high regard by Chennault. The group quickly departed the docks and headed for the Metropole Hotel built just a few years earlier where the group celebrated and tossed back numerous drinks. At the Metropole he also met an old acquaintance, Roy Holbrook, a former Army Air Corps pilot now employed by the Central Trust Company of China as an aviation instructor.

Growing up in the small Louisianan towns of Gilbert and Waterproof and a man who had never travelled overseas, Chennault was certainly overwhelmed by the sights, sounds, people, and politics that China forced upon him. Fortunately, he would be shepherded along the way by a diverse group of individuals. Chief among this assembly was William Henry Donald, an Australian journalist that consulted with Chinese warlords in the past few years and even Chiang Kai-Shek himself.

Donald was born in Lithgow, New South Wales in 1875 and began working for several newspapers in Australia beginning in 1901. In 1911, he moved to Shanghai and became a key editor for the economics monthly *Far Eastern Review*. At that time Donald became friends with Charlie Soong, who was the father of T.V. Soong and the Soong sisters.

A watershed moment in Chennault's life would be the first meeting with Madame Chiang Kai-shek, the second most powerful figure in

China. and the fourth wife of Generalissimo Chiang Kai-shek. The initial introduction was not arranged by Donald, part of Chiang Kai-shek's inner circle but with Roy Holbrook. Mei-ling Soong would be one of the most influential women in the 20th Century. She is best described by author Johnathan W. Jordan in his book *American Warlords* as "… an articulate, Wellesley-educated power broker, was an Oriental blend of Eleanor Roosevelt and Marlene Dietrich, a rare woman whose sharp mind and vague sexual charm mesmerized westerners in equal measure." [5]

Chennault was brought by Holbrook to the French settlement in Shanghai to meet Madame Chiang Kai-shek. When first introduced he was expecting someone much older and not a beautiful woman dressed in a modest French frock. And when she spoke English it was in a warm southern drawl garnered from her early years spent in Georgia and Chennault was instantly captivated.

Soong May-ling giving a special radio broadcast. She was the fourth and last wife of Generalissimo Chiang Kai-shek. (LOC)

Clare Boothe Luce, wife of *Time's* publisher Henry Luce, meets with Madame Chiang as the Generalissimo looks on. Mrs. Luce would later become Ambassador to Italy. (Alamy)

"I reckon you and I will get along all right in building up your air force," Chennault told her.

"I reckon so," she replied.

Chennault would later write in his diary, "She will always be a princess to me."

Madame Chiang would also be well known to Americans thanks to her friends, publisher Henry Luce and his wife Claire Booth Luce. Luce launched both *Fortune* and *Time* magazines and acquired *Life* magazine in 1936. Chiang Kai-shek and Soong Mei-ling would appear eleven times on the cover of *Time* between 1927-1955. Luce intended to help the Washington D.C. China lobby, which included T.V. Soong, and inform Americans of the plight that faced China as they battled Japan.

With all her grace and charm Madame Chiang stayed focused on the job at hand and wanted to know exactly what was the state of the Chinese Air Force. She told Chennault that she wanted the unvarnished truth of the air force status. Madame Chiang knew that the air branch was rife with corruption and politics and she promptly instructed Chennault to begin his survey in Nanking and have a report ready for her in three months.

Madame Chiang provided Chennault with two Douglas BT-2 training aircraft for transportation. The BT-2 was a 1920s-designed biplane powered by a 510HP Packard 1A-1500 Vee engine, which could be best described as unreliable and that is being charitable. Only 29 examples of this engine were ever built. It is not known if Chennault (or the Chinese) were privy to the unreliability of this engine at the time. To help him along Chennault enlisted his old wingman Billy MacDonald along with mechanic Sebie Biggs Smith. Madame Chiang also provided Chennault with a personal interpreter, Colonel P.Y. Hsu, who remained by Chennault's side for the next eight years. Chennault during his lifetime would never be able to speak Chinese except for a few basic words and phrases.

Chennault would later write, "Flying to Nanking, I had my hand on the throttle again for the first time since the Air Corps grounded me the previous autumn. It felt good to be in the air again with Billy on my wing and a broad muddy river below that could have easily passed for the Mississippi."

After landing in Nanking, Chennault faced an entirely different scenario than the one he encountered in Shanghai. The city with rife with anti-Japanese rhetoric and that the local population believed a fight with the Japanese invaders was imminent. Chennault was not immediately concerned about potential Japanese aggression but the abysmal condition of the Chinese Air Force due to the complete control by the inept, back stab-

A Douglas O-2H (BT-2) observation plane at the NACA Langley Research Center at Hampton, Virginia on 10 January 1934 for evaluation. (U.S. Navy)

bing, and corrupt Italian officials. The Italians totally hoodwinked both the Generalissimo and H.H. Kung while aiding and abetting the Japanese.

Chennault soon discovered that the "official" inventory of 500 usable airplanes in the Chinese Air Force arsenal was just a meager 91 available for first-line duty. The Italian manufacturing plant at Nanchang was producing Fiat fighters that became firetraps in combat and Savoia-Marchetti bombers, so obsolete they were only suitable as transports. It might have been at this time that Fiat became synonymous with the old saying, "Fix it again Tony." In addition, aircraft demolished or no longer airworthy were never removed from the official inventory. It was a scam of epic proportions and Chennault wondered how the Gimo would take the sobering news.

More foreign ineptitude became evident at the Italian flight school in Loyang. It was here that Chennault learned the graduation rate was 100 percent. Under the Jouett mission years earlier only qualified students were advanced while the rest were quickly washed out. Since many of these students were from influential families high in the Chinese society pecking order, Chiang Kai-shek faced a flurry of anger from these folks. In China "face" was everything. The Italians "solved" the problem by graduating everyone and that made Chiang Kai-shek quite pleased. No complaints were forthcoming from the families who sent their sons off for aerial training although an inordinate number of them would be killed in training mishaps and if they survived they were so inept they would be killed during combat or on bombing missions. Face was everything.

Although Jouett was washing out students at a high rate, it was not just because of their flying ineptitude but for medical conditions. Unlike the Italians the Americans retained a flight surgeon to determine who was physically fit to fly. Chinese students were often subject to syphilis, tuberculosis, and internal parasites that rendered them useless as competent pilots. Chennault could only shake his head at the current level of incompetent pilot training.

Totally perplexed by local politics, the saving of face, Chinese society, and their culture in general, the Louisiana farm boy persisted and knew that if the Chinese Air Force was to survive and become an effective fighting force it would be by the American way – or no way at all. Events would ramp up in earnest while Chennault was in Loyang inspecting the facilities and personnel. On July 7, 1937, the Japanese attacked Chinese military personnel in what became known to Westerners as the Marco Polo Bridge Incident, effectively starting the second Sino-Japanese war and a déjà vu moment reminiscent of the Mukden Incident of 1931.

What occurred on that date can be traced back to the Boxer Protocol established on September 7, 1901. At that time China granted legations in Beijing the opportunity to station guards at twelve specific points along railways connecting Beijing with the port city of Tianjin to ensure communication between the capital and the port. By this time Japan expanded their military forces in China from 7,000 to more than 15,000 men far exceeding the number dictated by the Boxer Protocol.

Even after 80 years what happened at the Marco Polo Bridge is subject to debate. Around 11PM on the night of 7 July, Chinese and Japanese forces exchanged gunfire outside of Wanping, a small walled town about 10 miles south of Beijing. During this event, a Japanese soldier went missing and his commander demanded permission to enter Wanping to search for him and the Chinese promptly rejected the request. At some point the young Japanese soldier returned to his unit but both sides continued to mobilize.

The Japanese asked to enter the town to investigate his disappearance. No historical records indicate why a simple interrogation of the soldier was made to unearth his desertion. Once again, the Chinese refused the Japanese commander to enter Wanping and within hours both sides clashed at the walled enclave and this also included Marco Polo Bridge located 1,000 feet to the north. Japanese Foreign Service personnel met with their Chinese counterparts in Beijing and drew up a truce. Military commanders during the fighting took no heed and the skirmishes escalated resulting in the expulsion of Chinese forces from the area and a Japanese military victory. The Second Sino-Japanese War, albeit undeclared on paper, began in earnest, but like so many others in history from a relative insignificant incident.

Chennault immediately sent a telegram to the Generalissimo offering his services which were graciously accepted and he was directed to take over command of the combat flight school at Nanchang. It was here that Chennault would meet up once again with General Mao Bangchu (also translated as Mao Pang Tzu). Mao was an excellent pilot and a fine example of Russian training. Mao and Chennault stayed at the Burlington Hotel in Nanchang where the food was terrible but at least the beer was cold. The two would have many future arguments but remained friends over the years.

Mao met Chennault in January 1936 at the Pan-American Air Show in Miami, Florida and the last aerial performance of the Three Men on a Flying Trapeze. Mao was truly impressed with the performance and invited the trio to meet him on none other than William Pawley's yacht. Mao asked the trio to travel to China to become flight instructors. Chennault suggested Williamson and McDonald to go but held off committing himself. Also in attendance aboard Pawley's yacht was another friend of Chennault's, Roy Holbrook.

Mao Bangchu who would later run afoul of the Taiwanese government after the war and flee to Mexico. (Wikipedia commons)

Conditions at the airfield were horrible, with clouds of swirling dust occasionally matted down by an early evening thunderstorm. There were a few good pilots left over from Jouett's training mission, but most fell under the auspices of Italian training and were totally incompetent ruining many airplanes and often killing themselves in the process. But they did save face. After a short period of time at Nanchang, Chennault characterized the flight school and readiness of the Chinese combat and bomber pilots in his diary "…a nightmare."

In short order Chiang Kai-shek summoned both Chennault and General Mao to his summer capitol at Kuling among the mountain pines on the west shore of Poyang Lake. The Gimo wanted an update on his "500 aircraft" that comprised the Chinese Air Force arsenal. The pair arrived on 23 July and mounted a pair of hired sedan chairs lifted by coolies for the trek up the rocky slopes to the Generalissimo's bungalow. Mao, drenched in sweat, knew it was a day of reckoning. [6]

The pair were greeted by the Generalissimo and Madame Chiang. After the usual preliminary introductions, the Gimo turned to Mao.

"How many first-line planes are ready to fight?"

"Ninety-one, Your Excellency," Mao replied. [7]

Chiang exploded and began strutting about while voicing a torrent of words in Chinese at Mao who looked like he was about to melt like the wicked witch in the Wizard of Oz. Then Chiang turned to Chennault and asked the same question. Madame Chiang interpreted while he essentially gave the same answer and he continued for another twenty minutes giving his assessment of the Chinese Air Force until Madame indicated to him to stop. Chiang recapturing a calmer demeanor then left the room but did not return. But Mao was spared and his head did not roll down the mountainside into Poyang Lake. And the Gimo finally received an honest assessment of his air force for the first time since he had been in power and it came from a Westerner and something that would serve Chennault well going forward.

Chennault still did not have any written contract with the Chinese and determined to rectify this situation immediately. If you wanted to cover your ass you made damn sure it was in writing. Three days after meeting with Chiang he posted the following letter to the Aeronautical Commission with conditions he knew Madame Chiang would agree to:

Subject: Terms of Contract between the Aeronautical Commission and Col. C.L. Chennault.

To: The Senior Secretary, Commission on Aeronautical Affairs.

1. Upon returning here from Nanking, I had a conference with Mr. Holbrook with regards to the terms of my contract with the

Aeronautical Commission. He informs me that he forwarded the terms agreed upon before my departure from the United States to you by letter dated May 27, 1937, copy of which he furnished me. These terms were accepted by me and approved by Madame Chiang Kai-Shek and Dr. Kung.

2. The only features of the contract which are not definitely stated are included in paragraph 6 of Mr. Holbrook's letter: "Other features of contract satisfactory to both parties which are included in contract with American Military Advisors." While I am not acquainted with the features referred to in above quotations, I would like to have the following additional terms definitely included in the contract:

    a. Salary to be paid by the rate of U.S. $1,000.00 per month, exclusive of all taxes or deductions. Monthly payments to be made on the first day of each month following the last day of the month during which salary is unpaid. Payments to be deposited in the Chase Bank, Shanghai, to the credit of C.L. Chennault. Salary to begin on the date of sailing from the United States and to terminate on date of departure from China. In this case, the date of sail was May 8, 1937, via President Garfield from San Francisco, and receipt of first month's salary, U.S. $1,000.00, and travel expenses, U.S. $600.00 is acknowledged.

    b. The Chinese government shall provide an airplane of the type specified by Col. Chennault for the purpose of making flights on official business, flights for demonstration and instructional purposes, and flights for the maintenance of flying proficiency. The airplane shall be serviced and maintained by the Chinese government without cost to the party of the first part, and shall not be held liable for its damage or loss while being employed for the purposes named.

    c. The party of the first part shall be entitle to the travel allowances authorized for foreign aviation advisors when required to travel from his usual place of duty by official orders or instructions. The provision shall apply from date of arrival in China to the date of departure from China, travel allowance from the U.S. to China and from China to the U.S. having agreed upon in paragraph _ of this contract.

    d. This contract shall be subject to cancellation by either party upon ninety days written notice. In case of cancellation by either party, the party of the first part shall be paid in full to the last day of the notice period and shall then be paid the travel allowance agreed upon in paragraph _ of this contract. (Allowance for return to the U.S. from China.)

NOTE: The provision exempting my salary from income tax or other deductions is included because I accepted the salary offered, U.S. $1,000.00 per month, as the minimum net offer which I could consider. This agreement was reached before the passage of the Income Tax law and the payment of the tax will result in a considerable reduction from the net terms agreed upon. If payment of the tax cannot be waived, my salary should be increased by an amount equal to the tax.

3. After considering this matter, I have come to the conclusion that this contract should be signed immediately so that there can be no possibility of a misunderstanding by either party. If cancellation is desired by either party at the end of the period agreed upon for making a survey of military aviation in China, it can be obtained by exercising the cancellation option. It is requested that you have the contract drawn, submitted to the Aeronautical Commission for approval, and forwarded to me for signature without delay.

4. My address until further notice is: Central Aviation School, Hangchow.

Thank you and the members of the Aviation Commission for the courtesies extended to me during my recent visit, I am
Most sincerely,
C.L. Chennault
Colonel, Aviation [8]

    Chennault certainly covered all of his bases. Although he was an intelligent man, Chennault was certainly no lawyer and it appears he had retained some cooperation in composing the document, perhaps enlisting the aid of his friend W. H. Donald and a local attorney. With the money involved in the Chennault contract and the salary of the average American worker at just $1780 yearly, China welcomed the birth of a true aviation mercenary.

Mercenaries and Americans?

CHENNAULT MAY HAVE NOT been the only aerial warrior for hire by China. On 6 August, a curious affair was taking place in California as the *Los Angeles Times* reported that a local entrepreneur and soldier of fortune named Russell L. Hearn had recruited 182 American pilots and a similar number of mechanics to fight on behalf of the Chinese. [9] Hearn was purportedly associated with a one-time war lord in Manchuria named Marshal Chang Tso-lin.

The official Japan news agency, *Domei*, took note of this activity and reported that the Japanese government was considering lodging a protest about this activity and stated that it was in direct conflict of the United States Neutrality Act. The American Ambassador in Japan, Joseph Grew, immediately telegraphed Hull saying in part:

> *I told the Minister [Japanese Foreign Minister] that as he must well know the American Government will do everything in its legal power to discourage or deter Americans from fighting in foreign armies. I also pointed out that the Neutrality Act is a domestic matter and that its interpretation by foreigners is difficult.* [9]

This story was immediately picked up by the wire services and published by newspapers across the Unites States. The State Department immediately took steps to prevent American citizens from joining the Chinese Air Force stating that "...the prohibitions imposed on American citizens by Revised Statutes, Section 4090 and 4102, are still in force." Within days passports for American citizens were further restricted indicating that, "This passport is not valid for travel to or in any foreign state in connection with entrance into service in foreign military or naval forces." [10] Madame Chiang Kai-shek was incensed and informed the State Department that to prevent American instructors to teach Chinese pilots to fly American made planes was "unneutral."

What is interesting is that the story of Russell L. Hearn exploded in a blinding flash on the front page of papers across the United States and disappeared just as quickly. The story hit the news services and a couple of days after it first appeared, the story of Hearn and his attempt to recruit mercenary pilots and mechanics for China vaporized into thin air. No further reference to him appears in newspapers or in government documents. Chenault does not mention his name in his memoirs that he published several years later and there is no evidence that any pilots or mechanics ever travelled to China as part of this enterprise. Was this a ruse by the China lobby, the United States government, or some type of scam perpetrated by the man named Hearn? Right now, it is just a footnote lost to history. One thing is clear – Chennault continued his quest to obtain more American pilots for the Chinese effort even though Cordell Hull and the State Department attempted to blunt his efforts.

As Chennault continued to entice more American pilots to join the Chinese cause the Japanese bombed Shanghai on 13 August. Seeking immediate retribution Madame Chiang turned to Chennault and asked if he could draw up an attack plan. With his limited knowledge of the opposing forces and the time restraints placed upon him, Chennault suggested Curtiss Hawk dive bombers attack the Japanese cruisers and that Northrop light bombers take out the armored cruiser *Izumo* (sometimes transliterated as *Idzumo*). [11] The *Izumo*, anchored at Whangpo, on the edge of Shanghai was essentially a hotel and meeting place for Japanese naval officers. Despite his resume, Chennault's first operational mission

The Japanese cruiser *Izumo* off Oahu February 25, 1925. (NARA)

would be a total failure and a day that would become known in China as "Black Saturday."

With bad weather over Shanghai the mission should have been aborted but the Chinese pilots decided to fly under the overcast at 1,500 feet. The Chinese bombing training was based on dropping ordnance on a target at a fixed airspeed at an altitude at 7,500 feet. They all failed to make the necessary adjustments and wound up dropping bombs on the International Settlement killing over 1,000 people and wounding another 1,200. The *Izumo* wasn't even scratched.

The Chinese fighter pilots fared better the same afternoon shooting down three Japanese Model-96 bombers over Jianjiao, four Model-94 bombers elsewhere, sixteen bombers over Hangzhou and another fourteen over Nanjing. Over a three-day period, Chinese fighters brought down a total of 42 planes, earning respect for their aerial exploits and shaking up the confidence of officers within the Japanese Navy and the perceived superiority they had on paper over the Chinese.

It was only a couple of weeks later the CAF bomber pilots once again showed their ineptitude. After the bombing of Shanghai, the Dollar Line ship SS *President Hoover* was diverted from Hong Kong to Shanghai to evacuate American nationals from the stricken city. A 30-foot US flag was draped topside near the stern to denote her neutrality to both the Chinese and Japanese. That did not deter the Chinese bombers. On a mission to attack the Japanese troopship *Asama Maru*, Chinese pilots managed to drop two bombs on the *Hoover*, killing one man and wounding several others while structural damage was minimal.

Chiang Kai-shek, who was friends with the late Robert Dollar took the attack personally. The Generalissimo was so infuriated he reportedly threatened to execute the officer responsible only to learn it was his new hire, Claire Chennault who orchestrated the operation. It is interesting to note that this mission, and several similar ones, are never mentioned in Chennault's biography published in 1949. It also did not dissuade the Generalissimo to give him a $10,000 bonus shortly thereafter.

In September, Madame Chiang presented Chennault with his own personal airplane, a Curtiss Hawk H75-M-Special she purchased from Pawley three months earlier at a cost of $55,000. This was a sleek fixed gear monoplane developed in 1935 and powered by the unreliable Wright XR-1820 producing 850 horsepower but had the selling point that it could be fitted with several different engines. Fast and maneuverable the Hawk H75 could also double as a light bomber and was especially effective on reconnaissance ventures. The Curtiss Hawk would be the precursor to the

P-36 Mohawk and later the P-40 Tomahawk.

Chennault went further and added additional armor plating around the pilot seat. This was truly the earmark of future American planes as vital protection of the pilot was incorporated in their designs. On the contrary, the Japanese opted for a lighter aircraft weight with minimal pilot protection and this would prove to have disastrous consequences for them in the upcoming years. American warplanes could withstand a tremendous amount of battle damage, whereas the Japanese planes would be turned into heaps of unrepairable scrap even if they manage to return home after a mission.

Chennault's Hawk 75 was superior to the principal fighter for China at the time, the Hawk III, an export version of the U.S. Navy's Curtiss BF2C-1 biplane, without the metal wings that model employed. It was discovered during flight tests that the metal-structured wing produced serious vibration inflight and at least one plane disintegrated during a power dive. Curtiss returned to the traditional wood wing structure on the Hawk III. Powered by Wright SR-1820F-53 Cyclone engine producing 785 horsepower at takeoff, it had a maximum speed of 240mph at 11,500ft. Between March 1936 and June 1938 China purchased 102 of them of which all but twelve were assembled by CAMCO at their Hangzhou facility.

A Curtiss Hawk 75 in Finnish service. About 1,000 were built and it was a commercial success for Curtiss. Unlike the Hawk Special it featured retractable landing gear. (NARA)

In mid-September Japan resumed their aerial attack on Nanking and the bombers were now accompanied by a new fighter, the Mitsubishi A5M-Type 96 (named as "Claude" by the Allies in 1942) from the Japanese Navy's Second Combined Air Flotilla. Japan's first carrier-borne aircraft was an open cockpit all metal monoplane powered by a Nakajima Kotobuki radial engine producing 615 horsepower. The only Chinese aircraft that could seriously engage them at the time was the Russian Polikarpov I-16 and the Curtiss Hawk III. The difference would be the expertise of the pilots involved and the Japanese flying the Claude fighters were among the best.

With the new Mitsubishi A5M and superb pilots the Japanese easily ruled the skies over Nanking. But a major problem was much closer to home. And as Pogo the possum quipped in the classic 1971 cartoon, "We are the enemy and he is us." Pogo might have well been describing the Chinese airmen flying advanced aircraft at the time.

On one occasion Chennault watched as eleven dive bombers took to the air from the Nanking airfield. A few hours later while having tea with Madame Chiang the pair observed all undamaged eleven planes return and circle the field to land. Within minutes five crashed while attempting to land and four pilots were killed. Madame Chiang, with tears in her eyes said, "What can we do, what can we do? We buy them the best airplanes money can buy, spend so much time and money training them, and they are killing themselves before my eyes. What can we do?" [12]

Chennault knew the answer was with better training – United Army Corps style training - yes better training and perhaps a good dose of American pilots to pave the way. The Generalissimo couldn't wait for the Chennault effect to kick in and moved his government inland, first to Hankow and a few months later to Chungking. This would be about 2,000 miles from Nanking and allow for the building of new airfields unfettered from Japanese aerial attacks so that training could resume. It also would have reinforced the Chinese doctrine developed over many years to "absorb" the Japanese rather than confront them.

On 29 September, Clarence E. Gauss, the American consul general at Shanghai, telegrammed his superiors at the State Department with his concerns about the activities of their new Chinese aviation advisor. Gauss indicated Chennault attempted to recruit local American pilots to fly Martin planes to bomb Tokyo and receive $25,000 each for the flight. If they happen to sink a Japanese aircraft carrier in the course of their duties, they would receive a $200,0000 bonus. [13]

Where Gauss got this information is not known. In Chennault's memoir, *The Way of a Fighter* there is no mention of this proposal. And with his recently signed contract providing him a stipend of $1,000 a month for his services it is highly unlikely that he could authorize such exorbitant amounts even if the proposal was practical or even possible.

With an undeclared Sino-Japanese war both Roosevelt and Hull engaged in a juggling act involving the United States Neutrality Act. Roosevelt instituted a partial embargo against both China and Japan which would still allow for American ships to transport aircraft and munitions to China. Hull would handle the problem of American civilians who would like to travel to China to be employed as pilots or aviation advisers.

The situation quickly escalated when the Japanese learned that an American vessel, the S.S. *Wichita*, was to depart Baltimore, Maryland on 28 August bound for China with nineteen Bellanca aircraft and other assorted war materiel on board. Newspaper accounts characterized the aircraft as "bombers" but when queried by the State Department, designer Giuseppe Bellanca insisted these were cargo aircraft originally designed to carry U.S. mail. Powered by a single 900 horsepower Pratt and Whitney engine and a crew of three, the planes could carry a 1,000-pound payload for 1,000 miles, at 280 miles-per-hour. Presumably these planes could be converted to a bomber configuration and possibly strike the Japanese homeland. Three days before the planned departure of the *Wichita* the Japanese Navy announced a blockade of the Chinese coasts and announced that the *Wichita* would be intercepted because it carried military airplanes.

Hull was incensed by this blockade statement and informed both Japan and China that the Neutrality Act did not apply since there was no declaration of war between the two Asian countries. Another mitigating factor is that the *Wichita* was owned by the United States government but operated by a private business, the American Pioneer Company. The proposed shipment of aircraft to China also brought the ire of American isolationists and several peace societies. Commerce Secretary Daniel C. Roper fanned the flames in a press statement saying:

> *The* Wichita *is a vessel owned by the Federal Government but leased to American citizens. It is therefore not under the direct control of the Federal Government. Under their own statement, we have no reason to believe that the Japanese embargo will be enforced against vessels which are bona fide under the supervision of citizens of this Nation.* [14]

American pacifists were infuriated and telegrammed the President with their displeasure. Ultimately the Unites States caved in and the cargo of 19 planes along with two cases of revolvers on board were off loaded from the ship when it docked in San Pedro, California to refuel. President Roosevelt was in Hyde Park at the time but upon his return to Washington, D.C. and conferring with Hull the following press statement was released on 14 September:

> *Merchant vessels owned by the Government of the United States will not hereafter, until further notice, be permitted to transport to China or Japan any of the arms, ammunition, or implements of war which were listed in the president's proclamation of May 1, 1937.*
>
> *Any other merchant vessels, flying the American flag, which attempt to transport any of the listed articles to China or Japan will, until further notice, do so at their own risk.*
>
> *The question of applying the Neutrality Act remains in status quo, the Government policy remaining on a 24-hour basis.* (15)

The appeasement of the Japanese by the Americans would have repercussions for years to come culminating with the attack on Pearl Harbor. The British also bowed to the Japanese will when the British Board of Trade suggested that British ships allow Japanese naval officers to board their merchant ships for inspection. The Japanese would continue to exploit the weaknesses shown by the Americans and British sensing that neither country had the testicular fortitude for a war in the Pacific.

The Partial American Embargo

WITH THEIR AIR FORCE in tatters and a "partial" American embargo in place, even the calculating Pawley could not sell enough aircraft to the Chinese to satisfy their needs. On August 21, 1937 Chinese officials pivoted quickly and signed the Sino-Soviet Non-Aggression Pact and sought out aid from the Soviet Union who were unencumbered by any perceived embargo. Truly a shame, as the Chinese would have preferred getting as many American planes, and pilots, as possible. Aircraft, pilots, and war munition would be secretly sent to China as part of "Operation Zet." Russia also realized supplying China could help blunt the Japanese expansion into Northeastern Asia. For the next two years Soviet aircraft and pilots would dominate the skies over China. Yet Chennault would remain - Perhaps in the background, but continuously planning and eventually emerging as

China's best hope.

On 14 September, Chinese Ambassador Wang Zhengting met with Roosevelt to express country's displeasure over the partial embargo enacted by the United States. Wang knew it would hurt China immensely, especially in acquiring American military aircraft, while the Japanese simply considered it a slap on the wrist for China being shut off from weapons and munitions. Yet it did mean that the scales of war were decidedly tipped in favor of Japan.

Chinese ambassador Wang Zhengting. (LOC)

Roosevelt reminded Zhengting that, had the Neutrality Act been fully invoked, China would receive absolutely no material aid. Yet the President was not about to leave beleaguered country completely high and dry. Roosevelt was constantly juggling the politics of foreign aid to presumed allies amongst his own military, pacifists, isolationists, and his own State Department. Ever the crafty politician, Roosevelt had an ace up his sleeve and showed it to Zhengting – the United States could still send some military aid but via a third party, one not involved in the Sino-Japanese conflict. The materials could then be forwarded to China. The Chinese ambassador recognized a glimmer of hope from this correspondence and thanked the President.

This partial embargo would hurt China much more than Japan. Roosevelt essentially caved into Japan's demands fearing a provocation occurring on the high seas that would pull the United States into a conflict with Japan. Japan took note of this reluctance on the part of the United States and became more aggressive with their military and political policies. With the decline of American warplanes entering China towards the end of 1937 the Soviets ramped up their assistance to the beleaguered nation.

Initially, Chennault was not actively involved in helping the Chinese obtain military aircraft but was instead engaged in aggressively recruiting American aviators to provide instructional assistance and suppling advisors to the Chinese government to assist them in interacting with American officials. Opposing Chennault was Secretary of State Cordell Hull whose office refused to furnish passports to anyone travelling to China, except under special circumstances, where it was endorsed, "This passport is not valid for travel to or in any foreign state in connection with entrance into or service in foreign military or naval forces." [16] This proclamation from Hull was enough to spook four American instructors in China who promptly left the country and returned home.

Chennault persevered and continued to seek out American aviators to support China and managed to corral Gerald Lee Cherymisin, a five-year veteran and second lieutenant in United States Army Air Corps. Offered a $550 a month stipend from the Chinese aviation bureau, Cherymisin resigned from the Air Corps and travelled to San Francisco to begin his voyage to China. Informed he would not be issued a passport by the State Department, the local Chinese consul informed him that none was needed and he just needed to provide a birth certificate along with other identification. Cherymisin boarded the S.S. *President Coolidge* for Hong Kong and was eventually passed through customs with no problem, albeit without a valid United States passport.

As the United States vacillated on what to do in the Far East as displayed by employing a partial arms embargo against China, the Japanese took full advantage of the perceived reluctance of the United States to fully enter the fray. On December 12, the Japanese attacked and sunk the American gunboat USS *Panay* (PR-5), anchored 28 miles north of Nanjing on the Yangzi River.

The *Panay* was launched in November 1927 and was built by the Kiangnan Dockyard and Engineering Works, Shanghai. With a length of 191 feet, her job was to protect American civilians, property, and shipping along the Yangzi River. Three Yokosuka B4Y Type-96 bombers dropped eighteen 130-pound bombs, two of which hit the *Panay*. Nine Nakajima A4N Type-95 fighters then continued to strafe the stricken vessel until she sank with the loss of three men and the wounding of 43 merchantmen and civilians.

USS *Panay* (PR-5). (Naval History and Heritage Command)

In a typical fashion that continues to this day involving such violent incidents, Ambassador Grew formally protested Japan's actions over this deadly event. The Japanese quickly apologized for the sinking of the *Panay* stating it was a mistake and promptly offered the American government two million dollars for compensation. As Dorothy Berg, a historian and expert in Asian affairs would later state, that it exemplified the attempt of Japan to eliminate American interests in China while President Roosevelt would not take any actions that could possibly lead to war. The

Panay affair is just another event that would forge a link in a long chain that would culminate in the United States for their desire to attack Japan with Chinese marked American bombers and Japan's decision to attack Pearl Harbor four years later.

On December 13, 1937, just a day after the Japanese attack on the USS *Panay* a seminal event took place as the Japanese attacked the capitol of the Republic of China, Nanking, and destroyed the city and its residents. In the pursuing six weeks mass murders and rape of her citizens committed by Japanese soldiers involved a low estimate of 40,000 as stated by Japanese, to as many as 300,000 by Chinese estimates. It became known worldwide as the Nanking Massacre or the Rape of Nanking.

During 1937 as Chennault focused on the training of Chinese airman, he would occasionally submit requests for suitable aircraft to the Aeronautical Affairs Commission for purchase. Unbeknownst to Chennault these requests were first reviewed by the minister of finance, H.H. Kung before being forward to T.V. Soong for approval. Yet Kung had a sweet deal with Pawley and any American aircraft purchased by China had the stamp of Pawley on it, which included his commission and a cut to Kung.

Pawley stayed on Kung's coattails during 1937 as Kung was his cash cow in China. Pawley followed him throughout Europe and even helped establish a London office to facilitate arms sales to China. The affair was becoming so transparent that even Secretary of the Treasury Henry Morgenthau, Jr. was informed of the possible ramifications. Still as 1937 ended, Pawley didn't face pressure from the Chinese government or Morgenthau but from the Japanese. Moving around China was no longer as it once was, and Pawley wrote:

> *I went down with Allison and Juan [Trippe] in a Vultee bomber-all guns ready and we expected to meet Japs but were lucky and landed just as the alarm was given. I ran for a car and went to the Wall gate and saw the Japs drop bombs on the field. Our ship was not hit, several others were. The next day we went to take off at 7 AM, but just as we were taking off, we got an alarm and had to wait at the Wall. This happened 3 times, and at 11:30 we started. 10 minutes out we saw 3 Japs in bombers, but they didn't trouble us as they were going to bomb Nangking [sic]. We got here OK, and that's the last time I'll do that.* (17)

And with that one event, making easy money wasn't so laid-back anymore. Viewing this event today it is hard for someone to consider the extent that a person would endanger himself to consummate a sales deal involving some airplanes. But remember this was late 1930s and China, and that the allure of the all-American dollar during a depression satisfied the risk for the reward. Soon after the event Pawley left China for the United States and this meant Kung remained to deal with the "little" mess that was left behind, if only temporarily.

Fourteenth International Squadron

As 1937 ended, China was in dire straits. Chiang Kai-Shek's armies were decimated by the Japanese and both Nanking and Shanghai had fallen to the invaders. Both qualified pilots and front-line aircraft were in short supply. For that reason, the Chinese abruptly decided to seek out mercenary fighter and bomber pilots to replenish their diminished ranks. Whether this idea emerged from the Generalissimo or Madame Chiang is not clear, but it is certain that Chennault did not initiate this idea, nor did he endorse it. Chinese consulates around the world were ordered to seek out prospective pilots. Chennault himself reached out to a couple of CNAC pilots he knew, Julius Barr (Madame Chiang's personal pilot) and Royal Leonard and see if they might be able to recruit some experienced pilots in the Philippines or back in the United States who they were familiar with. Those pilots that came forward to "volunteer" to fight for China did include a few exceptional pilots. For the most part they were either inept, inexperienced, or over-the-hill. It was a motley group of men and the whole idea was doomed from the start, but Chennault promised the Madame he would do his best to pull it all together.

The group consisted of an assortment of Americans, Germans, Frenchmen, and one Dutchman. Those with experience included Vincent Schmidt who flew combat missions during World War I, and in Mexico, Spain, and Ethiopia. Another seasoned pilot was Jim Allison who sided with the Republicans in Spain and locked horns with the Germans and Italians. Other Americans included Elwyn Gibbon, George Weigle, Ray Whitehead, and Tommy Walker. These pilots would become the newly constituted Fourteenth International Squadron. Chennault weeded out the deadbeats early on but quickly found himself in the difficult position of trying to turn this group of misfits into a cohesive fighter force. Promised $1,000 (Chinese) for downing each Japanese fighter along with a base salary, most pilots ultimately spent more time in seedy bars or whorehouses than in time aloft.

Former transport pilots were the most competent to fly bombers with minimal training required and this included Gibbon, Weigle, Allison, and another American named Lyman Woelpel. Chennault trusted Schmidt in his abilities and made him a squadron commander and lead instructor for bomber pilots. For the rest of the fliers, he hoped they would limit their time on "Dump Street", a collection of dive bars and whore houses along with an abundant supply of Japanese spies that infested them. As the liquor flowed so too did the military plans for those within earshot.

Chennault did not believe that the Fourteenth International Squadron had much of a future. This was evident as one of the Frenchman was killed on his first time aloft as he came in for what would be evidently a very poor landing after a short training flight. Nonetheless, training continued and Chennault reluctantly planned their first mission for January 23, 1938.

The attack would incorporate several Vultee V-11G single-engine bombers that the CAF possessed. The initial order for the bomber was placed way back in 1935 but the kits did not arrive to the CAMCO facility in Loiwing until the latter part of 1937 where they were assembled. The V-11 was obsolete before it even went into the air. It was derived from the unsuccessful V-1 passenger transport, crewed by two under a massive greenhouse canopy and mustered a cruise speed of just 188 miles per hour from her single Wright R-1820-G2 Cyclone 850hp engine.

30 Vultee V-11 aircraft were ordered by China, but only 25 were assembled at Loiwing before the plant was bombed by the Japanese. (SDASM)

The initial bombing target Chennault planned for the mercenary pilots was an airfield near Anyang and would comprise four Vultee bombers for the attack. Two of the bombers turned back to base before reaching their target and another plane crashed for unexplained reasons. One bomber managed to make it to Anyang but couldn't locate the airfield and returned home with all its bombs intact.

In the next few weeks several small missions were conducted targeting rail heads, airfields, and bridges. These were token efforts by the fourteenth although for unknown reasons two French pilots prepared for attacking Kagoshima on the Japanese mainland with incendiary bombs. This plan may have been formulated by Chennault who always favored the bombing of Japanese cities with incendiary ordnance since his initial visit, but the idea never matured – at least at this time - and the intended bombing run, that may have been hatched over several drinks at a bar, never took place. [18]

The end of the volunteer squadron came quickly – not in the air but on the ground. Chennault planned a mission to bomb troop depots at Tsinan. The day before the planned attack the Vultee bombers were refueled, armed, and neatly lined up on the runway so that they would be ready for their predawn takeoff. One or more of the pilots must have blabbed about the mission at one of the many bars on Dump Street and within hearing of a Japanese spy on that day because the Japanese attacked the airfield at sundown. Just one bomb was needed to cause a chain reaction and destroy every plane on the line. Chennault would later write: "What was left of the Chinese bombing force vanished in five seconds of flame and dust. With it went the jobs of the International Squadron pilots." [19] The mistake that was called the Fourteenth Volunteer Squadron and was officially disbanded on March 22, 1938.

Soviet Volunteer Group

FOLLOWING THE MARCO POLO BRIDGE INCIDENT in July, China and the Soviet Union signed a non-aggression pact on 21 August. Although it did not explicitly state that the Soviets would provide material and military assistance it was generally recognized between both parties that aid would be forthcoming. Dictator Joseph Stalin keenly understood his country's position during this time - A potential threat from the west with the German Nazi regime and to the east Japan. China would become a superb foil to blunt potential Japanese aggression at a minimal cost to the Soviet Union.

In September the Soviet Orgburo (a parallel government group to the Politburo and with extensive power) secretly dictated that a military air mission would be sent to China. They ordered that 155 fighters, eight Yakovlev UT-4 trainers, and 62 bombers be sent to China as soon as possible. The aircraft included:

Polikarpov I-15 – The biplane fighter, first flown in 1933

was nicknamed Chaika (Seagull) for its gulled upper wing. It fought for the Republicans in the Spanish Civil War but with a top speed of 220 miles-per-hour by 1938 it was truly obsolete and had no place in modern aerial warfare.

Polikarpov I-16 – First flown in December 1933 this aircraft was a revolutionary design that featured a cantilevered monoplane wing and retractable landing (the first operational aircraft of this type in the world) and had a top speed of 326 miles-per-hour. Soviet pilots nicknamed the plane "Ishachok" (donkey) for its stubby appearance. In early 1941 it could still match the current production German Messerschmitt Bf 109 with the right pilot at the controls.

Tupolev ANT-40 – With the service name of Tupolev SB, it was the most advanced Soviet bomber at the time. This twin-engine aircraft was first flown in 1934 and had a top speed of 280 miles-per-hour and a range of 1429 miles with a crew of three on board. The bomb bay could retain six 220-pound bombs and two 550-pound bombs on wing racks.

In October, after a brief ceremony in Moscow, 450 Soviet pilots and mechanics assembled for the huge delivery of aircraft to China. Although dubbed the "Soviet Volunteer Group" they were all preselected by Soviet Air Force commander Aleksandr Lotionov and his deputy Yako Smushkevich. In the Soviet Union no one ever volunteered and just went to wherever their orders told them to go – even if it was to pick up stakes from the Spanish Civil War and continue another fight in China. Upon their arrival in China half of the aircraft were turned over to the Chinese Air Force who desperately needed them as their entire flying inventory was perhaps just 100 serviceable aircraft. The presence of the Soviet pilots also bolstered the morale of the Chinese pilots who started to acquire a defeatist mentality. And in short order the Soviets would flex their aviation muscle against the Japanese.

On 23 February, three Chinese squadrons of Soviet SB-2 bombers with a mix of Soviet-Chinese crews launched a raid on Songshan (Matsuyama) near Taipei on the island of Formosa (now known as Taiwan). This is the base where many Japanese bombers have departed from to attack the China mainland. After-action reports vary from the bomber crews failing to find their targets to the destruction of twelve planes on the ground and three hangars. This would be the first transoceanic military action taken by the Chinese Air Force, but not the last.

Bomb Run on the Japanese Homeland

WHILE THE SOVIETS RAMPED up their support of the Chinese Air Force in late 1937 and throughout 1938, six Curtiss-Martin B-10 bombers were delivered to the Chinese in February and August of 1937 of which three were immediately assembled. The Chinese export version was designated Model 139WC and was powered by two Wright R-1820-33 radial piston engines developing 775 horsepower each and provided the aircraft with a maximum range of 1,243 miles and a cruise speed of 193 miles-per-hour. With enclosed cockpits, rotating gun turrets, an internal bomb bay, and retractable landing gear it became a base design for all future bombers in the United States for decades to come. One thing that could not be overlooked even by the casual observer is that it was one damn ugly looking airplane to see in the sky.

The Martin B-10 in flight would never win a beauty contest. (Wikipedia commons)

Just two months after disbandment of the Fourteenth Volunteer Squadron, the Chinese would conduct an extraordinary aerial mission and an event hardly mentioned by aviation historians – the bombing of the Japanese homeland itself. This mission, relegated to the dustbin of history, would have an implicit impact on Japanese military strategists in the upcoming years even after the attack on Pearl Harbor.

It is not known who initiated the idea of the aerial bombing mission, but it was certainly not Chennault. Earlier in February a mission was planned that would have two French pilots from the Fourteenth target Kagoshima with incendiary bombs, but the plan was scuttled for unknown reasons. The Chinese had a number of SB-2s at their disposal but decided to use the American made Martin B-10 twin-engine bomber that had a better range

The B-10 entered service in 1934 and was the first all-metal monoplane bomber to be used by the United States Army Air Corps and faster than many contemporary fighters at that time. With a crew of three the B-10 had a cruise speed of 193 mph and range of 1,240 miles, and a bomb load of 2,260 pounds. It also incorporated forward thinking concepts such as enclosed cockpits, retractable gear, and rotating gun turrets. When it was introduced, General Hap Arnold described it as the airpower wonder of its day, obviously based on its performance and not appearances.

Heading the bombing mission was Captain Hsu Huan-sheng, a squadron leader of the ill-fated all volunteer 14th Squadron and the second plane piloted by 1Lt. Teng Yan-po, leader of the 19th Squadron. The 19th had flown Heinkel HE 11 A-0 bombers in 1937 and there is little doubt that these two pilots were the most experienced medium range bomber pilots in the CAF.

On 19 May, the two Chinese Martin B-10s, serial numbers 1403 and 1404, jammed with propaganda leaflets departed for the Kyushu and Honshu region of Japan with their intent of dropping their flyers over five different cities. Ideally Chennault would prefer dropping incendiary bombs, but Generalissimo Chiang Kai-shek in a naïve attempt at propaganda had opted to drop leaflets and a message of goodwill to the Japanese people detailing the atrocities perpetrated by the Japanese Army on Chinese civilians. The leaflets would land on deaf ears.

It was a token gesture by the Chinese and the propaganda leaflets had left no discernible effect on the Japanese civilians. Experts have later stated that the Chinese simply could not have on board bombs for a long-range mission. This is not true. The Chinese could have substituted a similar weight in incendiary bombs but chose not to do so. The Japanese military on the other hand was concerned by the potential lethal bombing of their homeland by the Chinese and ordered all cities to maintain blackout conditions at night and this order would be enforced for the next eleven months.

There is little doubt that both Chennault, Soong, and the Generalissimo were informed of this successful mission and would like to take this accomplishment further by using incendiary bombs against the Japanese. As history has shown the next attack against the Japanese homeland would not take place until 1942 when Jimmy Doolittle led sixteen B-25B Mitchell medium bombers to strike the heartland of Japan. Yet the seed of the idea that Japan could be bombed, and effectively, took hold and our cast of characters acting on behalf of China would soon promote this idea to the highest leaders within the United States government, albeit with mixed results.

Chennault versus Pawley versus Patterson

Throughout the summer of 1938 CAMCO continued to receive crated Curtiss-Wright Hawk 75 airplanes as they arrived in Hong Kong, where they were shipped to Loiwing by rail and boat. The assembled product was less than desired as their top speed was just 255 miles per hour at 8,500 feet. Factory specifications stated 275 miles per hour at 10,500 feet.

CAMCO personnel in a photo that was taken at the Loiwing factory's opening. William Pawley is second from left, at rear. Eugene Pawley, his brother, is at the rear on the right. (Topdeadcenter at English Wikipedia)

The summer of 1938 would be the start a a full-fledged feud between Chennault and Pawley. It started with the assembly of the Hawk 75s at Pawley's Loiwing factory and Chennault's claims that the flight specifications fell well short of Pawley's performance statements. Pawley in turn said it was due to Chennault's modifications of insisting on a larger battery and fuselage changes.

Chennault would also blame Pawley for the recent Japanese advances because the salesman was able to block the acquisition of his competitor's (Seversky) pursuit planes. Chennault even wrote to Curtiss-Wright stating, "Personally I would welcome a radical change in the methods and attitude of Mr. Pawley as I am confident that it would be for the benefit of China." Of course, based on Pawley's sales performance, Curtiss-

Wright had no intention of replacing him.

With the continuous coverage by American newspapers of the incessant bombing of Chinese civilians and swayed by public opinion, the State Department finally decided to act against the Japanese. Joseph C. Green, Chief of the Office of Arms and Munitions Control, Department of State, sent a letter to 148 individuals and manufacturers who export aircraft and airplane parts. In part Green stated:

> *In view of the fact that the Secretary's statement definitely condemned bombing of civilian populations from the air, it should be clear to all concerned that the Government of the United States is strongly opposed to the sale of airplanes or aeronautical equipment which would materially aid or encourage that practice in any countries in any part of the world. Therefore, in view of this policy, the Department would with great regret issue any licenses authorizing exportation, direct or indirect, of any aircraft, aircraft armament, aircraft engines, aircraft parts, aircraft accessories, aerial bombs or torpedoes to countries the armed forces of which are making use of airplanes for attack upon civilian populations.* [20]

What is incredulous is that the United States implemented a partial Chinese embargo of aircraft months before placing an embargo, albeit an informal one, on sales to Japan. In 1938 the State Department issued export licenses for aircraft sales to Japan to the tune of approximately $9 million. This would drop to less than $800,000 in 1939.

Pawley's main competitor in China was Allen L. "Pat" Patterson, president of the Consolidated Trading Company. The Canadian born Patterson, a World War I pilot, could be considered an "old China hand," arriving in China in 1935 and forming the Airmotive Company in Shanghai. Once again blurring the lines between private enterprise and government bureaucracy, Patterson served as Bureau of Air Commerce inspector with direct access to the State Department in Washington, D.C. at the same time.

In 1937, Patterson would heed the U.S. Embassy directive that all Americans leave Nanking as soon as possible. He made his way safely to the gunboat *Panay* and was onboard when it was attacked by Japanese aircraft. He survived with no injuries and would later return to China representing Chance-Vought, Boeing. and other aviation interests.

Pawley was enraged when he learned that Patterson's Consolidated Trading Company managed to cobble together a credit line of

$12,800,000 for "his" trading ally, H.H. Kung in February 1939. It was a convoluted deal that would provide China with the following aircraft:

    50 Seversky EP-1 pursuits
    50 Ryan STC-4 two-place primary trainers
    50 North American NA16-4 basic trainers
    25 Chance Vought SB-21 dive bombers
    20 Ryan STC-P4 single-place pursuit trainers
    4 Seversky STC-4 biplane pursuits

The sheer size of the order would be an incredible boost to the Chinese Air Force. The model EP-1 was the export version of the Seversky P-35, the first single-seat fighter for United States Army Air Corps to feature all-metal construction, retractable landing gear, and an enclosed cockpit. Powered by a Pratt & Whitney R-1830-45 Twin Wasp radial engine producing 1,050 hp with a cruise speed of 260 mph. Armament consisted of two 30-caliber M1919 and two 50-caliber Browning machine guns. The aircraft could also carry 350 pounds of bombs. U.S. Air Corps deliveries were completed in 1938 at which time the aircraft was already considered obsolete.

The Seversky EP-1. Fighter. The company damaged its reputation with the American government after selling 20 SEV-2PA-83 fighters to Japan. (NASM)

As China sought out to purchase military American aircraft, on display was the incomprehensible foreign policy of the United States in Asia. This is evident with the Seversky A8V-1, a two-seat version of the P-35 with a rear gunner. Twenty of these variants were sold to the Japanese Imperial Navy and ultimately saw action against the Chinese. During

World War II the allied code name for the A8V-1 was "Dick."

The Chance Vought SB2U-1 was a carrier based, two-seat, single-engine monoplane powered by a Pratt & Whitney R-1535 Twin-Wasp Junior radial engine rated at 825 hp. The fuselage was a mixed bag of steel tube construction and covered with aluminum panels. Aft of the rear cockpit the fuselage was covered with fabric. The folding cantilever wing was of all-metal construction. It could carry a single 1,000-pound bomb and had a maximum speed of 250 mph.

Vought-Sikorsky SB2U-1 "Vindicator," a scouting bombing plane, June 23, 1938. Note the "Tophatters" squadron insignia. (NARA)

Within hours after the Patterson contract was signed Pawley got all the details from one of his stooges on the Commission of Aviation Affairs. He then took immediate action to thwart the Patterson contract and ginned up his rumor and innuendo machine to make Kung pause and rethink the whole deal. He continued the gossip that Chennault was getting a commission on every aircraft that China purchased from someone besides Curtiss Wright.

Pawley also informed Kung that because of Patterson's huge commissions that China was paying exorbitantly more for these planes than similar aircraft from Curtiss Wright. He also spread doubt that Consolidated Trading Company could fulfill the contract obligations. Word of these charges filtered back to Patterson's creditors (Hong Kong and Shanghai Bank) and this made them more nervous than a cat in a roomful of rocking chairs.

Cordell Hull got wind of these shenanigans and on 19 May he informed Ambassador Johnson to block Pawley's attempt to hijack the lucrative contract from Patterson. The following day Hull had his special advisor, Stanley K. Hornbeck, contact Chinese Ambassador Hu Shi to put pressure on Kung to sign the Patterson deal. Kung simply responded that the Seversky planes did not meet specifications even though both the United States Army and Navy had placed an order for them.

Stanley K. Hornbeck, special assistant to the Secretary of State. (LOC)

Hull once again took the softball approach and related to Ambassador Johnson how the United States purchased a great number of Seversky P-35s (EP-1) which have operated satisfactorily and are still in service. Other behind the scenes negotiations took place, but it was to no avail. China informed Patterson in August that the contract was null and void and that they would be ordering 100 aircraft from Curtiss Wright. This must have been a tremendous blow to Patterson, but he had no recourse. Pawley had won even with the intervention by the State Department. It truly showed how ineffectual diplomatic efforts were against bribery or "squeeze" as it was referred to in China.

In his book, *The Flying Tiger – The True Story of General Claire Chennault and the U.S. 14th Air Force in China*, author Jack Samson relates a few interesting statements from Allen L. Patterson and recorded in

1982. The 82 year-old former aircraft salesman was still residing in Hong Kong. Patterson did not hide his animosity that still lingered stating:

> *"I got the order for the 50 P-35s with funds etc. But Bill Pawley pulled such unbelievable stunts to kill it, that H.H. Kung finally cancelled the order and gave me additional North American NA-16 aircraft. However, the order for the P-35 to Seversky Aircraft did result in the company getting financed and changing its name to Republic Aircraft Corporation. It almost broke Chennault's heart.*
>
> *The story of what Pawley did would take a book to tell."*

Even with the Curtiss-Wright contract in 1939, China fell to third place as a country to import American aircraft with Russia picking up the slack. Japan was not at ease though. On the 18 April, as the Gimo launched a new offensive against Japanese forces and the *New York Times* related how the Chinese had been strengthened by the importation of American aircraft. The *Times* reported the "…arrival of airplanes from the United States, Russia, and other countries could raid Japan troops on the 1,300-mile front and on the island of Hainan." The Japanese military noted this and took the necessary precautions.

In the fall of 1939 T.V. Soong had the opportunity to meet with the Secretary of the Treasury, Henry Morgenthau, Jr. and the two soon became close friends. Morgenthau respected Soong and as China enlisted a new and powerful ally to help the country with aircraft and war material to blunt the aggression of Japanese military interests.

Morgenthau was not your typical Treasury Secretary and often delved into areas normally reserved for the State Department or the military establishment. Born on May 11, 1891, he was the grandson of wealthy German Jewish immigrants and educated in private schools. He was involved with agriculture early in life near the Roosevelt estate in upstate New York and he entered the Roosevelt administration in Washington, D.C. early on and was appointed Treasury Secretary in 1934. Morgenthau was instrumental in promoting many of Roosevelt's New Deal initiatives and later financing the ability of the United States to conduct World War II. He often met with Cordell Hull and not only discussed global politics with him but help influence them as well. This is something that would not occur today, nor did it occur with any Treasury Secretary that succeeded him in 1945 to the same degree. It is not just a testament on how Morgenthau used his position of power but how affairs were conducted within the Roosevelt administration during this turbulent time. Less known is the meticulous diary he maintained daily, with the help of his personal secretary that detailed not only events in Roosevelt's inner circle but with interactions of many influential people outside of the White House including Soong.

On 27 December, Twen-ling Tsui, First Secretary of the Chinese Embassy, spoke with Joseph W. Ballantine, Assistant Chief of the Division of Far Eastern Affairs, inquiring about the Chinese government's desire to obtain American aviators as instructors for their school in Kunming. This appears to be the first overt attempt by the Chinese to draw in American aviators to support the Chinese Airforce.

Ballantine quickly passed the buck to his immediate superior, Maxwell McGaughey Hamilton, a Princeton graduate. Hamilton spoke with Tsui and promptly informed him that the United States government would look unfavorably in any attempt to recruit active Navy or Army aviators or reservists. But he added he had no problem if they wished to pursue American civilians. He also suggested that Tsui reach out to Colonel Jouett at the Aeronautical Chamber of Commerce for assistance. In conclusion Hamilton also suggested speaking with Colonel Chennault who he was told was employed by the Chinese as an aviation adviser and instructor. It is not known if Chennault and Tsui were working independently or coordinated their activities at this time. [21]

On January 17, 1940, Rear Admiral Walter S. Anderson forwarded a cryptic memorandum from Intercontinent vice-president Bruce Leighton to his boss the recently promoted (August 1939) Chief of Naval Operations Admiral Harold Rainsford Stark.

> *Attached hereto is a memorandum prepared by Mr. Bruce G. Leighton, formerly of the United States Navy, and now Vice-President of the Intercontinent Corporation, which has been engaged in aircraft manufacturing and sale in China for the past ten years. His plan appears to offer the possibility of immediately so strengthening Chinese resistance to Japan at relatively little cost to the United States, as to eventually cause Japan to abandon her policy of armed aggression on the continent of Asia in open violation of treaties.*
>
> *W.S. Anderson* [22]

What is interesting about the Leighton memorandum is that it is undated, unsigned, and not directed to any person or government agency. Leighton's following memorandum appears to be the boilerplate form that most people within and outside the United States government would work with to provide aviation support to China. Leighton states:

> 1. Assuming that it is in the interests of the United States to prevent Japan gaining control in China, it is then in the interest of the United States to give immediate support to China, with the objective of denying to Japan and retaining in friendly Chinese hands, the military and naval bases and economic resources which Japan, if successful in China, will undoubtedly use for further aggression in the Pacific.
>
> 2. Japan's present military position in China would be very vulnerable, if China had properly organized and equipped mobile air forces to conduct effective operations against Japanese supply lines in Hankow, to Canton and to the Nanning area, all of which are essentially waterborne.
>
> 3. Chinese Government authorities are anxious to establish such an organization, but their present Air Force has not the equipment, training, and organization and pilots required.
>
> 4. The present force required can be placed at, say, 100 bombers, 100 pursuit, and 10 transport, with auxiliary portable ground communications and mobile supply service equipment. Its cost would approximate $25,000,000.00. Effective operation would require a staff, which is organized and trained in accordance with Western operating doctrines, and with a fair proportion of Western-trained pilots in lead positions, say, 50 U.S. pilots.
>
> 5. I am confident that the Chinese are in a position to make a 20% down payment for the necessary supplies, and to pay the balance over a period of four years in equal monthly payments covered by promissory notes of the Chinese Government and the Central Bank of China as joint makes. I believe that American banks would finance credits to China up to $25,000,000.00 if U.S. Government banking agencies would indicate their willingness to cooperate.
>
> I am certain that there are among U.S. Army and Navy reserve

pilots adequate numbers who would welcome an opportunity to engage in such a venture, provided they were not discouraged from doing so by the U.S. Government.

6. I believe that the interests with which I am connected could arrange all the essentials of establishing bases, supplying equipment, training personnel, and organizing maintenance facilities, under commercial contracts with the Chinese Government, without any direct participation by the U.S. Government. [23]

How Admiral Stark immediately treated the memorandum from Leighton is not known. What is acknowledged is that Stark would later submit to President Roosevelt in November 1940 a war operations strategy named the 'Plan Dog' memorandum. Stark considered that the United States would be drawn into a two-front war – Germany and Italy on the European front and Japan on the Pacific side. Stark urged a Europe first approach and in general a defensive strategy against Japan. The report was well received at the time and it may have been a contributing influence on what future support China would receive from the United States. Ironically, Stark himself would later be a target for the intelligence failure that immediately surfaced after the Pearl Harbor attack. [24]

Admiral Harold R. Stark. (U.S. Navy)

At the same time as Leighton delivered his "sales" pitch to Admiral Stark he was interviewed extensively by Major Rodney A. Boone, USMC. Boone was a subordinate of Arthur McCollum, who headed the Office of Naval Intelligence. Neither one was a lightweight in the events to be played with this China affair. In 1941 both men were just two of thirty-six Americans who would have been cleared and have access to read decoded Japanese diplomatic and military intercepts. Not even the powerful influence peddling Secretary of the Treasury, Henry Morgenthau would have this access to such vital information - President Roosevelt held his cards close to his chest.

In Boone's extensive interview he related the following from Leighton:

> *Commander Leighton advances the idea that, if Japan gains complete control of China, she will make aggressive movements in other parts of the Pacific area. In order to be in a position to meet these aggressive movements of the United States is compelled to maintain a huge Navy and keep most of it in the Pacific. By so strengthening the Chinese Government as to permit them to defeat Japan, or, at least, carry on the war for years, Japan would be weakened and the threat of other aggressive actions in the Pacific would be moved. He argues that a small, efficient group of planes, consisting of 50 dive bombers, 50 twin-engine bombers, 50 pursuits and 10 transports, could make the Japanese lines of communications untenable.* [25]

Boone did not offer any opinion in his memo and only related what Leighton told him. It was a slick salesman routine as the former Navy commander peddled Pawley's wares under the guise of national interests and protecting the United States. While Leighton worked the Navy angle, his boss Pawley was elsewhere in the Nation's capital presumably lobbying on behalf of China, Curtiss-Wright and himself.

At the same time, Chennault toured the Curtiss-Wright plant in Buffalo and soon arrived in Washington, D.C. to brief an Army officer on the Chinese Air Force. And of course, Soong continued to schmooze Morgenthau. Add in an assortment of military and civilian figures involved and there was a significant amount of people interested in getting aviation aid to China but all in an uncoordinated effort.

The extreme animosity between Pawley and Chennault still festered as the pair, along with Leighton, toured several aircraft manufacturing plants in California. As the trio departed Los Angeles in Pawley's plane on 1 February, bad weather induced carburetor icing and it appeared quite possible that the plane may soon make an emergency landing or crash. Pawley turned to Chennault and said "Claire, it looks like this might be it." Chennault nonplussed simply stated he regretted that both their bodies would be found together in the wreckage. [26] The pilot made a forced landing and soon after they continued to San Francisco where Chennault left the pair and continued his trip to China via a Pan Am Clipper. Just how history would have been altered had those men perished during this flight is open to conjecture.

Pawley ramped up his marketing of aircraft to China in April 1940 by sponsoring an essay contest for American university students with a 1,500-word essay about "Our Stake in the Future of China." The first-place prize recipient would be rewarded with $1,200 and a round trip to China if it was safe to do so. Judges of the essay included Henry Luce, Pearl Buck, Theodore Roosevelt, Jr. and Frank Knox that further blurred the lines between private enterprise and the public sector.

Frank Knox served in Cuba with Theodore Roosevelt's famous Rough Riders, the 1st US Volunteer Cavalry Regiment. In World War I he rejoined the Army attaining the rank of Major. In 1930, Frank Knox became publisher and part owner of the *Chicago Daily News*. In 1936 he ran alongside Alf Landon as the Republican nominee for vice president as the duo got crushed in the Presidential election. Roosevelt appointed him Secretary of the Navy in July 1940 in an effort to build bi-partisan support for his foreign and defense policies following the defeat of France. Knox, a rabid anti-isolationist, was keen on expanding the Navy and believed in the country being prepared for war – all attributes that Pawley took mental notes on.

In July 1940 China had a good inventory of aircraft but with the Soviet Union no longer sending pilots she had an acute shortage of experienced aviators. Yet for unknown reasons the Generalissimo did not tackle the problem quickly and only reached out to Chennault three months later to address this situation. And on 19 August, Chennault faced a more immediate challenge – the first appearance of the Mitsubishi A6M2 Zero fighter over the skies of China - an aircraft that easily sped pass any Chinese fighter by 50-100 miles-per-hour.

The A6M2 was a long range and nimble fighter for the Imperial Japanese Navy and was referred by its pilots as "Reisen" (zero fighter), "0" being the last digit of the imperial year 2600 (1940) when it first entered service. For the next several years it achieved a 12:1 kill ratio against en-

Knox (second from right) confers with Admiral James O. Richardson (right), Admiral Harry E. Yarnell, USN (Retired) and Admiral Harold R. Stark (far left). (U.S. Navy)

emy aircraft until the Allies produced faster and stronger aircraft eclipsing the plane's performance and exploiting the inherent weaknesses the Zero possessed.

For the Chinese, the results from this new fighter the Japanese put forth was unprecedented. On 13 September, thirteen Zeros led by Lieutenant Saburo Shindo surprised 27 Soviet-built Polikarpov I-15s and I-16s as the Chinese fighters thought they were engaging an unescorted flight of Mitsubishi G3M (Nell) bombers. The Japanese Zero pilots shot down all the fighters without a single loss to themselves. The Chinese would continue engaging unescorted bombers or those escorted by Nate fighters, but the Zeros continued to whittle down the CAF.

On 12 October, Major General Mao Bangchu, director of the Chinese Air Force Operations Division and Chennault, now debilitated from bronchitis, listened to the urgent request for planes, volunteer pilots, and ground crews from the Generalissimo. Chiang desperately wanted American support to stem the bombing of Chinese civilians by the Japanese. It was suggested the pair travel to the United States on his behalf and put on a full court press to obtain planes and pilots.

The following week Chiang met with Ambassador Nelson T. Johnson about the potential closing of the Burma Road, China's lifeline, by the Japanese. Chiang told Nelson, "I strongly hope that before the severance of communication facilities American planes can be procured in plentiful quantities. It is also hoped that American volunteers will be able to aid us in carrying on hostilities."

It would have seen to be the most opportunistic time to launch this mission as the Tripartite Pact (also known as the Berlin Pact) was signed in Berlin on 27 September forming the Axis partnership. This agreement linked Germany, Italy, and Japan militarily even with the principals located on opposite sides of the world. The purpose of the arrangement was apparently directed primarily at the United States and the Soviet Union as the Pact provided for mutual assistance should any of the signatories suffer attack by any nation not already involved in the war.

Chiang Kai-Shek believed the Tripartite Pact also strengthened his position to obtain as much war material as possible. Not satisfied with just Chennault and Bangchu seeking aid, a week later he met with the American Ambassador Nelson on 18 October. Chiang reiterated his fear of the closing of the Burma Road and the demoralizing effect that Japanese bombers were taking out on the civilian population. Nelson said he'll see what he could do but also stated that the United States could not even provide pilots for Great Britain. Nelson probably knew this was not entirely true as Americans could enlist in Canada and then travel to Great Britain to join the fight against the Nazis.

Closer to home, Stanley Hornbeck, Secretary of the Navy Frank Knox, Morgenthau, and even the President were on board to help China with American pilots. State Department head Cordell Hull was not part of that group at this time and his office had in October, advised that all Americans leave the Far East as soon as possible. On 19 October three passenger ships departed the United States to advance the evacuation of Americans overseas. That same day Knox asked Hull about aiding Americans that wished to travel to China and sent the following memo:

> *I am told there are a considerable number of American aviators who would be glad to volunteer their services to China in the present War with Japan if they could be absolved from any penalty for such action. Is it at all possible that we can handle this matter of American flyers going to China as we have handled the same situation with respect to young men volunteering for service in Great Britain in the present War there?* [27]

Hull stated in a reply memo that "the present policy of the Department of State is to refuse passports to persons who state that they desire to go abroad for the purpose of enlisting in the armed forces of a foreign state." Hull mentioned the "Canada option" where Americans fighting for England enlisted in Canada. It is interesting that none of the parties involved explored this opportunity in the upcoming months to circumvent Title 18. U.S. Code and the Nationality Act of 1940 for Americans entering the armed forces of a foreign state.

But the tides and winds were shifting closer and closer to war. The limited embargoes placed on Japan on scrap metal and aviation fuel the past summer had no discernible effect in negotiations between the two countries. And then in October, Roosevelt got a whiff of a rumor seeping from the head of the Japanese Press Association that if the United States withdrew all their military assets from Midway Island, Wake Island, and Pearl Harbor, that there would be no need for Japan to go to war. Roosevelt bellowed, "God! That's the first time any damn Jap has told us to get out of Hawaii! And that has me more worried than anything in the world." The President would not make this public and keep it to himself saying, "…because it will only stir up bad feelings in this country, and this country is ready to pull the trigger if the Japs do anything." [28] Going forward the United States would continue to put the screws to the Japanese both financially and through material resources.

As the United States continued to provide China with military aircraft and aviator expertise it was imperative that this information be withheld from Congress and more importantly, the American people. Perhaps Michael Lomasney's quote "Never write if you can speak; never speak if you can nod; never nod if you can wink," took hold of government officials in the deep state, civilians, and the manufacturers that provided the products to be exported to China and would continue until the attack on Pearl Harbor.

Lindbergh and the Isolationists

ISOLATIONISM AND NON-INTERVENTIONISM were rampant throughout the United States and embraced by many folks on both sides of the political aisle. And it should be remembered that in his Farewell Address, President George Washington advocated non-involvement in foreign wars and politics. But the world was shrinking as faster ships cruised the oceans and aircraft plied the skies.

The isolationist movement began shortly World War I when citizens made claims of arms manufacturers and bankers pushing America into the war to increase profits. And then Congress rejected U.S. membership in the League of Nations which emboldened their movement even more. With the onset of the Depression and as things began to unravel overseas, Congress passed several "Neutrality Acts" further keeping the United States out of foreign affairs. Roosevelt believed the country needed to be involved in future world dealings but essentially his administration was handcuffed by Congress. Aid to foreign allies was meager and cloaked with layers of bureaucracy and a myriad of government agencies.

University of California (Berkeley) students conduct a one-day peace strike on April 19, 1940, to protest American foreign intervention. (NARA)

Although many groups were involved in the isolationist and non-intervention movement, the America First Committee was in the forefront and would be elevated even further with a new leader – the first man to fly solo across the Atlantic Ocean – Charles Lindbergh – and like many other heroes throughout history saddled with feet of clay.

There is no doubt that Charles Augustus "Slim" Lindbergh was a true American hero as he flew the Ryan Airlines built Spirit of St. Louis solo from New York to Paris in May 1927. After that event took place he was probably the best known and most popular human being to exist on the face of the planet at the time. He is also synonymous with the anti-interventionist movement prevalent in the United States prior to Pearl Harbor and during his lifetime he would be tarnished as pro-fascist, a racist, and anti-Semite - Characterizations that are still disputed to this day. He was certainly not the figure displayed by Jimmy Stewart on the silver screen in the 1957 movie, *Spirit of St. Louis*.

Charles Lindbergh and the Spirit of St. Louis. (LOC)

In 1932, Lindbergh's son was abducted and subsequently murdered near Hopewell, New Jersey. The intense public pressure and media scrutiny that followed forced him and his wife Anne to seek refuge in the United Kingdom from 1936-1938. It was at this time that Lindbergh met Joseph Kennedy, the United Kingdom ambassador and a rabid anti-Semite with pro-fascist leanings.

At the bequest of the United States military, Lindbergh being a reserve Colonel, was asked to visit Germany and evaluate their aviation potential. Lindbergh did this on several occasions, and although his reports exaggerated the capability of the German Luftwaffe, they were still very much needed. During one visit while having dinner with several German luminaries, Hermann Göring presented the "Lone Eagle" with the Commander Cross of the Order of the German Eagle.

Lindbergh stated that America should not send aid to countries after Hitler's invasion of Czechoslovakia and Poland. He equated assistance with war profiteering: "To those who argue that we could make a profit and build up our own industry by selling munitions abroad, I reply that we in America have not yet reached a point where we wish to capitalize on the destruction and death of war." Lindbergh would become a spokesman for the non-interventionist movement America First Committee and speak to huge crowds at locations like Soldier Field in Chicago and Madison Square Garden in New York.

Unbeknownst to both Lindbergh and Göring, the Roosevelt administration and the United States were making moves to counter the aspirations of both Germany and Japan – Isolationism be damned. As Lindbergh continued to resist American involvement overseas, Chennault persisted in confronting the Japanese. But even Chennault underestimated the Japanese military by answering the following question from an Associated Press reporter:

Interviewer: Do you think this war will last long?
Chennault: No. I don't think so. I don't think it will last more than two years. I think the Chinese has [sic] got the Japanese worn down. The Japanese tried two big offensives this year and failed. [29]

1. A street is Boston (Lomasney Way) is named after him. Another great honor is a cocktail called a "Ward 8." It was concocted at the Locke-Ober restaurant, in Boston in 1898 to honor his contribution (and his ward) in sending him to the Massachusetts General Court.

2. The Role of Defensive Pursuit, Air Force Historical Research Agency (AFHRA), Document Number 248.282.4.

3. Chennault, Claire L., The Way of the Fighter, The Memoirs of Claire Lee Chennault. New York: G.P. Putnam Sons Chennault, Claire L. & Hotz, R. B. (1949), Pg. 32.

4. Chennault was never informed about the Doolittle Raid. The upper echelon of the United States military believed a possible intelligence "leak" could endanger the mission. Fifteen aircraft reached China and all crashed landed. The Japanese Army conducted a massive sweep through the eastern coastal provinces of China, in an operation now known as the Zhejiang-Jiangxi campaign, searching for the surviving American airmen and inflicting retribution on the Chinese who aided them. Eight flyers were captured and three executed. If Chennault's aerial radio net had been deployed several of these bombers could have been directed to safe airfields or retrieved quickly if their location was known.

5. Jordan, J. W. (2016). American Warlords: How Roosevelts High Command Led America To Victory In World War II. New York: NAL Caliber (2015), Pg. 253.

6. Martha Byrd, in her book, Chennault: Giving Wings to the Tiger, Tuscaloosa, Alabama, University of Alabama Press (2003) has this date as 10 August, Pg. 73.

7. Chennault, Way of the Fighter, Pg. 41.

8. Samson, Jack, The Flying Tiger: The True Story of General Claire Chennault and the U.S. 14th Air Force in China, Guilford, CT, Lyons Press (2012), Pg. 24-26.

9. The Los Angeles Times also reported Heard as a retired Army general.

10. Foreign Relations of the United States Diplomatic Papers, 1937, Volume III, 793.94/9204: Telegram, Tokyo, August 6, 1937—4 p.m.

11. The 434-foot Izumo was built in Elswick, England and launched on September 19, 1898. She would see service during the Russo-Japanese War, World War 1, and World War II. She was near-missed several times by American bombers in July 1945. The shockwaves from the bombs exploding caused the ship's seams to separate and the rapid flooding caused her to capsize four days later.

12. Shultz, Duane, The Maverick War: Chennault and the Flying Tigers. New York: St. Martins Press (1990), Pg. 67.

13. Clarence E. Gauss to the Department of State, September 29, 1937, File 893.20/627, RG 59, NARA.

14. Xu, Guangqiu, War Wings: The United States and Chinese Military Aviation, 1929-1949. Westport, CT: Greenwood Press. (2001), Pg. 122.

15. Department of State, Press Release, September 18, 1937, Vol. 17, No. 416, P. 227.

16. The Secretary of State to the Consul at Hong Kong (Donovan), August 21, 1937, FRUS, 1937, 4: 522.

17. Carrozza, Anthony R., William D. Pawley: The Extraordinary Life of the Adventurer, Entrepreneur, and Diplomat Who Cofounded the Flying Tigers. Washington, D.C.: Potomac Books (2012), Pg. 48.

18. Avions n°4, June 1993. Retrieved: 02 October 2016. ISSN 1243-8650.

19. Samson, Jack, The Flying Tiger, Pg. 39.

20. The Chief of the Office of Arms and Munitions Control, Department of State (Green), to 148 Persons and Companies Manufacturing Airplane Parts, Washington, July 1, 1938.

21. Memorandum by the Chief of the Division of Far Eastern Affairs (Hamilton) Of a Conversation with the First Secretary of the Chinese Embassy (Tsui), Washington, January 3, 1940.

22. Office of the Chief of Naval Operations, Document Op-16-F-2.

23. Ibid.

24. After the Allied invasion of Europe, Stark faced a Court of Inquiry about his actions prior to the Pearl Harbor attack. The Court decide that Stark did not provide enough information to Admiral Kimmel who was relieved of duty 10 days after the attack. Admiral Kimmel endorsed the decision but in 1948 asked that his endorsement be removed. Controversy and conspiracy theories abound around the Pearl Harbor attack to this day.

25. Office of the Chief of Naval Operations, Document Op-16-F-2.

26. Carrozza, Anthony R., William D. Pawley, Pg.62

27. Department of State, FRUS, 1940, 4: 677-8.

28. FDR, recording, October 8, 1940, Franklin Delano Roosevelt Library.

29. National Archives and Records Group Administration, RG. 59.

Michael Lemish

Part Three:
The End Game – And Time Runs Out

"There is much noise on the stairs, but no one enters the room"

Old Chinese saying

China Lobbies Hard for Aircraft and Pilots

THE NIGHT CHENNAULT returned to Washington on 1 November 1940, Soong met him for dinner, without Major General Mao Bangchu, and introduced the Colonel to newspapermen Joseph Wright Alsop, Jr. of the *New York Herald Tribune* and Edgar Ansel Mowrer of the *Chicago Daily News*. Both men were Washington insiders with China experience and the reporters were skeptical of Chennault's plan for a volunteer air force. The pair related how England was pushing for every possible aircraft coming off America's assembly lines. Also, the reporters related, everyone around the nation's capital and the American citizens considered Germany the immediate threat and Japan a minor annoyance.

Unlike today, top newspaper reporters like Alsop [1] and Mowrer, wielded their share of power and influence and were highly connected to many Washington insiders. Mowrer [2] for instance, joined the *Chicago Daily News* after being hired by the owner, Frank Knox, who would become President Roosevelt's Secretary of the Navy. Mowrer would also be part of the newspaper's Tokyo bureau. And Alsop, through his mother, was related to President James Monroe and Theodore Roosevelt. And it was because of these family ties that Alsop was well connected to the Washington elite that surrounded President Roosevelt.

The evening soured even more when Chennault told the pair of reporters the capabilities of the new Japanese Zero fighter that appeared over the skies of Chungking just a couple of months earlier. Whereas Chinese efforts previously focused on obtaining American aircraft based on older designs but still comparable to Japanese fighters, this new aerial threat meant that American first-rate fighters would be needed to counter the best aircraft Japan sent aloft. But as dismal as things looked, Chennault was not dissuaded from his quest and attempted to enlighten the War Department to the Japanese threat.

Newspaperman Joseph Alsop (right) would later become the historian for the A.V.G. (LOC)

A year earlier the Chinese had captured a Japanese Nate (Type 97) intact that was brought to Chengtu where Chennault flight tested the plane and made scrupulous notes about its performance. He forwarded this information to the War Department and got a thank you note in reply and that "aeronautical experts" stated that it was not possible that a plane could be built with those specifications. Chennault also provided information about the first series of the Japanese Model Zero fighters.

Now perhaps these reports were misfiled, or more likely someone decided to throw them into a waste basket. Chennault had made his enemies over the years and in American military circles the Chinese recruited "mercenary" was considered as "he's not one of us." As such, some military officers would turn away from what Chennault had to offer so as not to advance his stature as a forward-thinking military aviation strategist. So, it is with little surprise that when the Japanese attacked Pearl Harbor the Army and Navy had virtually no information about the Japanese planes that were attacking them from above even though Chennault had provided this information nearly a year earlier.

Nakijama KI-27, code name "Nate" by the Allies. It was one of the last fixed-gear fighters built by Japan. Chennault forwarded its performance to the War Department that was summarily dismissed by so-called "experts." (Alcherton)

While Soong was the top lobbyist for China in Washington, D.C. Chinese Ambassador Hu Shih occasionally dipped his toe into the murky waters of appropriating American pilots and war materials for his country. On 31 October 1940, he reached out to Joseph C. Green, chief of the Division of Controls on how he might be able to obtain combat aircraft for his country. Green suggested the Chinese ambassador contact Philip Young, chairman of Roosevelt's Liaison Committee and an assistant to Morgenthau. Green believed that small orders of aircraft (i.e. under 50) could be added to the existing British production orders already in place and in the following memorandum explicitly stated how Green felt and what could be accomplished.

Memorandum of Conversation, by the Chief of the Division of Controls (Green)
[Washington,] November 7, 1940.

Dr. T. V. Soong, President of the Central Bank of China, called at my office this morning by appointment. He referred to my recent conversations with the Chinese Ambassador and Mr. Arthur Young in regard to the purchase of military planes by the Chinese Government. He said that he had now been authorized by his Government to act as its agent for the negotiation of the necessary contracts. He added that his Government desired to obtain at least a few planes immediately. I replied that this Government was very anxious to make it possible for the Chinese Government to obtain a few planes immediately. I added that in view of the needs of the Chinese Government we had been somewhat surprised that it had placed no orders for combat planes in this country this year. Dr. Soong said that the failure of the Chinese Government to place orders heretofore was due to the fact that it had relied upon the U. S. S. R. to furnish it with combat planes, but that as it had been disappointed in the number of planes furnished by the U. S. S. R. it has now resolved to place orders in this country. Dr. Soong asked whether I could make an appointment for him to see Mr. Philip Young, Chairman of the President's Liaison Committee.

In Dr. Soong's presence, I called Mr. Young's office by telephone and made an appointment for Dr. Soong to see Mr. Young tomorrow afternoon.

I told Dr. Soong that Mr. Young was fully informed of the desire of the Department of State that arrangements be made which would permit the delivery of at least a few planes to the Chinese Government in the immediate future and that I felt sure that if an order were placed Mr. Young and his committee would find it possible to make the necessary arrangements. Dr. Soong then asked my advice as to how he should approach Mr. Young.

I suggested that he should be perfectly frank with Mr. Young, place the entire problem before him, and discuss it with him freely in all of its aspects. I added that I felt that he and his Government could fully rely upon any advice which he might receive from Mr. Young and his committee in regard to the types of planes for which it would be most advantageous for the Chinese Government to place orders.

Dr. Soong then mentioned the Thai planes now in

Manila. He said that he hoped that his Government might be able to purchase those particular planes.
I replied that that might be the solution, but I pointed out that those planes were dive bombers of an extremely powerful type. I added that for many reasons I thought that it would probably develop from his discussions with Mr. Young that it would be far more advantageous to his Government to acquire other planes rather than the Thai planes at Manila.

Joseph C. Green [3]

Green followed up with the request from Soong with Morgenthau's assistant, Phillip Young, in the following memorandum:

Memorandum of Conversation, by the Chief of the Division of Controls (Green)
[Washington,] November 25, 1940.

Mr. Philip Young, Assistant to the Secretary of the Treasury and Chairman of the President's Liaison Committee, called me by telephone late this afternoon. He said that he had just concluded a very satisfactory discussion with the Chinese Purchasing Mission. He said that the Mission's misgivings in regard to the P–40 planes, which had been caused by misinformation as to the speed of those planes and fear lest they would not be found suitable for use in the high altitudes of Western China, had been removed; that the Mission had presented a list of types of planes which it hoped to be able to purchase, and that this list had included P–40s to the number of from 50 to 100.

Joseph C. Green [4]

And on another Chinese tangent, Major General Mao Bangchu presented his own request to the President Liaison Committee (the civilian agency presumably covertly headed by Phillip Young) coordinating foreign arms purchases. The Chinese wanted 500 combat planes delivered in 1941, including 20 percent spare parts and material to build 14 major airfields and 122 landing strips

Although Secretary Knox preferred American fighter pilots to fly on behalf of China instead of simply supplying aircraft, Secretary Hull vacillated and was not fully committed to the proposal. He did relent in part to allow his office to provide passports to these "businessmen" that wished to travel to China. Hull told Stanley Hornbeck and Maxwell Hamilton to inform Soong and Ambassador Hu Shi that "…the Department of State would probably issue passports to American citizens who desire to proceed to China for the purpose of serving as aviation instructors." Clearly Hull wanted to steer clear of any words that included "fighter" or "combat" in his memorandums.

Soong took Chennault's plan and on 30 November proposed to Morgenthau that if the United States provided 500 planes and an appropriate number of American pilots and mechanics that the Japanese army could be driven from China and her navy severely weakened. Furthermore, an attack on the Japan homeland would damage their industrial production and demoralize Japanese civilians. Giving the abysmal state of the Chinese ground forces, it was pure fantasy that Soong believed that a strong Chinese air arm alone could drive the Japanese from China.

The following Tuesday, 3 December, Morgenthau spoke with the British ambassador Philip Henry Kerr (Lord Lothian) about diverting aircraft destined for Great Britain to China. Lord Lothian was an appeaser and can be remembered for saying after Neville Chamberlain signed the Munich Agreement with Hitler in 1938, that he had done "…a marvelous job…" Morgenthau pressed Lord Lothian and stressed that these bombers could target Tokyo and industrial centers in the Japanese homeland. In his diary Morgenthau stated:

> *I told Lothian that I am going to try to get, for the Chinese, three or four-engine bombers and train their crews here with the understanding that these bombers are to be used to bomb Tokio [an obsolete spelling used prior and during the Second World War] and other big cities. He seemed very enthusiastic and said that it might change everything. He said he would take it up with T.V. Soong.* (5)

It is unknown where Morgenthau thought the United States were producing three-engine bombers. After talking with "his people" Lothian came away unimpressed with this proposal as Great Britain was not at war with Japan and apparently the British had no appreciation of Japan's future intentions in the Pacific. Lord Lothian suggested that the Treasury secretary go back and discuss the proposal again with Soong. As with the

Americans, the British adopted blinders and became focused on the immediate threat at the time – Adolph Hitler and Nazi Germany.

In one of the best books available about American and Chinese aviation interests during this period, *War Wings: The United States and Chinese Aviation, 1929-1949*, author Guangqiu Xu states:

> On December 4, Hornbeck hinted that military aid may be available and encouraged Hamilton [Chief of the Division of Far Eastern Affairs] to "do something toward helping China in the matter of aviation instructors" because Washington sent "officers of the Army and the Navy as instructors to certain Latin American countries and recently sent eleven officers to the Netherlands East Indies… [A]n investment of the services of a few of our officers by way of helping the Chinese prepare for an ultimate offensive would…be a sound and a profitable investment. Hamilton suggested at the end of December, that "Colonel Chennault would undertake the employment of American personnel" and that the War and Navy Departments would assist largely in providing lists of qualified personnel and the State Department would finally issue passports for them to go to China. (6)

On the 8 December, after having lunch with the President, Morgenthau and Soong left together in a car along with their wives and then the Treasury Secretary remarked, "Well to ask for 500 planes, is like asking for 500 stars." But he intimated that the United States could provide some long-range bombers and Americans to fly them, and that this was the President's idea. Soong was elated and said that the bombing of Tokyo would have a profound effect on the Far Eastern theatre. Morgenthau asked Soong, "Would you be afraid of their bombing you?" And he replied, "They are doing it any way." Morgenthau further recorded in his diary that same day:

> I thought this could be done by January, and it would be possible to arrange to hire pilots who are experienced in flying this kind of bomber. He [Soong] said he thought that would be necessary because it took the English a long time to fly these ships.
>
> If the Chinese would do this, I am convinced that overnight it would change the entire picture in the Far East. (7)

Later on that same day Soong forwarded to Morgenthau a summary (marked SECRET) of the current military situation in China and what could be expected in the future. Soong stated in part, "According to the political strategic necessities of the war in Asia and Europe it will be possible to take a decision as to the advisability of carrying the air war to Japan proper."

Soong continued his push by stating the process should begin within two weeks so that both Chinese mechanics and American pilots could start an intense three-month recruitment and training period and be ready for a spring offensive. He called the recruitment of pilots and securing aircraft as the "Special Air Unit." A week later Soong sent Morgenthau a hand-written note from his home in Chevy Chase, Maryland accompanied by a detailed map that showed every airfield and its location in possession of the Chinese Air Force. Soong also made sure to include a postscript that said, "This map is of course very secret and is for your personal information only."

Hull and Morgenthau met early on the morning of 10 December. Apparently, Hull was pivoting 180 degrees and wanted to join the camp that advocated bombing Japan. Morgenthau says:

> I called on Hull this morning at 20 minutes of nine. He came in with a mouth full of breakfast and he said that he said to see the doctor at eight. Before I could even open my mouth, he said, "What we have to do Henry, is to get 500 American planes to start from the Aleutian Islands and fly over Japan just once." He said, "That will teach them a lesson." Well his opening remarks took my breath away, and then he said, "If we can only find some way to have them drop some bombs on Tokyo." I asked, "Well, who do you mean?" and he said, "The Chinese." So I said, "Well, Cordell, you leave me speechless. I didn't know you felt that way." Then I said I have a confession to make. I said, "Sunday I suggested to T.V. Soong in the greatest of confidence and secrecy that he wire Chiang Kai-Shek that we could make available to him a limited number of long distance bombers provided that they were used to bomb Tokyo." So Cordell said, "Fine." But, he said, "that proviso doesn't have to be part of the contract, does it?" I replied, "of course not." So he said, "How would get them over there?" I answered, we are letting them fly planes from San Diego to Halifax. Couldn't we let them fly to Hawaii and

the Philippines and then to their destination in China?" and Cordell said, Absolutely. I will be for that." Hull said they have the airfields in China within 600 miles of Tokyo, and I said, *"I know that."* Then he said, *"But couldn't we fly them to the Philippines ourselves in order to make a demonstration to Tokyo, and then let the Chinese take title for them in the Philippines? I replied, "It might be worked out but I think it is more difficult."* (8)

Chiang Kai-shek continued to pressure President Roosevelt for additional help and sent a telegram to him on 12 December thanking him for his "generous and timely announcement of a substantial loan to China has infinitely increased China's powers of resistance, strengthened its social and economic structure, and enhanced the confidence of the army and the people in its final victory over the aggressor." The generalissimo continued to push

Generalissimo Chiang Kai-Shek at home with Madame. This photograph was taken for *Life* magazine. Notice how the photograph of President Roosevelt was carefully staged in the background. (LOC)

Roosevelt and urged him to communicate with Soong as he needed a strong air force to help stem Japanese aggression.

Just four days later the generalissimo sent a telegram to Morgenthau about his wishes to secure the Boeing B-17 bombers and what he intended to do with them:

> ...I am most interested to acquire as many of your Flying Fortresses as you could spare, which from our air bases could effectively bomb all the vital centers of Japan and harass their fleets and transports. The effect of this upon the Japanese people who are already much divided and dispirited will certainly be far-reaching.
>
> The Flying Fortresses should be complemented by a proportionate number of pursuits and medium bombers, so that the air force thus constituted could also support the counteroffensive which I am preparing with a view of taking Canton and Hankow, and of forcing the Japanese to recall their troops, transports, and airplanes from the contemplated attack on Singapore, the safety of which is vital to us as to the British. (9)

On Wednesday, 18 December, Soong called Morgenthau on the phone and according to the Treasury Secretary in his notes stated:

> T.V. Soong called and said that General Chiang Kai-Shek feels the only way to stop the Japanese from going down and attacking Singapore in April is for the Chinese to attack Japan and Chiang Kai-Shek is ready to do so provided that we can provide him with Boeing [B-17] bombers and the escort planes necessary to accomplish it. He said it is important that they be given material to build up a ground organization. He left me with a map, which he says is very secret, which shows the various airfields in China. There is a big airfield in Chekiang which he says is only 500 miles from Japan.
>
> He is leaving at my house tonight a more detailed memorandum on just what General Chiang Kai-Shek said. I promised him I would lay the whole thing before the President sometime tomorrow. He also asked if I could deliver to the President a personal message from General Chiang Kai-Shek rather than go through the State Department and I said

I could. (10)

And later in the day Morgenthau made another diary entry stating:

I told T.V. Soong that Cordell Hull has brought up the question himself of the advisability and feasibility of bombing Japan from China. When Hull did this, I told him of my conversation with Soong. I also told Soong that not only did Hull approve the plan of their having these bombers with which to bomb Japan, but also approved the idea of having them fly from the West Coast via Hawaii, Wake Island, and the Philippines directly to China. I told him that Hull was the only person who knew of this besides myself, but I would be in touch with the President tomorrow.

He told me that he had information that the Germans and Italians expect to go right ahead with their campaign, irrespective of temporary reverses that they are having in Greece and Africa. (11)

The following morning Morgenthau met with President Roosevelt for forty minutes to discuss several matters and culminating with what has been called the "Chinese problem."

I had a chance to go over the whole Chinese thing with the President, and he is just as thrilled as I am. I said, "Don't you think, Mr. President, that this may have even a more far-reaching effect than the campaign in Greece?" He said, "Much more. Much more." I asked him if he wouldn't take it up with Cabinet with Stimson, Knox, Hull and myself and he said he would. (12)

On a late Friday afternoon 20 December, Morgenthau, along with his assistant Philip Young, met with Soong. In attendance with the three men was Morgenthau's secretary, Henrietta Stein Klotz, who he once called her "the watchdog of the Secretary of the Treasury." Morgenthau had the following conversation with the head of the Chinese lobby:

Morgenthau: He [the President] was simply delighted, particularly with the one about the bombers. Yesterday, after Cabinet, I ask for a chance, and the President had Hull,

Stimson, and Knox stay, and we had your map out, and the President gave it his approval. I said, "should we work it out and come back?" and he said it was not necessary. He said, "The four of you work out a program." Just how we are going to do it, I do not know, but I wanted you to know that the President was delighted. I am meeting again with these gentlemen on Monday. I wanted you to get word to Chiang Kai-shek that he has the approval of the President, and the President said he had been dreaming about this for years...I understand that the Japanese Navy has a new kind of fighting ship which takes off from an aircraft carrier, which is so much better than anything you have.
Soong: I understand that they do not take off from the decks of ships but from the water.
Morgenthau: This Colonel Chennault, where is he?
Soong: He is here now in Washington.
Morgenthau: I have not told anybody about this outside of Mr. Young and Mrs. Klotz. I have told them because I need their assistance. I said, and I hope you will back me up, that if they could get a man who knew how to fly these four-engine bombers, that China would be glad to pay up to $1,000 a month in United States dollars. Was that too high?
Soong: No. Not at all.
Morgenthau: What are your plans for the next two days? Something might break over the weekend.
Soong: I will be available at any time.
Morgenthau: Find out whether a four-engine flying boat will be any use to you.
Soong: It is the best news I have had since I came here.
Morgenthau: I am going to put all of my energy behind this because it has to be done at once. (13)

With Morgenthau pumped up from the meeting with Soong he placed a quick call to Frank Knox shortly after the Chinese lobbyist departed and the always dependable Mrs. Klotz dutifully provided a transcript.

Morgenthau: I see. Well, I am delighted. Now, Frank whenever you're ready on that hush-hush thing we've been talking about...
Knox: Yeah. I'm worried about that. I wanted to talk with

you about that today but the President kept me busy on this other thing.

Morgenthau: *Well, when are you going to be ready?*

Knox: *I'll be ready anytime. We must do it quickly if we're going to do it at all.*

Morgenthau: *Well, shall we do it Monday morning in Hull's office?*

Knox: *Yeah*

Morgenthau: *Whoever's there we can "shush" them all out after we get through dividing up these three hundred Curtiss P-40s.*

Knox: *Where-what office, Henry?*

Morgenthau: *I sent you a list-I don't know whether you've got it. There are three hundred Curtiss P-40s which can be ordered…*

Knox: *Three hundred Curtiss P-40s.*

Morgenthau: *Yeah.*

Knox: *For the British.*

Morgenthau: *Well, for anybody. They've got the engines.*

Knox: *Well, by God, we ought to grab some of those for the Chinese.*

Morgenthau: *Well, that's the point, and I sent you a list of all the requests from all the countries for the various things.*

Knox: *When did you send it to me?*

Morgenthau: *Oh, two days ago.*

Knox: *Well, then I've got it here. There's a lot of stuff here I haven't had a chance to…*

Morgenthau: *Two days ago-at the point-I mean, I'm sick and tired of all this hemming and hawing, you see, and I thought I'd lay the whole thing and what you're going to do with the new order. See?*

Knox: *Yeah.*

Morgenthau: *And I'll keep pushing for these foreign orders and playing nurse to them until the President tells me not to.*

Knox: *Uh-huh.*

Morgenthau: *I suppose, as far as I know, he wants me to continue this as I have.*

Knox: *Why sure. I don't know why not. There's nothing in this new set-up [sic] that interrupts that. You're, as I've recognized your efforts, to help the British get what they want.*

Morgenthau: Or any other foreign country where it doesn't interfere with our own progress.
Knox: That's right.
Morgenthau: Well, there are three hundred Curtiss P-40s that this fellow can still make. The English have got the engines 'cause they've cancelled the Lockheeds, you see. Now, we've got the Greeks and Chinese and South Americans-I sent the whole list over and I thought the four of us would get together with Hull at 9:30. Did you get that note?
Knox: I got that note. Hull called me up about it. That's the one-9:30 A.M. at Hull's office. Okay. I got that.
Morgenthau: Now, what we'll do is this, when we get through with that. I'll ask Hull to ask the other people to step out and we'll talk about this hush-hush [author's italics] mission.
Knox: All right. That's fine.
Morgenthau: How's that?
Knox: That's okay.
Morgenthau: Thank you.
Knox: All right Henry.
Morgenthau: Good-bye. (14)

The "hush-hush" thing talked about was of course the idea of providing the Chinese with American bombers to hit Japan. The concept of bombing Japan continued to gain momentum as more people piled on to the prospect and things were looking good for both Chennault and the Generalissimo, et al. Morgenthau called a conference at his home the day after speaking with Knox. The early evening conference included Soong, Chennault, General Mao, and Phillip Young. It was at this meeting that Chennault delivered definitive plans for bombing Japan. In the meeting (presumably recorded by Mrs. Klotz) the Secretary asked what kind of bombers China needed. Chennault suggested either the Lockheed Hudson or the Flying Fortresses but indicated that the Hudson could not reach Tokyo. They could, however, without escort pursuit ships, conduct nighttime bombing runs against Nagasaki, Kobe, and Osaka.

The tactical discussion continued, and Chennault indicated that 130 pursuit ships would be needed to defend the bomber bases and another 100 to keep the Burma Road open. Morgenthau asked what crews were needed for the bombers and Chennault replied that one American pilot and bombardier and about five mechanics for each aircraft were required. Morgenthau at this time told the group that the Army would release men if they were paid $1,000 a month and apparently Soong and Mao thought this was just.

Chennault also inquired if the bombers could be flown into China from the Philippines and Morgenthau stated that this problem had already been solved. The Secretary also inquired as to whether incendiary bombs could be used since the Japanese cities were built principally from paper and wood. Chennault indicated that yes they could be deployed and since they were lighter than ordinary bombs that would mean a longer range for the bombers.

The party obviously separated that evening on an upbeat note, but one wonders how many martinis Morgenthau had imbibed, if any. The Secretary of the Treasury all but guaranteed that either Flying Fortresses or Hudson bombers were in the pipeline on their way to China via the Philippines and this was simply not the case. Morgenthau vastly overstated exactly what the United States was willing to provide China and severely overstepped what he was capable of delivering as the United States Treasury Secretary. The people within the United States government favoring a direct attack on the Japanese homeland from Chinese bombers were about to be dealt a crippling blow and this would come from another government faction.

Several influential individuals were not on board with what Morgenthau and Hull envisioned, namely Secretary of War Stimson and Chief of Staff General George Catlett Marshall Jr.. On the 23 December a meeting was made to discuss the covert bombing of Japan and in attendance were Morgenthau, Hull, Knox, Stimson, Admiral Harold Stark, and General George Marshall. Up to this time there is no record of Marshall being involved in any discussions regarding the potential bombing of Japan with American planes, adorned with Chinese insignia, and flown by Americans. General Marshall was born in Uniontown, Pennsylvania in 1880 and over the years he advanced through the Army ranks and responsibility but had limited combat experience as a platoon leader during the Philippine–American War. During World War I, he had roles as a planner of both training and operations, excelling in both positions. In 1938 he was assigned to the War Plans Division of the War Department Staff and eventually replaced General Malin Craig when he retired in 1939 to become the Army Chief of Staff.

In his book, *Flying Tigers – Claire Chennault and the American Volunteer Group*, Daniel Ford relates the meeting of Knox, Marshall, and Morgenthau [not mentioning Admiral Stark] and states:

Stimson also had second thoughts. The bombing scheme was "half-baked," the Army Secretary [sic] decided, so he asked Marshall, Knox, and Morgenthau to his home that Sunday – a beautiful afternoon, virtually a second Indian summer – "to get some mature brains into it." The brains were Marshall's, and the Treasury Secretary immediately capitulated to the general's cool logic. By Monday morning, only fighter planes were still on the table for China. (15)

Later Stimson would record in his notes, "As usual, the demand boils down to land planes for our army and threats to deplete us more. The proposition as it was made the other day was rather *half-baked* [author's italics]. It hadn't been thought out. It was the product of Chinese strategists rather than well-thought-out American strategy and I called this meeting to try to get some mature brains into it, before we got committed to it."

The so called "Chinese strategists" put forth by Stimson was essentially Chennault's plan and in time his strategies would be proven sound. Stimson sided with Marshall and believed providing bombers to China would provoke the Japanese to attack an unprepared United States that was not in a viable position to take on Japan militarily.

This was indeed a watershed moment in American history that nullified, if only temporarily, the possibility of China possessing B-17s or Lockheed Hudsons, that could bomb Japan, but no clear reason is ever given. And it also raises the question of why Morgenthau and Hull, who had spent an inordinate of time on this endeavor would fold so easily as a house of cards that someone breathed on. There is more here to see to meet the eye and unfortunately the recorded history of these events do not clearly present the answer. Historians can interpret the written record that is available to them but unfortunately cannot interview the dead. What Marshall brought to the table to derail this effort, a secret operation endorsed by the President himself, has yet to be uncovered.

But there are several possibilities. Roosevelt wanted desperately to go to war with Germany and Japan and he knew that with the isolationist sentiment throughout the country that Congress would never issue a Declaration of War. By supporting Great Britain, he hoped to goad Hitler in declaring war on the United States. And by ratcheting up the embargoes against Japan they too would be lured into war. General Marshall and Henry Stimson were certainly aware of this strategy but may have believed American made bombers (even in Chinese markings) raining incendiary bombs over Japan as such an overt action that Congress and the American people would see through this charade.

Although it could conceivably be something entirely different and more personal. Be assured that both General Marshall and Hap Arnold did not like Chennault. Chennault was an outsider, a renegade, and not part of the clique, and someone to be distrusted. Just a few years later, during World War II, Marshall would call him "disloyal and unreliable" because of his direct dealings with Chiang Kai-shek. Hap Arnold would later refer to him (Chennault) as a "crackpot." Toss in Vinegar Joe Stilwell (Chennault's superior in China during World War II) who later referred to him as a "jackass." These opinions did not occur overnight but were cultivated after many years of being associated with Chennault and one wonders if these views influenced the decision not to supply China (and Chennault) with heavy bombers. It is also interesting to note that an aircraft dubbed "Andrew's Folly" just a few years earlier would become such a hot commodity.

General Henry Harley "Hap" Arnold was born on June 25, 1886 in Gladwyne, Pennsylvania, into a prominent family with both political and military ties. His earliest flying instruction was from the Wright Brothers and he was an acolyte of General Billy Mitchell. He rose in rank to become Chief of the Air Corps from 1938 to 1941. He also despised Chennault well before the first flight of the Flying Tigers. In his book, *The Maverick War: Chennault and the Flying Tigers*, author Duane Schultz states:

> *"They saw him as a mercenary, fighting for economic gain as well as personal glory. General Laurence Kuter recalled that, to Arnold, "Chennault was an anathema, and he could see no good in him at all." Whispered allegations circulated in Washington that Chennault was involved in the black market and that he had love affairs with Chinese woman. "How can you trust such a dissolute man?" said General Marshall.*

Neither Marshall nor Arnold never confronted Chennault about these perceived imperfections to his face. It is easy to see why such military men such as Marshall and Arnold would oppose anything Chennault recommended for the Chinese even if it was of sound military advice and strategic value. Yet there are those who would argue that Chennault's failings as alleged by Marshall and Arnold would also be assets in a foreign and hostile environment.

Marshall, along with other high-ranking Army officials also questioned whether Chinese pilots were capable of flying high performance

General Hap Arnold tangled with President Roosevelt over lend-lease aircraft shipments that peaked on March 20, 1940 when Arnold went public. Roosevelt gave him a personal warning and banished him from the White House for eight months. (USAF)

four-engine bombers effectively and that these prize aircraft would be lost through accidents or mishaps. Although that would become a moot point, Marshall would entrust these precious aircraft to his friend General Douglas MacArthur in the Philippines. This would prove to have disastrous consequences just a day after the attack on Pearl Harbor.

One also one has to question why Morgenthau and Hull caved in immediately and so easily after just a single meeting with Stimson and Marshall. The pair were essentially neutered in dealing with China and the two government officials quickly dropped the proverbial hot potato of providing long range bombers to China. Like a magician lifting a cloth to reveal an illusion, both Morgenthau and Hull disappeared from the Chinese airpower scene like the lovely lady on stage during a magical act.

The Chinese still continued to push hard in an attempt of getting as much American aviation assistance as possible. Soong was a shrewd operator and he knew how big government worked and didn't work. There were fiefdoms, powers struggles, and often compartmentalization of information and a simple fact that remains to this day, that often the right hand does not know what the left hand is doing. Soong looked to take advantage of this foible and figured that if you throw a dozen darts against a wall some are bound to stick. Soong then made a quick pivot towards the British.

Soong approached the British Chargé d'Affairs Neville Butler in Washington, D.C. and suggested the formation of a British-American air force to operate in China in the interest of the Chungking Government. This was audacious on his part but also a non-starter as neither Great Britain nor the United States were in any state of war with Japan. Perhaps Soong simply decided to reach for the stars but settle for a few planets as a consolation prize.

Butler spoke with Sumner Welles, the Undersecretary of State, about Soong's proposal. Both agreed that this was not possible for both political and practical reasons and that each government should continue to take parallel action. Welles also indicated to Butler that the Chinese were not satisfied with the aircraft they were receiving and were only interested in the most modern planes being manufactured by the United States. So, it appears possible that Soong may have been applying gentle

Undersecretary of State Sumner Welles shakes hands with Cuban dictator Colonel Fulgencio Batista as General Malin Craig, then Army Chief of Staff looks on. (LOC)

pressure to persuade Great Britain to give up some of the planes they were receiving from the United States for possible shipment to China.

Essentially what Marshall was saying that Japan was a serious military threat to the United States yet on the other hand did not demand that America take a military response with a buildup of forces in the Pacific. Although the proposal to provide bombers appeared dead, it was really on life support – in just a few months Dr. Lauchlin Currie would soon breathe life back into the "half-baked" idea.

As cold rain showers swept across Washington on New Year's Day 1941, Secretary Morgenthau held a conference at his home. In attendance was Soong, Chennault, General Mao, and Phillip Young. According to the conference notes, the Secretary broke the news to those in attendance that the bombers were not available. Those present must have been stunned, given what Morgenthau had stated in their previous meeting. The secretary did offer a consolation prize. The notes of the meeting stated:

> *Secretary Morgenthau opened the conference by stating that it looked very doubtful if any of the long range heavy bombers could be made available to the Chinese. He added that, although the idea had the backing of the President, the Army felt it just couldn't release any of these ships at the present time. The Secretary said, however, that there was a good possibility of getting some P-40 pursuit ships, and he inquired from Dr. Soong how many ships they would have in order to start operations. Dr. Soong and General Mao carried on quite a conversation discussing the various uses and tactical maneuvers for which the P-40 would be used and then decided that probably twenty-seven ships would be required.* [16]

Yet it appears even with the B-17s off the table, Cordell Hull and the President wanted to string along General Kai-Shek for the ride. Nineteen days after the Gimo's telegram to President Roosevelt, Hull finally sent a reply via Ambassador Johnson:

> *My Dear General Chiang:*
>
> *I have your telegram of 12 December. I and other officers of this Government have been and are giving close and sympathetic attention to the situation in the Far East with a view to continuing to proceed along the lines of our announced*

policies. The Chinese Ambassador and Mr. T.V. Soong have been in frequent communication with various officers of this government. Recently, following the taking of solid steps of assistance to China (including large-scale loan and credit arrangements), officers of the Department of State discussed with Dr. Hu and Mr. Soong various aspects of the matters mentioned in your telegram, and you may be assured that it is our earnest intention to do everything we appropriately and practically can. Franklin D. Roosevelt. (17)

For several years the United States had the opportunity to provide the Chinese with war materials to help stem the Japanese advances. Yet the supplies came slowly and in meager amounts, with the promise that more was always on the way. For the Chinese it must have been frustrating and evoked an old Chinese saying, "There is much noise on the stairs, but no one enters the room."

Stepping into the void would be Dr. Lauchlin Bernard Currie. Although he was not involved in foreign affairs and not familiar with China, President Roosevelt decided to dispatch his administrative assistant to examine the current economic and military situation in China. The Canadian born economist, although never confirmed as a Communist, was considered an "agent of influence" by Moscow and also worked closely alongside Harold White in their respective departments of the Treasury and Federal Reserve. Being considered at a minimum a "democratic-socialist," Currie could influence Washington and help the Soviet Union blunt the

Lauchlin Currie would eventually move to Columbia and never return to the United States. (NARA)

aspirations of Japan to attack their country from the East by enabling the Chinese.

At this point the Generalissimo looked forward to meeting Currie, who Roosevelt sent to China to examine the current military and economic situation. Dr. Currie subsequently visited the country from 28 January to 11 March 1941, without, it would seem, having actually explored the scope and degree of completion of the various projects presented to him by the Chinese. Currie returned to tell the President that in anticipation of increased U.S. support the Generalissimo was rushing completion of airfields for the B-17s, making plans to centralize administrative control of the Burma Road, and assembling troops at strategic points to receive American weapons. Currie also presented Chinese requests for technicians, advisers, and further financial credits for the beleaguered country - and his continuing efforts would soon bear fruit.

Hemingway the Spy

WHILE THE GENERALISSIMO pushed every available button in his quest to acquire the much-vaunted B-17, a much more subdued event outside of government circles was taking place in the state of Idaho. Journalist and war correspondent Martha Gellhorn, the third wife of author Ernest Hemingway, was soon to embark on a trip to China. Gellhorn's plan was to report on the Sino-Japanese conflict on assignment for *Collier's* magazine.

Although Gellhorn lived off and on with Hemingway for four years they did eventually marry in December 1940. She asked Ernest if he would be interested in accompanying her on a visit to China. At first Hemingway balked at the proposal since he had never been to Asia and knew little about the country or culture. He soon relented and decided it might be a great adventure, but he would like to make the trip as a journalist and not just a simple tourist. Hemingway decided to reach out to his old fishing companion and magazine editor Ralph Ingersoll and asked him if he could travel as a correspondent.

Ingersoll was at *The New Yorker* and then *Time* before leaving in 1940 to launch a left-wing afternoon tabloid in New York named *PM*. Unlike other papers at the time they added a splash of color on page one and accepted no advertising and presented a daily political cartoon from Theodor Seuss Geisel, better known as Dr. Seuss.

Like so many other folks, Ingersoll had met Hemingway at the Key West bar Sloppy Joe's in 1934. After introductions and a few drinks, the two soon became good friends and went fishing together with Ingersoll spending time at Hemingway's house on Whitehead Street and probably nursing a hangover on several occasions. Hemingway in August 1940 discussed being a war correspondent in China with Ingersoll and the pair struck a deal in December. Ingersoll needed Hemingway more than the other way around. Gellhorn's assignment with *Collier's* magazine was also a big plus for the hard-drinking writer. Being friends with Elenore Roosevelt, Gellhorn helped smooth the path as she was usually able to obtain a letter of introduction from the President before she travelled abroad on various assignments. The letter from the President would be an asset as neither Hemingway nor Gellhorn had any inkling or familiarity of what was taking place in China at the time. For the pair of writers, China represented both an adventure and an opportunity to enhance their resumes.

Treasury Secretary Morgenthau caught wind of Hemingway's intended trip and in January 1941 and had his right-hand man Harry Dexter White reach out to the hard-drinking writer. Morgenthau intended to use Hemingway to garner more information on what was taking place in China as the United States was supplying the Generalissimo with vast amounts of money and he wanted to ensure that it was being spent appropriately. Hemingway would be a spy, not in the style of 007 James Bond, but someone who could obtain information outside of government influence. Besides, Morgenthau was not entirely friendly with Cordell Hull, the Secretary of State, distrusted him, and could not count on his office to receive accurate intelligence regarding overseas affairs.

Harry Dexter White was born in Boston, Massachusetts and was a noncombat Army Lieutenant during World War I. He did not start attending college until the age of 30 and he earned a Ph.D. in economics from Harvard University eight years later. White joined the Treasury Department in 1934 with an invitation from economist Jacob Viner and he became very important dealing with monetary issues. Unbeknownst to the White House or Morgenthau is the fact that White also had a potential part-time job as a spy for the Soviet Union, although historians are conflicted on this point. White did hire many aides outside normal civil service requirements that were either Soviet spies or Communist sympathizers.

White was also quite familiar with China and her policies both internal and external and in 1936 authored a 44-page memorandum on her financial situation. In March 1939 he advised Morgenthau that "the time is ripe to propose to Congress the extension of a $100 million ten-year credit to be used by China for whatever American products she wishes." Morgenthau had agreed which is why he was more than anxious almost a year later to have Hemingway have a peek on how the money was being spent but also on the status of the conflict the Nationalists had with both the Japanese and the Communists. With demands constantly increasing from the Generalissimo for more money and material the Treasury Secretary not only wanted to cover his backside but also needed vital information if he needed to turn the spigot off.

Harold Dexter White (left) testified against accusations of being a Soviet agent. Immediately thereafter he suffered two heart attacks and died at the age of 55. (International Monetary Fund)

White relayed Morgenthau's desires to Hemingway in a letter dated 27 January. It was the same day that Hemingway and Gellhorn left New York for Los Angeles on their first leg of the long journey to China. It would still be many weeks before the Treasury Department received any reports from Hemingway and in the end, they would be paltry at best.

Morgenthau had no qualms about the Treasury Department enlisting Hemingway to conduct such a spying mission. There were few restraints placed upon him by the Roosevelt administration on the activities he dabbled in. The powerful Treasury Secretary had even contacted the head of the FBI, J. Edgar Hoover, to provide surveillance on T.V. Soong and his activities.

As it turns out, Hemingway did not like China nor the culture and formed his opinions well before his arrival in Hong Kong. Writing in her memoirs, Gellhorn constantly calls Ernest the "Unwilling Companion," or "U.C." for short. The pair had met with Madame Chiang and Hemingway hit it off immediately with the fiery woman while Gellhorn raised the issue of lepers begging in in the streets. Madame erupted in anger and said "… unlike westerners we would never lock lepers up in isolation from other people." The visit by the couple to China was not a pleasant one but they would still deliver their stories to their respective publications.

Martha Gellhorn and Ernest Hemingway with unidentified Chinese military officers, Chungking, China. (JFK Library)

Hemingway would pen seven pieces (two that focused on Chinese aviation) about his observations in China for the New York based *PM* publication, but not until his return to New York in June 1941. It is not known if he met with or communicated with Morgenthau upon his return. The articles all had datelines of Hong Kong, Rangoon, and Manila, but were culled from notes that he amassed while visiting China. The precursor to the articles would be an interview by his editor, Ralph Ingersoll (edited by Hemingway) prior to their publication.

In Ingersoll's interview with Hemingway, published 6 June, he writes: "Must America Fight Japan? Hemingway told us why it's just a matter of timing. As far as America is concerned, time itself is fighting on our side. As for Japan, time is running out on her – and no one, not even the Japanese, knows when the last strategic moment will have to come. Or whether she should extricate herself from China at any price before challenging us." And Ingersoll wrote this six months before Pearl Harbor.

In his first piece, regarding Chinese aviation and titled *China's Air Needs*, Hemingway totally eviscerates the quality of Chinese pilots. He states how they regaled Dr. Lauchlin Currie in flying formations during his visit only to be shot down several days later while engaging the Japanese. Hemingway states, "Any real American aid to the Chinese in the air would have to include pilots. Sending them planes keeps them happy and keeps them fighting. It will not put them in condition to take the offense successfully." [18]

In his next piece titled *Chinese Build Air Field*, the novelist and reporter left little to doubt what the Chinese intended, or wished to do, in the immediate future as Hemingway writes:

> *It started with the Generalissimo talking about Flying Fortresses. With some of those big four-motor Boeings the Chinese could fly over Japan at an altitude where neither Japanese anti-aircraft nor pursuit could bother them and bring to Japan the horror that she had spread through China in the past four years. There were no Chinese who were qualified to be checked out on Flying Fortresses as pilots, but none of those present brought that up. That was a thing that could presumably be arranged later. Someone did point out, though, that there was not a single airfield in China which could handle a Boeing B-17.*
> *At this point in the conversation the Generalissimo made a note. "What do they weigh? He asked.*
> *"Around 22 tons," told him with more or less accuracy.*
> *"Not over that?" asked the Generalissimo.*
> *"No. But I will check."*
> *The next day construction on the airfield begins.* [19]

It's amazing that this vital military information made it to publication and with little doubt that Japanese took keen interest in this activity. And construction of the airfield, in Chengtu, did begin immediately and was headed by a 38-year-old engineer, Chen Low-khan, a graduate of the University of Illinois. Building of the airfield began on the 8 January 1941 and was expected to be completed within ninety days.

The great writer travelled to Chengtu to see the construction firsthand. Hemingway related how no mechanized equipment was used, but instead wrote how 100,000 workers, working 12-hours shifts, transformed a 1,000-acre field to produce a runway over a mile long with a width of 150 yards. Over 5000 wheelbarrows and 200,000 baskets, slung on carrying sticks, were used at the time. Roughly 150 three-and-a-half to ten-ton concrete rollers were employed to smooth the runway pulled with the only power available, humans.

Hemingway noted that the workers were always singing, and he asked an engineer what is that song. Hemingway relates:

> *"It is only what they sing,"* the engineer told me. *"It is a song they sing that makes them happy."*
> *"What do they sing now?"*
> *"Now we have done what we can do. Now come the Flying Fortresses. Now-we-have-done-what-we-can-do! Now-come-the-Flying-Fortresses!"*
> *"You can send somebody who can fly them,"* an engineer said.[20]

Obviously, the Chinese engineer was referring to American pilots for the B-17s. There is little reason to believe that Hemingway fabricated any parts of the story. If Hemingway confided in Morgenthau, the Treasury Secretary did not relate this in his detailed diaries. Yet the story was laid out for the public and for those within the Roosevelt administration to read. It meant the Chinese were serious about dealing a serious blow to the Japanese homeland and was planning on American aid. It is also possible that Hemingway had a dual purpose in making the trip to China. Some historians have also speculated that Hemingway was recruited by Soviet intelligence agents during this time and given the agent code name "Argo."

Tomahawks for Chennault

WITH THE BOMBERS OFF the table (temporarily), Chennault and Soong would have to settle for 100 P-40B Tomahawks that would eventually be the nucleus of the American Volunteer Group (A.V.G.) better known as the Flying Tigers. Now how these aircraft were acquired by China is a convoluted story involving a number of different characters. As with all matters involving the delivery of war material to China, the Tomahawks were unnecessarily delayed for months and this would have serious ramifications leading up to the attack on Pearl Harbor.

The P-40 Tomahawk can trace its roots back to 1938 when a radial engine in a P-36 Hawk was replaced with an Alison V-1710 V-12 liquid-cooled, supercharged engine. The first flight took place later that same year in October. The Army Air Corps adopted the name Warhawk while the British and Soviets took on the name Tomahawk. Many variations ensued but the British ones destined for China were fitted with six .303-caliber machine guns.

Curtiss XP-40 prototype. (USAF)

The Tomahawk was agile at low and medium altitudes but with just a single stage supercharger it performed poorly at high altitudes and the service ceiling was 29,000 feet. The planes destined for China did not have the capability of a detachable belly tank or wing bomb ranks and the fuel tanks were not truly self-sealing. The plane cruised at 270MPH and had a maximum speed of 360MPH, but its best attribute was its ability to dive swiftly without fear of tearing off a wing. Chennault would later impress upon his pilots not to dogfight with Japanese fighters but use the advantage of the Tomahawk's impressive dive capability and the structural integrity of the planes not to shed their wings in a high-speed turn. Soong had an open checkbook but finding suitable aircraft would be problematic. Soong and Chennault travelled to the Curtiss-Wright plant in Buffalo, New York, where Chennault met an old friend, Burdette Wright, the Curtiss vice-president. Wright came up with a proposition, where an additional assembly line could be launched and that the British could waive rights for 100 P-40Bs scheduled for production in favor of the newly designed P-40C. Soong and Morgenthau were able to convince the British to release the order and initial shipments of the planes was scheduled for February – that is until Pawley got wind of the sale.

With Pawley as President of Intercontinental Aviation Corporation he insisted that he held exclusive rights for all Curtiss-Wright aircraft sales to China and demanded that he receive his 10% commission which amounted to a whopping $450,000 for essentially doing nothing. At this point the shit hit the fan and the whole deal began to unravel as everyone scuttled about attempting to rectify the situation.

First up in this messy situation was Phillip Young who said that Intercontinent was the only company to assemble and maintain the aircraft, thus receiving an appropriate service charge and that Intercontinental should waive the commission. Pawley didn't blink. Another possibility emerged was that China would buy the aircraft directly from Great Britain, thus bypassing Intercontinent, but this was deemed unworkable. Morgenthau leaned on Young and told him to deal with Curtiss-Wright directly to get this situation resolved quickly. On the 16 January, Curtiss-Wright stated that they were willing to pay the 10% commission to Pawley. But Young dug in his heels and believed that since the United States government was involved no commission should be paid at which Pawley responded by threatening a court injunction. Curtiss-Wright was showing their intentions by starting to ship P-40s to Weehawken, New Jersey in preparation for delivery to China.

After an all-day meeting that took place on Wednesday, 29 January, Young hammered out a deal that would have Curtiss Wright pay $100,000 and Soong $150,000 to quiet Pawley. The first P-40Bs, a shipment of 36, would leave for Rangoon on 19 February.

Chennault would later paint an entirely different [inaccurate] version regarding Pawley's commission on the sale of the Curtiss-Wright P-40s to China. In his memoir, Way of the Fighter, Chennault wrote:

> In February the planes were on the New York docks ready for shipment to Rangoon. At this critical stage William D. Pawley, Curtiss-Wright salesman in China, entered the picture...
>
> Pawley's role in the A.V.G. project began with his demand that Curtiss-Wright pay him a 10-per-cent commission on the $4,500,000 purchase price of the one hundred P-40's [sic] being sold to China. He produced his contract with Curtiss, which called for the commission on all planes sold by Curtiss in China and threatened to get an injunction against shipment of the P-40's [sic] unless he was paid.

Curtiss-Wright refused to pay Pawley alleging he had nothing to do with the sale. Months were lost in futile negotiations until there was acute danger that the Chinese would lose the planes. Rather than pay Pawley, Curtiss-Wright was ready to sell them back to the R.A.F.

Secretary Morgenthau called a conference on April 1, 1941, for a showdown. The fight lasted all day. The Chinese were so desperate for the planes they offered to pay Pawley out of Chinese funds. Morgenthau refused to let them and concentrated on wearing Pawley down. Morgenthau threatened to take over Curtiss as a war emergency, but Pawley didn't scare. Finally the Chinese suggested a compromise where-by Pawley would be paid $250,000-considerably less than the $450,000 he wanted-in return for which Central Aircraft Manufacturing Company would assemble, test fly, and service the P-40's [sic] in Burma and China. CAMCO then had an assembly plant at Loi-Wing just across the Burmese border in China that was ideally located as a heavy maintenance base. Late in April, the planes were shipped aboard an old slow Norwegian freighter. The first plane was lost when a cargo sling broke, depositing a P-40 fuselage in the waters of New York harbor. (21)

Morgenthau kept meticulous notes and recorded Pawley's commission on January 30, 1941. In reviewing Morgenthau's notes, he only met Chennault twice on December 21, 1940 and January 1, 1941. Both meetings took place at Morgenthau's home. Several years later Morgenthau would later confide to Senator Claude Pepper in a telephone conversation that he never met Pawley personally. This indicates that anything written in Chennault's memoirs should be carefully reviewed for accuracy before recording it as fact.

With some aircraft already in the pipeline the daunting task began of finding American pilots and ground crews that would be willing to travel to China. The United States government would have to "officially" have nothing to do with the recruitment of American servicemen as this would be an overt violation of the Neutrality Act. Chennault suggested that a civilian company be formed to facilitate the recruitment of American fighter pilots for China. As it turns out a company was already in place – Central Aircraft Manufacturing Corporation – CAMCO – Hello again Mr. Pawley.

CAMCO - A Secret Operation to Reel in the Pilots

ACQUIRING PLANES FOR CHINA was one thing, getting American pilots and ground crew was an entirely different situation – namely it was entirely illegal and would be a flagrant violation of the Neutrality Act. Recruitment would need to be done covertly and on 15 February, General Marshall informed Undersecretary of State Sumner Welles that William Pawley would do it and use his company, CAMCO, as a cover. [22] How Marshall got involved in this murky operation is not known.

Pawley's lawyer, Robert R. Scott, informed his client of the illegality of this operation and that he could possibly be jailed in the future. Pawley was undeterred even if it meant imprisonment and worse, having to deal with Chennault. Arthur N. Young, a financial advisor to the Chinese government, stated the position of the United States in a 29 January memorandum saying: "…in practice the American authorities are prepared to close their eyes if it is possible to avoid raising issues with which they will be forced to deal [with]." [23] The dates of Young's memo, and Marshall conversing with Welles, indicate the planning and negotiation of the clandestine operation took at least a couple of weeks involving an unknown number of people.

Even though this illegal operation still needed President Roosevelt's approval, if only verbally, Pawley believed it was forthcoming and told his company treasurer, Octavio Cuevas, to send a telegram to his brother Ed in China:

February 18, 1941

Negotiating extensive training program requiring employment by CAMCO of approximately 250 [stop] 100 pilots 150 technical including mechanics clerks radio operators doctors nurses [stop]. British as to cooperate [stop] Air Vice Marshall [John] Slessor (spell in code) now Washington notifying Royal Air Force Far Eastern Commanding Officer Singapore to contact you through British Embassy Chunking regarding any local information he may require [stop] Royal Air Force London requested furnish several pursuit squadron leaders to instruct American pilots [stop] Possibly will arrange for several weeks squadron training in Burma [stop] P.T. Mao possibly familiar with part of program [stop] 100 P-40's purchased 35 being shipped immediately balance soon [stop] Intercontinent signed contract covering assembly and flight test Rangoon [stop] Special revolving fund being arranged New York payment of expenses this program [stop] British showing excellent cooperative spirit [stop] You can discuss this telegram with British Ambassador [stop] (24)

The idea of the United States providing China with aircraft, pilots, and potentially long-range bombers was intended to be accessible to a limited number of individuals. As it turns out this was not case. The Assistant Naval Attaché at the time in China, Major James M. McHugh, USMC, was privy to the deals that were going on between the politicians in Washington, Chennault, and the Chinese government.

McHugh had spent over twenty years in China and as an "Old China Hand," he had the ear of the Generalissimo and Madame Chiang. As an attaché, he was the eyes and ears of Ambassador Johnson and this totally irked another attaché, Colonel Joseph "Vinegar Joe" Stillwell. Because of his demeanor and relationship to the Chinese, Stillwell was not very effective in his position and despised McHugh's rapport with those in influential positions. The two would later lock horns in the upcoming war with Japan.

On 8 February, McHugh dispatched a telegram, presumably to his immediate superior Secretary Knox. He verified a large shipment of aircraft from the Soviet Union to China of which the majority were twin-engine bombers. He also informed Knox of a new airfield being built near Chengtu and that the Chinese were expanding several runways with improvements.

While the United States politicians wrung their hands, and hemmed and hawed over the Japanese "problem," Admiral Isoruko Admiral Yamamoto, with assent from the Naval High Command, ordered plans be drawn up for the attack on Pearl Harbor. As McHugh sent off his telegram, Admiral Ryunosuke Kusake, Captain Minoru Genda, and Deputy Chief of Staff, Captain Kameto Kuroshima, developed the operational attack plan.

While Japan took concrete steps for their future activity and territorial expansion, Washington vacillated on what to do and feared what their Japanese counterparts would do if provoked. Incredulously, while the United States knew that war with the Japan was on the horizon, sales of oil and gasoline continued until an embargo on these products was initiated on the 1 August.

The recruitment of active servicemen to serve in China still needed the President's approval. Despite the urgency of the situation, American bureaucrats moved at a speed that could easily be eclipsed by a 90-year-old with a walker. Soong had had enough and met with the "Cork," Tommy Corcoran, to ask him to persuade the President for his approval of the operation. On 15 April, Roosevelt signed a secret executive order that would permit a private corporation [CAMCO] and allow them to solicit U.S. military servicemen for employment in China. [25] A contract was already in the waiting, signed by both Leighton (Inter-continental vice-president who sent the cryptic memo to Admiral Stark a year earlier) and Soong. Chennault was depicted as the American supervisor. The CAMCO contract stated:

> *CAMCO would pay $600 a month "to render such services and perform such duties as the Employer may direct."*
> *Employment was for one year and would begin when the employee reported in person at a designated port of departure from the United States.*
>
> *All reasonable travel expenses would be paid by CAMCO "to the place in China" where the employee would be assigned. Expenses include: first-class railroad fare and berth, the cost of a passport and visas, the reasonable cost of hotels and meals "while awaiting ocean transportation," transportation to China, $100 for "contingent expenses," and "actual expenses" incurred on the trip to destination in China.*
>
> *CAMCO would pay $500 in lieu of employee's return transportation costs from China to the United States upon termination of the contract.*
>
> *CAMCO would have the right to terminate the contract "in the event of misconduct" of the employee for insubordination, revealing confidential information, habitual use of drugs, excessive use of alcohol, illness or disability not incurred in the line of duty as a result of employee's own misconduct, and malingering.* [26]

Pawley reached out to several individuals to join him as recruiters. Don't forget the United States was still in the throes of the depression and good paying jobs were hard to come by. First up was Richard Aldworth, a former Army pilot who at the time was recovering from a kidney ailment at Walter Reed Hospital. Eventually Pawley met him in New York City where he agreed to become a recruiter.

Next up was Captain Claude Bryant Adair (referred to in most publications simply as C.B. "Skip" Adair). Adair, a former Army pilot who spent time in China as a flight instructor, would later become the Flying Tigers supply officer. Next on board were Rutledge Irving, Harry C. Claiborne, and Fenton L. Brown. They fanned out across the country looking for potential candidates. All recruiters were given blank contracts to hand out for signatures, informed them of CAMCO's requirements and the "incentives" available to offer prospective pilots and ground crew.

This recruitment process, a Presidential mandate, would be stymied by low level bureaucrats and even high-ranking military personnel such as General "Hap" Arnold who opposed the entire idea. Secretary of War Stimson even needed to step in and tell Arnold to let these "recruiters" onto the Army bases. And Army base commanders often resisted the recruiters who were attempting to pluck the "cream of the crop." Ground crewmen who earned $84 a month with the Army could soon earn $300 a month for the same work in an "exotic" locale. Who could resist?

CAMCO recruitment for American volunteers began in April and by May, 243 applications were received. By June, 18 pilots, 58 ground personnel, and seven medical personnel had been recruited. By 30 May, ground crewmen set sail aboard the SS *President Pierce* of the San Francisco American President Lines. On 7 June, Chennault met the first contingent of volunteers at the Mark Hopkins Hotel located at the top of Nob Hill in San Francisco – ironically the fourth anniversary of the Marco Polo Bridge incident when Sino-Japanese relations took a turn for the worse.

Even with Soong approving a $500 bonus for each Japanese plane shot down recruitment was slow. Photographs of a beautiful countryside, colorful pagodas, and water buffalo were circulated at the hotel meeting. Chennault assured the men that their American citizenship was not in jeopardy. Then Pawley gave a short speech. James Howard, a Navy pilot and recruit, recalls the salesman saying:

> "As president of CAMCO, I welcome you to San Francisco where you will start your first leg of your trip to Burma. I spent many years in the Orient where we established an aircraft manufacturing plant. Because of the constant advances of the Japanese army, we have been forced to move our factory several times until it is now located in the town of Loiwing on the Burma-China border."
>
> "When do we get our P40s?" an anxious pilot asked.
> "I have a branch at my factory in Rangoon which is assembling

the planes from crates that are on the Rangoon dock. By the time you arrive in Burma your planes will be ready to fly." [27]

Pawley of course was stretching the truth a bit. Arrangements still needed to be worked out with the British War Office, and the recruits eventually would find out about their new home, Kyedaw Airfield. Boasting a 4,000-foot paved runway it was abandoned by the British because during the monsoon season the climate reeked of decaying vegetation and the insects were incessant and voracious. Even for the standards of Burma at the time, Kyedaw was at the bottom of the barrel.

Always the consummate salesman, Pawley passed out passports to his new employees, with occupations noted as clerks, clergy, bankers, and musicians, but none as pilots. The following day Chennault, along with Owen Lattimore, a special political advisor to Chiang Kai-shek, boarded a Pan American Airways Clipper bound for Hong Kong via Hawaii. On 10 July, the new volunteers boarded the MS *Jagersfontein* of the United Netherlands Navigation Company.

A Pan American Airways Martin M-130 "China Clipper" of the type that Chennault and Lattimore would have flown together to China. The starboard engines have had their cowlings removed for servicing. (NASM)

Two weeks later another group of pilots and ground support crew arrived at the Bellevue Hotel in San Francisco. Skip Adair courted this group and told them what to expect in China (sort of) and to keep tight-lipped about the operation. That really wasn't necessary as both the Japanese military and the American press was already quite aware of the A.V.G. Adair stressed that this is a secret mission and everything should remain confidential. Benjamin Franklin once stated, "Three may keep a secret, if two of them are dead." And there were a lot more than three people involved in this guerilla aviation operation besides those in the A.V.G. and all the government entities involved. Franklin would have been stacking the bodies like cordwood to keep this operation secret.

On 24 July the second volunteer contingent boarded the MS *Bloemfontein*, a sister ship to the MS *Jagersfontein*. A day earlier, the *New York Times* reported, "For the past few months, tall, bronzed American airmen have been quietly slipping away from east and west coast ports, making their way to China." While in route, the "…bronzed American airmen" aboard the MS *Jagersfontein* heard a Japanese broadcast stating that the ship would be sunk and never reach its destination. Currie had anticipated this and asked President Roosevelt to provide an escort. Two light cruisers were dispatched, the USS *Salt Lake City* (CA-25), nicknamed the Swayback Maru, and the USS *Northampton* (CA-26), named after the town in Massachusetts where President Calvin Coolidge was born, to accompany the Dutch ship. The Americans warships separated at Australia where Dutch military vessels continued the escort without incidence.

The Soviets Bail Out on China

WHAT MUST HAVE BEEN a crushing and demoralizing event for Chiang Kai-Shek and the Chinese Air Force is the decision by Joseph Stalin to end all Soviet aviation support to China. After the collapse of France, Stalin, expecting a possible two-front war, decided to make amends in Asia and secure his eastern borders. It is for that reason and several others that the Soviet–Japanese Neutrality Pact was signed in Moscow on 13 April.

The agreement favored both parties and the Soviet Union could focus on Nazi Germany to the west and the Japanese would have just a single front against its future antagonist the United States. The treaty was signed by Soviet Foreign Minister Vyacheslav Nikhailovich Molotov and Japanese Ambassador Yoshitsugu Tatekawa and Foreign Minister Yosuke Matsouka. In an unprecedented move, Stalin bid farewell to Matsouka at the train station and even hugged him! Concluding the man crush, Stalin then approached the German ambassador and embraced him saying, "We must remain friends and you must do everything to that end." [28] It is not known if alcohol was a factor, but it did send an important message to Hitler that Stalin was a major player on the world stage despite the Tripartite Pact that Japan had signed on to.

Of course, treaties are only as good as the paper they are signed upon and the men that stood behind them. That same day that the Soviet-Japanese Neutrality Pact was signed by the Soviets, they also agreed to respect the territory integrity regarding Mongolia and Manchuria. Stalin was gambling more than his Japanese counterparts and would take that risk. Eventually both countries benefitted by sticking to this agreement and the two losers, at least in the short view and for several years, would be the United States and China. Hitler sealed the deal when he launched Operation Barbarossa and attacked the Soviet Union on 22 June. Russian aid for the Chinese immediately evaporated.

For the three years that the Soviet Union actively supported China with aircraft and pilots and it eclipsed by leaps and bounds what the United States would provide during the same period. About 1200 aircraft were delivered, many of which were crewed by Soviet airmen. And the Japanese did not discriminate and would strafe parachuting airmen, whether Soviet or Chinese. About 200 Soviet pilots lost their lives during this time – split equally between combat losses and accidents. Stalin also believed that the United States would pick up the slack, further sucking their resources and enabling the Japanese to pursue their military efforts southward – and he was right in both cases and played his cards extremely well.

Goodbye American Isolationism – Hello China Defense Supplies!

ON 29 DECEMBER 1940 during a radio broadcast, President Roosevelt proclaimed the United States should become an "Arsenal for Democracy" and pushed for a bill for the United States to provide material aid (openly) for Canada, Great Britain, and China. The isolationists and interventionists, including many Republicans, but represented mainly by the America First Committee (AFC), led by Charles Lindbergh, denounced this speech and once again stated that this would draw Americans into another war on foreign soil. Often overlooked at this time was that two future Presidents supported the AFC initiative, namely John F. Kennedy and Gerald Ford.

In Lindbergh's testimony before the House Committee on Foreign Affairs the "Lone Eagle" proposed that a neutrality pact with Germany would be in the best interests of the United States. Roosevelt had told Morgenthau, "If I should die tomorrow, I want you to know this, I am absolutely convinced Lindbergh is a Nazi." [29] In a letter to Secretary of War Stimson Roosevelt said in part, "When I read Lindbergh's speech I felt that it could not have been better put if it had been written by Goebbels himself." [30]

Congress would approve the bill, mainly along party lines and a month prior to the Soviet-Japanese Neutrality Pact. President Roosevelt officially signed the Lend-Lease Act on 11 March. Formally designated as "An Act to Promote the Defense of the United States" it essentially ended United States neutrality in world affairs. The United States finally started to flex its industrial muscles and would provide war material to Free France, China, Great Britain, and the Soviet Union. This was a sharp departure from American isolationism that dominated United States foreign relations since 1931. But the lend-lease initiative did not make it legal for American citizens to participate as foreign combatants – this will still be needed to be part of a clandestine operation.

Dictators Benito Mussolini and Adolph Hitler in happier times when Charles Lindbergh advocated appeasement and an isolationist policy for the United States. (LOC)

President Franklin D. Roosevelt, 1941. (LOC)

On the heels of this new political directive, Lauchlin Currie updated Roosevelt on the Chinese situation and sent a telegram that included the following recommendations regarding military assistance:

Mr. Lauchlin Currie to President Roosevelt
[Washington,] March 15, 1941.

Report on Some Aspects of the Current Political, Economic and Military Situation in China

2. Military Aid.

I was given a complete list of the artillery, ammunition and ordnance raw material needs of the Chinese Army, amounting to $207 million. In addition, the Chinese would like as many pursuit ships and long-range bombers as we can spare. It was stressed continually that all these items were necessary in order to assume the offensive. I think that, in releasing matériel and pilots, you could arrive at a more definite understanding that an offensive will actually be undertaken. A first-class military diversion in China should have a decidedly deterrent effect on any contemplate Chinese are making great efforts to build a number of airfields that can carry the weight of our flying fortresses. I inspected one at Chengtu which was being built by 75,000 peasants with no power-driven machinery of any kind. The man in charge was a Chinese civil engineer trained at the University of Illinois. It was a marvelous job of organization and, so far as I could judge, completely adequate from the point of view of foundation and drainage. I was assured that a number of such fields were being built near the coast.

I questioned the Generalissimo and the various generals I met closely on the specific need for airplanes. It developed that the most pressing need is for pursuit ships and a few very long-range bombers (author's italics). While medium-range bombers would be useful, they are not so essential as the others. Pursuit ships are essential to protect troop concentrations in an offensive and to machine gun opposing troops.

The Generalissimo is very anxious to secure a few flying fortresses. He is under the impression, via T. V. Soong via

Secretary Morgenthau, that you promised some in March or April. If you did not, this matter should be cleared up.

I inspected an aviation basic training school, where an air show was staged for my benefit by the more advanced commissioned pilots. There was formation flying, landing and taking off without stopping and a dog fight. The cadets were a fine-looking group. I saw no evidence of any slackness and I was told that they were vigorously selected and trained. One defect I noticed is that they receive no training in motor mechanics. [31]

In his telegram, Currie mentioned "long-range bombers" twice and then followed up with "a few flying fortresses." This certainly reinforces Currie's position that China should be provided with the capability of bombing the Japanese homeland. Whether this was meant as an assist for China or possibly Stalin's Soviet Union is open to conjecture.

With Roosevelt's approval of the Lend-Lease plan that included China, it did not include (or condone) the employment of American citizens to fight on behalf of China. Even though recruitment of Chennault's pilots to fly the newly acquired Tomahawks that would be through CAMCO, another entity to cloak the acquisition of additional aircraft and pilots would be advantageous. This is when an acquaintance of T.V. Soong, a Polish doctor named Ludwig "Lulu" Rajchman, suggested that a separate private corporation be created to handle the potential questionable monetary transactions supporting the "Special Air Unit." Rajchman was the former head of the Health Secretariat at the League of Nations and was well known amongst the diplomats embedded in Washington. [28] Even with the passage of Lend-Lease, the formation of another company pursuing the interests of China simply added another wrap of obfuscation that the United States and China could hide themselves behind from prying eyes – whether that was internal or external. – even though it would be unusual for an American corporation to be housed in the Chinese embassy. CAMCO could legally and openly provide aircraft to China but someone else would be needed to provide cover for the pilots to fly those aircraft.

Several people relate that Roosevelt himself suggested the name China Defense Supplies, Inc. (CDS), although this is unlikely as the shadow enterprise was incorporated in Delaware. On paper it was a private corporate company, yet Roosevelt recommended that William S. Youngman be at the helm of the newly constituted company. Youngman, the former counsel for the Federal Power Commission immediately sought out Roosevelt's former speech writer and New Deal enabler Thomas Gardiner Corcoran. One of Roosevelt's close confidents for several years, the President called him "Tommy the Cork." Corcoran, along with Benjamin V. Cohen, jump started a number of New Deal initiatives and the pair were dubbed the "Gold Dust Twins" and featured on the cover of *Time* Magazine, September 12, 1938.

As an Irish Catholic, Corcoran, a fascist sympathizer and isolationist was not keen on increasing financial and material aid to Great Britain. Harry Hopkins once told Corcoran, "Tom you're too Catholic to trust the Russians and too Irish to trust the English. As a close advisor to the President he eventually found himself outside of the "inner circle." Yet his finger would stay in the political pie for years to come.

Tommy Corcoran (right) leaves the White House alongside Secretary of the Interior Harold Ickes after conferring with President Roosevelt. (LOC)

Several sources state that early in October 1940 Roosevelt asked Corcoran to resign from his administration and carry out a clandestine operation that was deemed "too politically dangerous" while in government service. This was months before the CDS would be officially incorporated and CAMCO began recruiting pilots and ground crewmen. Corcoran himself held no title within the newly formed enterprise except as "outside counsel." He would later describe China Defense Supplies as "an unorthodox operation...dubious according to the letter of the law." (32) Arrangements were then made to lease office space at 1601 V Street, Northwest, in Washington, D.C. to stay close to the makers and shakers within the Roosevelt administration.

But according to Hannah Pakula, author of *The Last Empress*, Corcoran stated that he was approached by Lauchlin Currie who said the President wanted to help Chiang. Pakula goes on to say that Corcoran said:

> *"Acting for the President, Currie then suggested that as a private individual ...charter a Delaware corporation to be known as China Defense Supplies. In fact it would be the entire Lend Lease operation for China. The civilian company, supported entirely with government funds, was in one respect a simple conduit behind a façade of utmost respectability."* (33)

Pakula incorrectly states that these alleged activities took place in the winter of 1941 when they probably occurred (if at all) in the winter of 1940 or the spring of 1941. Regardless of who pushed Corcoran to form the company, it certainly included an intriguing group of people.

First off is Roosevelt's uncle Fredric Delano as "honorary counselor" to the business and Corcoran's brother David as the CDS President and you have a poster child for the President's incestuous relationship with private companies during his administration. The CDS corporation would soon include William Brennan as the congressional liaison, Gordon Bradford Tweedy, who was also a "special counsel" and a member of the tax division in the Department Justice. Additional figures included Quinn Shaughnessy, a former Marine Corps intelligence officer and a trained Harvard lawyer. Also brought into this questionable operation was Whiting Willauer.

Willauer was born in 1906 in New York City, New York and graduated both Princeton and Harvard Law School. He practiced admiralty law in Boston, Massachusetts and become executive secretary of the CDS enterprises for three years and with little surprise entered government service as director of the Far East and Special Territories Branch of the Foreign Economic Administration from 1944 to 1945.

It is interesting that Willauer would later partner with Chennault after the war and form the Civil Air Transport enterprise. In the ensuing years, Civil Air Transport would be sold to the CIA and morph into Air

America and eventually become a clandestine aerial service for the spy agency during the Vietnam war. After World War II, Willauer became an ambassador to Costa Rica and Honduras. He was also part of the 1954 Guatemalan coup d'état that was a covert operation carried out by the CIA that deposed the democratically elected Guatemalan President Jacobo Árbenz. These future activities were no doubt cultivated by his work with the CDS before World War II.

Unlike war material aid to Great Britain, that seemed to be well choreographed, assistance to China seemed to be splintered among many different individuals with no single person or department to spearhead the effort. Currie was only an advisor and delivered his suggestions to the President and then that information filtered down on what was needed to take place with other governmental departments for action. No one had the courage or ambition to take the lead amongst several governmental agencies and everything moved forward at glacial speed. That "can do" American spirit that extended to the British seemed to evaporate when dealing with the Chinese. It appears even more apparent with the following memo from General Marshall to Hap Arnold:

March 28, 1941 [Washington, D.C.]

Confidential

The Secretary of War had two things up yesterday:

His first question was how far you had progressed in making arrangements for your trip to England. The second matter related to General Clagett's prospective visit to China. He approved the idea of General Clagett, and I will leave it to you to prepare the directive to Clagett. Mr. Currie [sic] (the official who reported the Chinese desire to have a high ranking Air Corps official visit there) stated there were three things the Chinese thought might be accomplished by this visit:

1. The officer could determine for himself the efficiency of the Chinese Air Force, from the viewpoint of its possible cooperation with us if we became involved in this war.

2. The officer could inform himself as to the adequacy of the new air fields to be constructed.

3. The officer could inform himself as to the fighting tactics and characteristics of the Japanese Air Force, from what has been learned by the Chinese Aviation Corps.

The visit would have an important psychological effect in that it would indicate to the Chinese that they were being considered as potential allies rather than beggars at the rich man's table. (This last phrase is mine) (34)

The last sentence in Marshall's memo to Arnold clearly indicates what the man really thought of China and her people. Several days later Soong presented China's aircraft requirements to Maj Gen James H. Burns, Executive Officer of the Division of Defense Aid Reports (precursor to the Office of Lend-lease Administration) and under the auspices of Harry Hopkins.

Gen. George C. Marshall, U. S. Army Chief of Staff and Gen. Henry "Hap" Arnold, Commanding General, U. S. Army Air Corps. (NARA)

May 1941 appears to be a pivotal month regarding the United States in possibly providing aircraft to the Chinese as a plethora of memorandums, letters, phone calls, and telegrams flew amongst the politicians and military strategists, seemingly with no single figure nor government entity taking the lead to ensure that this endeavor achieve success. On the 9 May, Currie wrote a memorandum to President Roosevelt about the aircraft requirements to China. Three days letter he then informed General Marshall of the proposal to supply China with 350 fighters and 150 bombers and that the whole affair was referred to the Joint Aircraft Committee who then passed it along to the Joint Army/Navy Board. On the 15 May, Roosevelt told Currie to proceed with the program for supplying aircraft to China, but reading the following telegram from Hap Arnold, it appears that Currie jumped the gun, without approval from the Commander in Chief.

May 10, 1941
MEMORANDUM TO: The Secretary of War.

SUBJECT: Aircraft Requirements of the Chinese Government

1. The Joint Aircraft Committee is in receipt of a request to give consideration to the Chinese aircraft requirements in the scheduling of future aircraft production. The request was from Mr. Lauchlin Currie (sic), Administrative Assistant to the President, and was transmitted to the committee by Major General J.H. Burns.

2. The results of a study which was prepared so as to show the scheduling possibilities are included in the enclosed chart. It is apparent that there is a wide discrepancy between the deliveries desired and the estimated deliveries which can be made on the basis of present production programs. Therefore, the only possible means of providing aircraft appears to be diversion from present Army, Navy or British procurement. The Chinese request also included indefinite numbers of replacement airplanes to maintain the combat squadrons at full strength and of additional trainers to expand the training program. No allowance is made in the attached study for additional aircraft.

3. It is the desire of the Joint Aircraft Committee that this request be referred to the Joint Board for policy to be used as a guide if it is thought necessary to divert from present pro-

curements. The Committee also requests that the British staff be invited to present their views to the Joint Board.

4. The Committee has been informed that there is urgent need for a satisfactory answer to the Chinese request and it is therefore asked that the Joint Board consider this case at the earliest possible moment.
(Signed)
Henry H. Arnold
Major General, U.S. Army
Senior Member, Joint Aircraft Committee [35]

Arnold's memorandum once again shows that no single person or group of people was willing to pull the trigger and get the ball moving to send combat aircraft to the Chinese. Part of this may still be the isolationist movement prevalent across the country. Another factor may be "War Plan Orange," part of a series of United States Joint Army and Navy military plans developed over the years since World War I. Broad-based for just about any worldwide scenario they were updated in recent years that took a "Europe first" approach.

Another consideration with lend-lease to China was Arnold's concern of slow delivery of aircraft to the Air Corps. This began in 1938 when aircraft production was given to the Procurement Division of the Treasury Department. Arnold and Morgenthau would be at each other over this process for two years. This battle climaxed when Arnold went public with his concerns and on March 12, 1940 and President Roosevelt personally warned him that if he didn't "play ball" he could wind up on Guam. Roosevelt then banished the General from the White House for eight months. That same day that Currie wrote to General Marshall and Lieutenant Colonel Edwin Elliot MacMorland, Chief of Ordnance within the War Department, and informed Marshall's secretary, Colonel Orlando Ward, that the question of providing China with aircraft would be placed with the Joint Army/Navy Board. This appears to be a redundant communication since Currie already informed Marshall. MacMorland states:

For the information of General Marshall, I am attaching a strategic estimate which I obtained from Mr. Currie, [sic] indicating the interest which the British should have in a strong Chinese air force on the flank of any attack on Singapore. I make this remark because I've heard that the British will be invited to attend the Joint Board Meeting, and if diversions are seriously discussed, it would very desirable to emphasize the importance of a Chinese air force to them [36]

As the proverbial Chinese hot potato was tossed about in Washington on 13 May the Northampton class cruiser, the USS *Houston* (CA-30) sailed the coast of the Philippine Islands. Built in 1929, it was the flagship of Admiral Thomas Hart, the commander of the U.S. Navy Asiatic Fleet in the Philippines. On board was Captain Williams Reynolds Purnell, the Chief of Staff of Admiral Hart's Asiatic fleet. And from the *Houston*, Purnell would forward a secret memorandum to President Roosevelt of what that Japanese military intended to do and what the response should be from the United States. Roosevelt must have certainly considered Purnell's observations as efforts for air support for the Chinese lurched ahead. Nothing had changed in six months as everyone was clamoring for four-engine bombers, and not just the Boeing B-17 but the Consolidated B-24 Liberator as well. The British of course were still looking for as much the material as they could get and General MacArthur wanted the bombers for the defense of the Philippines. And the previous March, air commanders in Hawaii continued to ask for a whopping 180 Flying Fortresses for air patrol around the islands. On it's face this appears to be a misapplied asset as the B-17 was designed for strategic bombing.

On 28 May, Currie sent to Secretary Knox a letter entitled, "A Short-Term Aircraft Program for China," proposing that sixty-six Lockheed Hudsons and Douglas DB-7s be shipped to China. He suggested that twelve Hudsons and twelve DB-7s be shipped immediately with the balance sent by the end of 1941.

A week earlier, the *New York Times* reported on U.S. training of the Chinese air force and the provision of "numerous fighting and bombing planes" to China by the United States. The subheadline read, "Bombing of Japanese Cities is Expected." The same day of the *Times* piece, the *Los Angeles Times*, ran with an Associated Press story headlined, "Million Men Wanted for Home Guards." Pearl Harbor was still six months down the road.

On Tuesday, 11 June, Major General Arnold met with both Currie and Chennault to have another discussion about the aircraft requirements for the Chinese government. A review was made of the Chinese requests, the actions taken to date, and what the Chinese expected from the United States soon. A slight pivot was made on the utilization of four-engine heavy bombers and whether or not the twin-engine Lockheed Hudson or Douglas DB-7 bombers would satisfy the needs of the Chinese. It appears that the idea of these bombers came from Navy Secretary Knox, who garnered the suggestion from Dr. Currie. From whom or how Currie gathered the information about these bombers is not known. Arnold made a summary of the entire conference and dispatched it in a memorandum that same day to Robert A. Lovett, the undersecretary of War for Air. Lovett was named to this position just this past April, a post that had been vacant since Roosevelt became President in 1933. Arnold updated Lovett as to the Chinese requests and the action taken to date – which was little or nothing. Arnold stated for just about every request either there was "no order, nor action, or no money." Obviously, there was a breakdown of communication between the Lend-Lease Administration and the military. It is interesting to note that in the last four sentences of the memo Arnold states:

> *The Chinese believe that bombers are very essential if the Japanese transport lines are to be attacked effectively. They call attention to the congested life lines, usually rivers, used by the Japanese for transporting their supplies deep into isolated sections of China. In one case, about 1,400 boats a month went up one river just for supply purposes. The A-20s or DB-7s can be used for this purpose; that is, destroying boats and trains on lines of communication. The Lockheed Hudsons have ample range to perform missions against targets in Japan. It is their desire to use incendiary bombs on the Lockheed Hudsons. Advance bases are available in Eastern China. It is 1,300 miles from these advance bases to industrial Japan. (emphasis added)* [37]

Both the Lockheed Hudson and the Douglas DB-7 (also refereed as the A-20 Havoc) were considered "light-bombers" and initial shipments from the factories went forth to the Royal Air Force (RAF).

The A-20 Havoc (company name Douglas DB-7) bomber initial design period began in 1937. Based on the aircraft performance of the planes flying in the Spanish Civil War it was determined that the plane was underpowered and subsequently Douglas engineers upgraded the aircraft to the 1,100 hp (820 kW) Pratt & Whitney R-1830 Twin Wasp engine. The French were interested and covertly attended the flight trials without the assistance of the Army Air Corps due to the rampant isolationism within the United states. The British examples went by the service name "Boston."

The DB-7 could cruise at 256 miles-per-hour and have an effective combat range of 950 miles. With a crew of three airmen, it featured six

A major shipment of DB-7s originally destined for France was retained by the United States and converted to A-20G attack planes. (USAF)

fixed forward firing 50-caliber Browning machine guns in the nose and two in in dorsal turret. A single flexible machine gun sprouted behind the bomb bay all while carrying a 4,000lb bomb load. It may not be a "flying fortress" but it sure did pack an offensive wallop.

Like the Douglas Havoc, the Lockheed Hudson can also trace its roots back to 1937. But that is where the similarities end. The Hudson had a crew of six and was powered by a pair of Wright Cyclone 9-cylinder radial engines each producing1,100 hp. The maximum speed was only 235 MPH and the bomb load was an anemic 750 pounds. Yet the British liked the design and placed an initial order for 200 aircraft - The largest order of any aircraft that Lockheed had ever received up to that time. Armament consisted of just two 30-caliber machine guns in the nose and two in a dorsal turret. The plane didn't poise much sting for an opponent but the upside over the Havoc was that it had twice the range of more than 1,900 miles.

A day before Chennault's departure from San Francisco with Owen Lattimore alongside on 9 July, he was informed that Roosevelt had approved the Second American Volunteer Group, that would be comprised of bomber pilots and ground crewmen. It would have made interesting conversation with Lattimore on the long flight. One hundred pilots, bombers, 181 gunners and radiomen would arrive in China by November 1941.

As Irish writer Johnathan Swift once quipped, "Promises and pie-crust are made to be broken." Chennault would be totally disappointed in the upcoming months with many unfulfilled assurances.

A Lockheed Hudson in Royal Air Force colors. This aircraft, named "Spirit of Lockheed-Vega Employees," was a gift to the people of Great Britain from the workers at the Lockheed-Vega plant in Burbank, California in December, 1940. (Alamy)

In the Lovett memo, General Arnold also indicated that part of the order included 144 Vultee P-48s and 122 Republic P-43 fighters. He goes on to say "Two [P-48s] are completed, ten are expected in June, and 25 per month thereafter until the order is completed in December." Even though the British agreed to release them (because they were unimpressed with the fighter) money had yet to be allocated from lend-lease to pay for them. An order was also on hold for the P-43 and Arnold stated one could be delivered in October the balance completed by February 1942.

The P-48 designation was based on Vultee's company name, the Model 48, and changed to P-66 Vanguard after Pearl Harbor. Powered by a Pratt & Whitney R-1830-33 14-cylinder twin-row radial piston engine developing 1,200 horsepower, the fighter had a maximum speed of 340 miles-per-hour. Vultee built 144 examples of the fighter.

The Republic (originally called the Seversky Aircraft Company) P-43 Lancer was powered by an R-1830-35 14-cylinder air-cooled radial engine with a General Electric B-2 turbo-supercharger generating 1,200 hp and driving a three-blade variable-pitch propeller. Many pilots stated the Lancer's performance was superior to the P-40 at higher altitudes. It featured four 50-caliber M2 Browning machine guns and had a maximum speed of 356 miles-per-hour. It did have excellent range but lacked self-sealing tanks and enough armor plating.

Chennault was expecting the P-66 Vanguard in November 1941 but would not see them until late 1942. (SDASM)

A Republic P-43 Lancer being repaired in China circa 1943. (LOC)

J.B. No. 355 (serial 691): The Joint Board Makes a Pivotal Move.

ON JULY 18, 1941 Acting Secretary of War Robert P. Patterson and Navy Secretary Knox forwarded the following secret letter to the White House:

Dear Mr. President:

At the request of Mr. Lauchlin Currie, [sic] Administrative Assistant to the President, The Joint Board has made recommendations for furnishing aircraft to the Chinese Government under the Lend-Lease Act. These recommendations are contained in the Joint Planning Committee report of July 9, 1941, J.B. No. 355 (Serial 691), which The Joint Board approved, and which is transmitted herewith for your consideration.

In connection with this matter, may we point out that the accomplishment of The Joint Board's proposals to furnish aircraft equipment to China in accordance with Mr. Currie's [sic] Short Term Requirements for China, requires the collaboration of Great Britain in diversions of allocations already made to them; however, it is our belief that the suggested diversions present no insurmountable difficulty nor occasion any great handicap.

We have approved this report and in forwarding it to you, recommend your approval. (38)

Just five days later President Roosevelt approved the J. B. No. 355 plan that yes, American planes and pilots would be made available to China. Roosevelt also added one caveat in his own handwriting, "OK- but restudy military mission versus the attaché method." And this simple handwritten note exemplifies President Roosevelt's acute cagiest acumen. If a military attaché method is employed the bulk of these activities can be cloaked under the diplomatic umbrella as advice and counsel by the United States embassy in China. The same day the President approved the aid plan for China the secretary of the Joint Board, Lieutenant Colonel William P. Scobey sent a memo to the Chief of Staff, General Marshall, Jr. of the President's decision.

Subject: J.B. No. 355 (serial 691) – Aircraft requirements for the Chinese government.

Reference our conversation at 2:00 o'clock this afternoon I find the records of the Joint Board show the following:

Approved by The Joint Board on July 12, 1941. This action is indicated in the minutes of The Board meeting on that date. Copies of these minutes furnished to the Plans Di-

vision, Office of Chief of Naval Operations.

Following Joint Board approval, the serial was transmitted by letter dated July 14, signed by Admiral Stark, Senior Member, to the Secretary of the Navy and the Secretary of War. The Secretary of the Joint Board was notified by memorandum dated July 16, 1941. Op-12S-CTB, that the Secretary of the Navy, Mr. Frank Knox, approved the serial on July 15, 1941. The War Department was notified of the action of the Secretary of the Navy by a memorandum for the Chief of Staff dated July 16, 1941.

The serial was approved by the acting Secretary of War, Mr. Patterson on July 18, 1941. Notice of the Acting Secretary of War's approval was transmitted to the Navy Department by a memorandum for the Chief of Naval Operations dated July 19, 1941.

Following approval by the Secretaries of War and the Navy, the serial was transmitted to the White House on July 18, 1941. It was returned to the Secretary of the Joint Board on July 23, 1941 endorsed by the President as follows:

"O.K. – but restudy Military Mission versus the attache method. F.D.R."

W.P. Scobey
Lieut. Colonel, G.S.C.,
Secretary. [39]

And just a day earlier, unaware of the Joint Board's decision, Madame Chiang Kai-Shek telegrammed Dr. Currie to continue to pressure the United States for action on China's behalf:

"Dr. Lattimore yesterday presented letter of introduction a contents of which is much appreciated. Received very favorable impression of Dr. Lattimore during interview. Owing to rainy season and reorganization, traffic on Burma Road will not appreciably increase until October, but unremitting efforts continuing.
Chennault plans start operations in Kunming by October 15th. Meanwhile hopes to enforce combat training in Burma if local authorities consent. Will you please try expedte [sic] bombing planes so necessary in counteroffensive. Your letter

sent through Dr. Lattimore received. Warm thanks for your efforts in China's behalf. (40)

On the heels of the Joint Board approval Dr. Currie provided a detailed and exhaustive report to President Roosevelt detailing the agreement of aircraft shipments to China. One wonders if Roosevelt even had time to bother and read it.

Washington, July 19, 1941.
Re: Chinese Aircraft Program.

Attached is a Report of the Joint Planning Committee, concurred in by the Secretaries of War and Navy, and the Joint Board, on the Chinese Short-Term Aircraft Program. It was prepared in response to my request for recommendations to you.

The recommendations are as follows:
a. With regard to Policy:

1. That the United States and Great Britain, subject to United States and British requirements, furnish material aid to China by providing aircraft of pursuit, bombardment, and training types, together with accessories, spares, armament and ammunition, in quantities sufficient for effective action against Japanese military and naval forces operating in China and in neighboring countries and waters.

2. That the United States provide a cadre of American instructor pilots in China aided by such technical personnel and equipment as may be necessary to the accomplishment of the training of Chinese personnel as flight and maintenance crews. This instructor cadre will render advisory assistance in the maintenance and employment of all training and combat aircraft, and equipment pertaining thereto, which has been made available to China by the United States Government.

3. That to aid China in the proper utilization of the large amount of material resources being furnished by the United States, the United States send a military mission to China to act in an advisory capacity.

b. With regard to the Short-Term Aircraft Program for China:

1. That aircraft, together with accessories, spares, armament, and ammunition be made available to the Chinese Government as follows:
(a) 144 Vultee 48 Pursuit, from stocks or production already allocated to China by the Joint Aircraft Committee.
(b) 125 Republic P–43 Pursuit, now on contract to the Chinese Government.
(c) 33 Lockheed Hudson, Medium Bombardment, from stocks or production now allocated to the British.
(d) 33 DB–7, Light Bombardment, from stocks or production now allocated to the British.
(e) Accessories and spares to be scheduled for production or made available from stocks controlled by the United States or Great Britain, as the case may be, to accompany each group of planes.
(f) Armament and ammunition from stocks or production controlled by the British.

2. That delivery of aircraft indicated in recommendation b (1), (a) to (d), inclusive, D. conditioned upon the diversion of adequate armament and ammunition to permit their efficient employment in combat.

The recommendations to which your attention is specifically directed are those dealing with the diversion of a limited number of medium and light bombers from the British, the diversion of a limited amount of armament and ammunition, now being produced in America for the British, and the proposal of a military mission.

On the diversion of bombers, armament and ammunition, I have prepared for you the accompanying directives which the Secretary of War can transmit to the Joint Aircraft Procurement Committee and the appropriate Ordnance Committee.

I had previously raised the question of a Military Mission to China with Mr. Welles. He feels strongly that all *our relations with the Chinese Government should be tied in with the Embassy, that increased military representation in China, if necessary and desirable, should take the form of appointing a Military Attaché of higher rank than the Colonel now there and of additional assistant military attachés assigned to different tasks, and that, finally, the lease-lend "expediter" in China should be a civilian. Mr. Hopkins concurs in these views. It so happens that one of the ablest officers in the Far East Foreign Service, John Carter Vincent, is now acting temporarily as Counselor at our Embassy in Chungking. He knows China, speaks Chinese, and is a close friend of Lattimore. His detail as lease-lend expediter would be agreeable to Mr. Welles and to me.*

I would suggest, as a possible way of reconciling the views of the State Department and the War Department, that the man the War Department has in mind to head the mission, General Magruder, be appointed Military Attaché with the understanding that in the event of hostilities, he would become head of a Military Mission. This is the arrangement the British have worked out in Chungking with their Military Attaché, Major-General Dennys.

I would also like to recommend that you approve the suggestion of detailing John Vincent as lease-lend expediter in Chungking.

Lauchlin Currie [41]

Currie pushed as hard as he could to provide the Chinese with the aircraft that they needed to combat the Japanese onslaught and he succeeded, at least on paper. The biggest names in the United States government were involved and approved of the plan and that included President Roosevelt, Secretary of War Stimson, Knox, Marshall, Turner, Arnold, and a host of other government and military officials. The problem was that no one was delegated specifically to advance JB 355 and the initiative wallowed in the murky waters of government bureaucracy. The Joint Board resolution in government circles became as cold and lonely as a nudist on an iceberg.

A month earlier (as previously noted) President Roosevelt, by Currie's recommendation, appointed Dr. Owen Lattimore to serve as the civilian American advisor to Chiang Kai-shek for a period of one and a half years. Although born in the United States, Lattimore was raised in Tiaujin, China and was fluent in Chinese and Russian. Lattimore had direct access to Currie and presumably other cronies within the State Department. Word quickly made its way to Chiang Kai-shek about the Joint Board's decision and on 28 July, Lattimore telegrammed Dr. Currie stating, "The Generalissimo sends hearty thanks for good bomber news." He also added, "Madame Chiang adds cordial personal greetings." (42)

Owen Lattimore meeting with Chiang Kai-shek. Lattimore and Currie conducted a lot of personal correspondence and both would be suspected as Soviet spies or "agents of influence" after World War II. (W.E.B. DuBois Library, University of Massachusetts, Amherst).

By all accounts the approval of J.B 355 should have the ball moving on several courts within different agencies of the United States federal bureaucracy. It would soon be discovered that this was not the case. It is not known if the military attaché in Beijing at the time, Lieutenant Colonel William Mayer, was aware of the approval of J.B. 355.

Mayer had lived and worked in China since the 1920s and that made him the archetypical "old China hand." Mayer on 8 August updated the United States War Department with the following telegram into the activities of Chennault in China but is unaware of the bomber situation:

Referring to your number 4, total of 188 Americans, of which

[??]1 are pilots, expected by Chennault to be at Rangoon by 22nd of August; balance 146 plus 20 pilots expected by September 15. So far 20 P-40's [sic] have been test flown. The main shortages are in same spare parts and 30 caliber ammunition which are unable to get. With regard to bombers released, he asks for shipment of incendiary bombs, preferring that these should precede bombers. In China none are available. For airplane interception urgently need 20 new radio direction finders for aircraft trips 22 thousand pound weight, following fields are suitable: Xiangtan which is located near Changehan, Henyang, Chekiang and Hunan, Liuchew Kwangai, Kweilin, Namyung, Kian Kiangsi. These all have radios, telephones and labor, but do not have any 100 octane gasoline. Also excellent fields at Chunchow, Chekiang, but near occupied territory, being only 30 miles there from. Regarding his request for 5 air officers to supervise use of lend lease equipment, would like to know if any action has been taken. Units training South Burma will not be permitted by local authorities. By October 15th Chennault thinks he can be ready for combat with 54 pursuits in 3 squadrons.

Distributed to General Magruder and the State Department [43]

As it turns out Chennault was nowhere near ready for combat operations on the 15th and would not engage the Japanese until December. And the bombers that Chennault was expecting were still not in the pipeline. Lend-lease favored Great Britain over China and not just by a small margin. Essentially for every ton of war material England received the Chinese collected 60 pounds. Truth was, that the United States was producing airplanes faster than Great Britain could find pilots to fly them. It was also during July that the British screwed China out of obtaining Lockheed Hudson bombers immediately – even though their initial request was for just thirty-three.

A reporter for the *American Aviation Daily* found 155 Lockheed Hudson bombers sitting on the tarmac at the Lockheed Air Terminal in Burbank, California. The reporter then asked a British official why the Hudsons could not be converted to transports that they so desperately needed and the official replied that England needed as many bombers as she could get. And quietly and with no fanfare the Hudsons were whisked off to the friendly environs of Canada and away from the prying eyes of reporters. And an action like this speaks volumes compared to words on paper carried in a diplomatic pouch or in a telegram. Chennault was expecting Hudson bombers and to strike Japan in November – a month before Pearl Harbor.

Lockheed PBO Hudson Patrol Bomber. (Naval History and Heritage Command)

The Clagett Air Mission

CURRIE HAD VISITED CHINA earlier in the year and would spearhead the lend-lease initiative. An American transportation expert was also dispatched to see what logistical improvements could be made regarding the Burma Road. American military officials viewed the CAF with skepticism, and Chiang knew this and asked that the United States provide a senior ranking officer to support an air mission to evaluate the CAF capabilities and offer recommendations. For a variety of reasons, principally because he was overwhelmed launching the A.V.G., Chennault was not a suitable person for this enterprise.

On 29 March Secretary of War Stimson tapped Brigadier General Henry Black Clagett, the future commander of the Philippine Air Force for the job. Clagett was no desk jockey, earning his wings at Kelley Field in 1917-18 and would be accompanied by Colonel Harold H. George, commander of the 31st pursuit group at Selfridge and a World War I ace. Lieutenant Colonel David D. Barrett was also part of the assemblage along with assistant naval attaché for air, Major Francis J. McQuillen, who was already in China and naval officer Lieutenant Commander E.O. McConnell. The group focused on training and the condition of airfields, particularly Chengdu, Chongqing, and Kumming.

Clagett disembarked from a Boeing 314 Clipper that landed in Canacao Bay, south of Manila on Sunday morning 4 May. Much worked needed to be done at his new Philippine command before going to China. This was also around the time that Hemingway was in Manila working on his stories for *PM*. The air mission members arrived in Chungking on 17 May and returned to the Philippines on 12 June aboard the SS *President Coolidge*. The mission was cut short by two weeks because Clagett and George became extremely ill and were hospitalized upon their return.

The Clagett air mission had three main objectives: 1. How well will China cooperate with the United States in the event of war. 2. The tactics and characteristics of the Japanese air force. 3. The adequacy of the airfields under construction. The open secret is that everyone knew, including Chennault, the sad state of affairs regarding the Chinese Air Force. The Chinese expected that the air mission would spark additional aircraft and pilots to bolster their meager forces. What transpired is confusing and irritating starting with Ambassador Gauss' telegram to Secretary of State Hull:

Chungking, June 12, 1941
[Received June 26.]

It will be observed from the Naval Attachés memorandum that, while invited repeatedly by the Generalissimo and Madame Chiang Kai-shek to criticize the Chinese air force, its organization, war plans, personnel, training, et cetera, the mission spokesman at the interview with the Generalissimo voiced no criticism and gave blanket approval on all points. Colonel George, the spokesman, impressed me most favorably during my brief contact with him. I am somewhat surprised that he gave so sweeping approval of the Chinese air force as is indicated in the memorandum.

It appears the mission discussed with the Generalissimo (1) the question of possible establishment of direct air communication between Chungking and the Philippine Islands and (2) plans for the training of pilots in the United States or the Philippines for heavy bombardment, medium bombardment, light bombardment and pursuit operations, recording certain views set out in the Naval Attaché's memorandum. (44)

The Generalissimo invited the Claggett mission to China to provide constructive criticism and how China can improve her air force. Instead all the Gimo heard was promises of support and that "all is fine." Exactly what was the game being perpetrated upon the Chinese and for what reason? Several historians suggest that General Marshall was looking to expand United States military influence in China and squeeze out Currie and Soong.

On the 10 April, well before the Clagett air mission, Major McHugh circulated a summary based on Major McQuillen's observations to several people:

> 1. Results of combat on 14 March, 1941, at Chengtu, between 31 Chinese fighters (Russian Type E-15-3) and twelve Japanese Type "Zero" fighters. Score: Chinese lost 15 planes and 8 pilots to 1 (possible) Japanese.
>
> 2. Faulty machine guns on Russian planes and poor tactics by the Chinese.
>
> 3. Overloading of Chinese Aviation Schools and slow progress of students.
>
> 4. Methods used by Russians in training Chinese at Ining, (Kuldga), Sinkiang.
>
> 5. Lack of Chinese teamwork. (45)

McQuillen totally disembowels the CAF to his American counterparts and yet the Clagett air mission paints a rosy picture to the Gimo and Madame Chiang Kai-shek. The mission did depict that many airfields were in excellent condition and could accommodate light and medium bombers and in some cases even the heavy B-17. And once again, like the Jouett air mission years earlier, Clagett did recommend to Madame Chiang that with American flight instructors and advisers training Chinese pilots that the CAF strength would be greatly improved.

Chinese military attaché Chu Shiming followed up on this recommendation in a letter to the War Department requesting that Chinese students travel to the United States for aviation training. The Lend-Lease Administration allocated $1 million to train the Chinese students. The first 50 students arrived at Thunderbird Field in Arizona in October 1941. After returning home McConnell wrote to Dr. Currie regarding China's bomber needs. How the two met is not known but it may have been earlier in the year when Currie visited China. McConnell did not believe the bomber allocations appropriate and suggested that the longer-range B-25 be added to the Chinese requirements since the plane could strike Tokyo and Yokohama from bases in East China.

This is the first time that the North American B-25 came up in

The B-25 design was named in honor of Major General William "Billy" Mitchell, a pioneer of U.S. military aviation. Nearly 10,000 B-25 bombers were produced by North American Aviation. (SDAM)

correspondence as a potential bomber for the Chinese. The Mitchell B-25 designed emerged back to 1939 when the Air Corps looked for a new generation of medium-range bombers. A prototype crashed in testing and the Air Corps ordered the DB-7 instead. The B-25 development progressed but did not reach production until 1942 and was the bomber of choice for the Doolittle raid on Japan.

Alas Poor J.B. 355 (serial 691), I knew You Well

AMERICAN AND JAPANESE RELATIONS deteriorated further on the 24 July when Vichy France, under control of Marshal Philippe Pétain, "agreed" to the occupation of her Indo-China colonies further putting a squeeze on China to the south. The Japanese took control of Cam Ranh naval base just 800 miles from the Philippines. Two days later Roosevelt countered by freezing all Japanese assets in the United States, which is often referred to at the time as the "oil embargo" and Great Britain, along with the Dutch Indies joined in. Effectively Japan lost 90 percent of her imported oil along with 75 percent of foreign trade. Roosevelt literally strangled Japan for oil and the country had just a three-year reserve and less than a year if she decided to go to war. Events were taking place politically to form the perfect storm.

By the tail end of August, no action was taken by the United States as directed by J.B. 355 – an initiative that began months earlier. Admiral Turner was not only perturbed by the lack of aviation assistance by the Navy Department to the Chinese but so pissed off that he phoned Lieutenant Colonel Scobey and laid into him. Scobey replied to Turner the same day in a memo and that he was in no way was he complicit in the inaction by the United States Navy. Scobey wrote in part:

> It was, and still is, my understanding that this action fulfilled the responsibility of the Secretary of the Joint Board. As far as the War Department is concerned, when it has received notice from the Secretary of the Joint Board of final approval, it becomes a matter for one or more agencies of the War Department to activate the approved recommendations ascertained in the serial.
>
> Naturally, I do not know the routine of implementing approved action in the Navy Department. In all cases, the Navy Department is furnished with two complete copies of every Joint Board; and where the various agencies of the Navy Department deem it necessary to have additional copies in order to accomplish action on a paper, I am happy to furnish their requirements. From past experience no additional copies of a joint report have been required by the Navy Department for most of the approved recommendations. In other cases, as for example Joint Basis War Plans, the Navy Department has requested as many as 50 and 60 copies. These are

always provided. The point I want to make is that I unfailingly provide to the Navy as many copies of an approved serial as they require of me.

May I say in this connection that my records of this case indicate that my action as Secretary in connection with this paper was complete. I feel that a failure on the part of either the War or Navy Department to implement approved recommendations is no fault of mine.

W.P. Scobey
Lieut. Colonel
G.S. Secretary [46]

Cudos to Scobey as he refused to fall on the sword on behalf of the War or Navy Departments. Instead he was smart enough to defy the bureaucracy and delivered a response, on written record, that would clear himself for the lack of action taken on J.B.355. It assured his current position, but once you "rock the boat" you poison the well for any possible future advancement of any significance. [47]

Yes, J.B. 355 (serial 691) was approved but who was intended to catch the pass and carry the ball into the endzone? Who specifically was ordered to ensure that the Chinese were supplied with the aircraft that that they requested? Was it Marshall, Arnold, Stimson, Knox, Stark, Turner, Lovett, Currie, or some mid-level bureaucrat? It appears to be none of the above, although Currie was certainly attempting to move the program forward as much as any civilian in government possibly could.

As JB 355 wallowed within the government bureaucracy, Chennault's A.V.G. was facing some serious problems. First off was that the P-40Bs were shipped without ammunition, which made them totally useless. Currie approached General Marshall who told him ammunition was in short supply and denied his request. Currie had to approach the President with the problem and ask him to intervene. Roosevelt immediately had the Army release 1,500,000 rounds for the Chinese. This was another indication that General Marshall was not inclined to support Chennault at all.

Spare parts were another issue as Curtiss-Wright moved production to newer models and not all parts were interchangeable. Chennault worked with Pawley to get spare parts and Pawley in turn worked his contacts in the Philippines. Only 99 Tomahawks would be assembled – the one dropped in New York harbor was used for parts.

Even though Roosevelt was providing China with war materials,

Before Pearl Harbor

he still sought to blunt Japanese aggression by dangling the proverbial carrot in front of them. On 26 July, he sent a telegram to Harry Hopkins, then in London and stated in part:

> *"...I have suggested to Nomura [Japanese ambassador] that Indo-China be neutralized by Britain, Dutch, Chinese, Japan and ourselves, placing Indo-China somewhat in the status of Switzerland. Japan to get rice and fertilizer but all on condition that Japan withdraw armed forces from Indo-China in toto. I have had no answer yet. When it comes it will probably be unfavorable but we have at least made one more effort to avoid Japanese expansion to South Pacific."* (48)

Soong was getting increasingly frustrated with the pace of American aviation assistance and sought out additional allies in his efforts. This included the head of the newly formed Office of the Coordinator of Information headed by William J. Donovan, better known as "Wild Bill" Donovan. (49) This agency would split within a year to form the Office of Strategic Services (OSS), the precursor to the Central Intelligence Agency (CIA). On 15 August, a Sunday and with temps in the eighties and a light rain in Washington, D.C., Soong met with Donovan to explain the plight of China in her fight against Japan.

A World War I Medal of Honor recipient, William "Wild Bill" Donovan was a soldier, lawyer, and diplomat. He is best known as the founding father of the OSS, the precursor to the CIA. (LOC)

Soong gave Donovan a review of the current military straits China was in and related how round-the-clock bombing was wearing down not only the military but civilians as well. Soong said in part, "… is the swiftness with which it is announced that deliveries of aircraft are being made to the Soviet Union, after repeated earlier promises of delivery to the Chinese have been excused as nonperformable [sic] because the aircraft simply does not exist." He continued to ratchet up the rhetoric stating. "…is the recent frank disclosure of the American policy of appeasing Japan with materials of war—the very material and gasoline that are presently bombing Chungking—in order to keep Japan from attacking certain American supply routes to the south. If planes are delivered to Russia now—even though the Russians are still our friends and allies—you must get planes to Chungking now or the Chinese will never understand." [50]

Soong did not mention Morgenthau but went on to say, "Last fall and winter we were offered a few bombers capable of raiding Japan. The offer was accepted but it did not materialize." And then Soong took a swipe at Marshall stating, "Through the exertions of the President, 100 Curtiss P–40's were released by the British last fall and eventually reached China, but the necessary spare parts and ammunition without which these craft are not fighting ships but only training ships, are just being arranged for now." [51]

The letter was blunt, forceful and a very accurate assessment of the situation and the promises of material aid put forth by J.B. 355. The feisty Soong, representing China Defense Supplies, laid out what could be accomplished if the planes promised were delivered and of course added, "Finally, we could attack the main industrial areas and fire the paper and wood cities of Japan." [52]

Donovan reported Soong's assessment to President Roosevelt and assigned James Roosevelt, the eldest son of Franklin and Eleanor, to urge the Chinese case with close Presidential aides such as Harry L. Hopkins.

Hopkins was another mover and shaker within the Roosevelt administration and part of the inner circle. James Roosevelt, a Captain in the U.S.M.C. at the time, sent the following poignant dispatch to Hopkins on 22 August and you'll notice how personal the correspondence is.

Dear Harry:

I know the enclosed has been described as just another hysterical letter from one of the three groups, British, Russian, and Chinese yelling for help. I do feel, however, very strongly that something definite, concrete, and honest should be done about it.

After all, from a long range point of view, when this war is over, China can be the greatest export market for many years to come that this country has ever seen. I am convinced from personal observations that they are going to have the fastest growing civilization when that time does come. All of this can be true only if they have been sold on our friendship and actual support. Unlike other countries, their tradition has been, and is, to remember their friends. Russia will throw us out of the window, England will use us for her own gain when she is strong and able to do so, but China will use us as a friend. Their ancestor religion may be responsible for this attitude, but let's not miss the chance of taking advantage of it.

Above all else, the most tragic part of the letter for the Chinese mind are the promises and telegrams specifying numbers and amounts all of which turn out to be just so much "bunk."

I specify this because after all I have been there and I do know the state of their mind and the things which mean much to them. If we miss the boat on this, someone should be very soundly kicked!

Sincerely,
James Roosevelt [53]

Harry Hopkins and FDR's dog Fala on the porch at Top Cottage in Hyde Park, New York. (FDR Presidential Library & Museum; photograph by Margaret Suckley)

Besides James Roosevelt's capitalist's views of China as an export market, he was spot on relative to all the countries involved (i.e. China, Russia, and Great Britain) and what the future may hold. The young Captain obviously did not anticipate China would fall to the communists. A copy of the correspondence was also sent to Undersecretary Sumner Welles who responded:

Dear Jimmy:

I thank you for sending me a copy of your letter of August 22 to Harry Hopkins together with its enclosure, Mr. T. V. Soong's eloquent letter of August 16 to Colonel Donovan.

I am glad to have your personal views on this important question. There seems to me to be no question that prompt assistance to China is of vital importance and should at all times be regarded as and be made a part of our program of giving aid to countries that are resisting aggression.

Yours sincerely,
Sumner Welles [54]

One wonders if the correspondence was indeed informal or were the veteran politicians just patronizing Roosevelt's son? And it only took a short time that yes, the United States did "…miss the boat on this…" and no, someone was never soundly kicked. Soong's correspondence to Donovan would indeed stand the test of time and it appears the proverbial "Chinese can" was once again kicked down the road.

Chennault was unaware of the sloth-like moves surrounding J.B. 355 and on the 4 September, he sent a letter to Soong detailing his plans on how the Hudson bombers can be transported to China in the most efficient and expeditious manner. Chennault offered two routes and he appeared to favor the northern route which would limit the involvement of the United States government. Chennault explained it succinctly writing:

One of your older CNAC pilots, who has been your personal pilot on a number of flights, is scheduled to return to the U.S.A. on leave about Dec. 1, 1941. He has stated to me that he will be available to lead a formation of bombers back along the Pan American route or north over the Alaska-Siberia route to any designated point in China, about the end of

December, 1941. He also states that he would be willing to accept command of the bombardment Group for subsequent tactical operations. Since the pilot is a very skillful navigator and is acquainted with most of the Chinese Airdromes, his services would be of great value to us.

It is proposed that a number of long-range bombers, say ten to twenty, be held at the factory and that crews of volunteer personnel be employed to fly the bombers from the factory to China. The bombers should be fully equipped with bombsights, radio direction finders, navigating instruments, oxygen apparatus, and bomb racks. Guns, ammunition and bombs should not be carried, but should be shipped to China in advance of the flight.

Permission to make the flight via Honolulu, Wake, Guam, and Manila would have to obtained from the U.S. government. It is not believed that a stop at Midway Island would be necessary. It would also be necessary to obtain information as to whether the runways at Wake and Guam will be available, say by Dec. 31, 1941.

From Manila these bombers could be flown at night so as to arrive at any designated airdrome in China just before dawn. If this plan is approved, I will instruct the CNAC pilot to call upon you for instructions after his arrival in the States. (55)

And, as previously noted, not everyone was in sync with the bomber plan. Currie telegrammed Madame Chiang Kai-shek on 5 September stating that, "British have agreed to diversion of 33 Hudsons and 33 DB–7s by end of year." Currie, usually a detailed oriented administrator, uncharacteristically kept the delivery of the bombers ambiguous as there were four months remaining in the year.

The total ineptitude of the United States government was evident when Sumner Wells, the Undersecretary of State, telegrammed the American ambassador in China, Gauss, the contents of which was to be forwarded to Madame Chiang Kai-shek on the 23 July:

For Madame Chiang Kai-shek from Lauchlin Currie. I am very happy to be able to report that today the President directed that 66 bombers be made available to China this year with 24 to be delivered immediately. He also approved a Chinese pilot training program here. Details through normal channels. Warm regards. [Currie.] (53)

The Chinese training program did move forward. As far as the bombers being delivered "immediately" it would appear to be determined what the definition of what Currie called "immediately" is. No bombers would be delivered to China in 1941. Promises as always are easily made but are more difficult to keep. One also questions why Currie did not send this information to Madame Chiang Kai-shek as he had a direct line to her instead of going through Ambassador Gauss. (56)

What is even more curious and disturbing is that Currie contacted Madame Chang on 6 August, indicating that the British may be willing to provide China with Hawker Hurricane fighters and Bristol Blenheim bombers. Author Alan Armstrong, in his superbly researched book, *Preemptive Strike: The Secret Plan That Would Have Prevented The Attack On Pearl Harbor* stated:

> *Currie dispatched a telegram to Madame Chiang to be relayed to Chennault with an intriguing question:* WOULD YOU BE INTERESTED IN HURRICANES IN 1942 WITH PERFORMANCE AS FOLLOWS: THREE THREE NINE MPH AT TWENTY-ONE THOUSAND FEET, CEILING THIRTY-THOUSAND FEET, TWELVE GUNS 303 OR FOUR CANNONS, TWENTY MM. IMMEDIATELY ANSWER. *Currie went on to relate:* HOPE TO GET SOM [sic] B-25S EARLY IN 1942.
>
> *A telegram from Currie to Madame Chiang for delivery to Chennault, dated August 26, 1941, clearly indicated that British involvement in China was contemplated. Dr. Currie cabled:* GOOD PROSPECTS OF OBTAINING FOUR HUNDRED HURRICANES WITH AUXILIARY TANKS, STILL NEGOTIATING WITH BRITISH FOR BOMBERS, AM WORKING ON YOUR SUGGESTIONS CONCERNING OTHER PURSUIT SHIPS. (57)

These dispatches raise more questions than answers provided. Why would Dr. Currie open up a conversation with a question to Madame Chiang stating, "Would you be interested in Hurricanes in 1942...?" when Currie was completely aware of the status of the Chinese Air Force with its limited inventory of aircraft? And Currie then goes forward to say that 400 Hurricanes could be made available from the British in 1942 when the United States could barely scrape together 100 P-40 Tomahawks culled from the British for the Chinese just a few months earlier. Although not specifically stated in the Currie telegram, Author Alan Armstrong also indicates that Bristol Blenheim bombers were also offered and that Curtiss-Wright salesman William Pawley was involved in the affair.[58]

The Hawker Hurricane played second fiddle to the Supermarine Spitfire in the public's eye during the Battle of Britain but accounted for 60 percent of the Luftwaffe's losses during this epic battle. The single-engine fighter had its deficiencies at higher altitudes but was no slouch against opposing forces at lower altitudes. The Bristol Blenheim was a light twin-engine bomber similar to the Lockheed Hudson and Douglas DB-7. Neither aircraft saw service in China.

How and where Currie got this information about the Hawker Hurricanes and Bristol Blenheim bombers and what his true intentions were, are unknown. No further documents from Madame Chiang or Currie refer to this offer and Chennault's autobiography makes no mention of the British largesse. Much like today, there were deep state operatives conducting business within the Roosevelt administration and the British government that did not divulge their secrets or record them during normal written correspondence and had their own agenda.

The American Military Mission (AMMISCA)

WHEN HITLER LAUNCHED HIS attack on the Soviet Union, code name "Barbarossa", on Sunday, 22 June, it shook the politicos in Washington, D.C. to the core. This meant that the Soviet Union would be preoccupied with the Germans in the west and that Japan could deal with China who could no longer count on any Russian support. Roosevelt, Welles, and Hopkins all agreed the Generalissimo needed additional support if they intended to keep China in the game and the Japanese occupied. Time to launch another military aid mission.

On 3 July General Marshall approved the American Military Mission to China (AMMISCA). The following week, Acting Chief of Staff, G-2, Brigadier General Sherman Miles, wrote a personal letter to Brigadier General John L. Magruder, then commanding Fort Devens in Massachusetts that he was being considered to head a lend-lease mission to China. Magruder, a World War I veteran, was the military attaché in China before Stilwell and would retain the position after Stilwell's tenure. And as with everything else involving China, just getting the mission going took more than two months as factions squabbled over Magruder's status and the objectives and goals of the mission. Often mischaracterized as the "second air mission" to China,

AMMISCA went further with the principal objective of facilitating the delivery of lend-lease aid, the possible arming of 30 Chinese divisions, and the effective use of such aid. Of course, this also included fighter and bomber aircraft, and the efficacy of Chennault's A.V.G.

The military mission to China was announced on 26 August yet Magruder and his entourage would not arrive in Chungking until 9 October and not meet with the Gimo until three weeks later. On 30 October, Madame Chiang Kai-shek telegrammed Lauchlin Currie about the meeting:

The following is a summary of the Generalissimo's interview yesterday with General Magruder:

The Generalissimo is deeply gratified at the arrival of the Magruder mission, which is unlike the German and Russian military missions engaged by the Chinese Government. The Magruder mission owes its origin to the American Government and is for the common interests of our two countries. The Generalissimo recognizes the friendliness of America's action, especially at this time of tension when all officers are needed by the home government. (59)

Magruder's team did go to work promptly and found out why lend-lease supplies were stacked up at the docks in Rangoon and Lashio before departing on the nine-foot-wide, 715-mile-long "highway" to Kunming. Toss in the usual corruption, but trucks had to pass through eight customs desks and more than a dozen checkpoints, and many broke down due to lack of maintenance before reaching their destinations

Magruder offered unspecified additional air assistance for the Chinese Air Force, although Chiang Kai-shek asked that the Americans takeover and manage the CAF, whereas Magruder declined, but he did endorse the idea of augmenting the A.V.G. What is not stated in the mission's original statement is that Marshall also wanted to break the coziness between the Generalissimo, Currie, Chennault, and others in the American government circles. That took place to a degree but only by the efforts of the Japanese in December.

What little aid was being provided to the Chinese was further diluted by logistical problems. In 1941, China received about $26 million in American aid or roughly 1.7% of what was provided to Great Britain, the Soviet Union, and other countries. Logistical problems and delivery issues could be rectified, but even so, that would mean only a paltry amount of goods would be delivered.

On top of that, *Chicago Daily News* reporter, Edgar Mowrer and correspondent Vincent Sheehan, accompanied General Magruder aboard a Pan Am Clipper to China and after arriving asked him about the United States providing bombers to Chennault and the Chinese Air Force. According to Jack Samson in his book *The Flying Tiger*:

> *Magruder argued that only a few bombers were available to China, that a few bombers could not materially affect the war's outcome, and that release of them might rouse Japan to further aggression. He also said that the bombers would need American pilots, their release would not fit the "defensive theory" of American policy. Pursuit planes, he said were permissible as defense, but bombers, as offense, were questionable to say the least. The evening broke up in the small hours. Both correspondents were due to leave the next day for Rangoon and from there on to Chungking.* [60]

So, let's get this straight. On 22 October the S.S. *Tulsa* sailed for China with 11,000 Thompson submachine guns, forty-eight 75mm guns, a hundred 50-caliber machine guns, a boat load of ammunition and thirty-five scout cars and yet Magruder was worried that some bombers might "…rouse Japan to further aggression." What further aggression could they be roused to? Did he also believe that the war materials aboard the *Tulsa* and Chennault's one hundred P-40s "…could not materially affect the war's outcome…"?

Chennault was having problems acquiring spare parts and ammunition, well before the A.V.G. even began combat operations. Exasperated and stressed out he telegrammed Currie on 22 October in both a conciliatory note yet also someone on a mission to support the Chinese.

> *COLONEL HOYT AIR MEMBER MAGRUDER MISSION JUST HERE SHOWED PROMISING EVIDENCES DESIRE HELP GROUP STOP GAVE HIM COMPLETE HISTORY STATUS REPORT INCLUDING ALL PRESENT NEEDS WITH PRIORITIES REOPENING MANY DEAD QUESTIONS SUCH AS SPARE PARTS VULTEE TURBOSUPERCHARGERS PEE THIRTYNINES STOP AIRMAILING YOU SOONG COPIES STOP TRUST CLOSE LIAISON EXISTS OR ARRANGEABLE BETWEEN YOU AND MISSION IN GROUP WORK STOP MIS-*

SION EXPECTS OUR COOPERATION STOP BYPASSING IT DANGEROUS BUT ABOVE ALL ANXIOUS NOTHING YOU DISAPPROVE STOP KNOW YOU WILL UNDERSTAND POSITION HOPE STEPS TAKEN AGREEABLE YOU STOP PLEASE ADVISE BEST COURSE FOR FUTURE STOP (61)

In his telegram to Currie, Chennault gave high praise to the Magruder mission but recanted this in his autobiography stating:

"The military observers regarded the group [A.V.G.] as an undisciplined mob. Official reports that went back to London and Washington and circulated around Rangoon were pretty bad. Probably the worst report was made by Colonel Ross Hoyt and Major Roy Grusenberg, of the American Military Mission to China, who were far too conventional to approve an unorthodox organization such as the A.V.G. and much too inexperienced to have any understanding of the value of our specialized tactics." (62)

Chennault would later say in his autobiography that Magruder "… was helpful to us within the limits of his power." But what is even more intriguing is that Chennault in his telegram to Currie mentions acquiring the Bell P-39 Airacobra, a single-engine fighter that would be used predominantly by the Soviet Union during World War II. And once again this is where we find a void in the historical record. This single commu-

The Bell P-39 featured a 37mm cannon in the nose and a mid-fuselage engine fit. It was the first U.S. fighter with tricycle landing gear. (Public Domain, U.S. Government)

nication between Chennault and Currie is the only mention of providing P-39s to China. This would indicate that we only know a fraction of what took place in the months leading up to Pearl Harbor and that includes the plan(s) to bomb Japan.

Time Runs Out – For Everyone

Harry Hopkins, Roosevelt's right-hand man became involved in the mess of supplying a handful of bombers to China. On 2 September, Hopkins sent a telegram labelled "most secret" to Sir Archibald Sinclair, Great Britain's Secretary of State for Air. The telegram was sent to the United Ambassador in Great Britain and shows that even getting a date for some bombers for China was a difficult enterprise.

> FOR SIR ARCHIBALD SINCLAIR.
>
> I WONDER IF YOU AND MORRE-BRABIZON AND PORTAL CAN HAVE A SUGGESTION TO MAKE TO HELP US OUT OF A DIFFICULY SITUATION TO MEDIUM BOMBERS FOR CHINA.
>   A RECOMMENDATION HAS BEEN MADE BY OUR MILITARY PEOPLE THAT 66 MEDIUM BOMBERS BE RELEASED TO THE CHINESE OVER A PERIOD OF THE NEXT FEW MONTHS. WHILE THEY RECOMMENDED 33 HUDSONS AND 33 DB-SEVENS I BELIEVE THE IMPORTANT THING IS THAT THEY BE SATISFACTORY MEDIUM BOMBERS IRRESPECTIVE OF THE PARTICULAR TYPE.
> THE PRESIDENT IS ANXIOUS GET THESE BOMBERS AND WE ARE SIMPLY NOT IN A POSITION TO RELEASE ANY ORE BOMBERS IMMEDIATELY OUT OF OUR OWN SHARE OF THE PRODUCTION, WHICH IS VERY SMALL.
> CHIANG KAI-SHEK WAS ADVISED INADVERTENTLY [emphasis added] THAT THE BOMBERS WOULD BE AVAILABLE.
>   I REALIZE HOW DIFFICULT IT IS FOR YOU TO RELEASE THESE BOMBERS BUT ON THE OTHER HAND WE ARE IN A DIFFICULT SITUATION IN REGARD TO THE CHINESE AND WE KNOW OF THEIR VERY URGENT NEED WHICH THE PRESIDENT BELIEVES SHOULD BE ME. I KNOW YOU HAVE GIVEN SOME CONSIDERATION TO THIS. I EARNESTLY HOPE THAT A WAY CAN BE FOUND TO GIVE

THEM THE BOMBERS WITH AMMUNITION.
THE CHINESE ARE ALSO MAKINKING A VERY URGENT RE-
QUEST UPON US FOR ONE HUNDRED TONS OF INCENDI-
ARY BOMBS. WE HAVE NONE. IS THERE ANY POSSIBILITY
THAT THIS REQUEST CAN BE MET FROM YOUR STOCKS?

HOPKINS [63]

What is interesting in the telegram is that Hopkins' states that "Chiang Kai-shek was advised inadvertently that the bombers would be available." Did Hopkins really believe that or was he playing a game with Sir Archibald Sinclair? Clearly not everyone was on board in providing the Generalissimo with bombers. It also sounds in the telegram that Great Britain was dictating the terms of lend-lease to the United States and not the other way around.

The ambassador in the United Kingdom, John Gilbert Winant (who replaced pro-appeasement ambassador Joseph P. Kennedy Sr.) telegrammed Hopkins on 9 September. Winant confirmed the British release of the bombers and that they would also make available to the Chinese 50,000 four-pound incendiary bombs. [64] These incendiary bombs were manufactured by Imperial Chemical Industries, headquartered in London. They consisted of cannisters filled with thermite, a combination of metal powder, which serves as fuel, and metal oxide. What is not known is if the intended recipients of these incendiary bombs were Japanese forces in China or mainland Japan itself.

As one can see it was not just a pain in the butt trying to get bombers for China but CAMCO was being stonewalled in their recruitment efforts at every military installation they visited for qualified bomber pilots. Hap Arnold told Currie he doubted if anyone was interested but did not object to the recruitment process – although it was apparent Arnold did not appreciate his pilots being poached with the lure of more money and with an imminent war between the United States and Japan on the horizon. Frustrated by their efforts (CAMCO) Currie once again turned to Roosevelt for relief and hoped he wasn't dipping into the well one too many times to accomplish the task at hand and sent a lengthy memorandum to the President on 11 September and stated that the British have agreed to release 66 bombers for China. Currie also said in part:

"General Magruder is proceeding shortly to Chungking with several regular army air officers. These will be attached to

the volunteer air force as observers and this in turn should enhance the morale, discipline and efficiency of the volunteer pilots. A short term of duty in China should afford invaluable experience to our pilots, similar to that gained by the Germans and Russians in Spain.

Recommendation. In the light of the foregoing considerations, would you care to authorize the acceptance by the Army and Navy, beginning in October of this year, of resignations of pilots and other personnel for service in China to the number necessary to fly the ships we are supplying to China until such time the Chinese have an adequate number of adequately trained pilots?" (65)

Currie followed up just two days later in another memorandum based on letters from Owen Lattimore and Major McHugh. Currie did not mention bombers or pilots but went right to Roosevelt's heart stating in part:

"When I was in China you were revered throughout China as the leader and symbol of righteousness in the world. It distresses me terribly to think that your enormous influence for good in shaping the destinies of a coming great people might be jeopardized. The condemnation of Nazi aggression and the recent silence on Japanese aggression have erected a bad impression in China." (66)

Currie was focused on getting pilots to China and even hit up Roosevelt again on 18 September stating:

I consulted General Magruder on this, but I'm afraid that I can't "work it out" with him. He concurs but think but thinks you will have to give a directive. I raised the subject with you on Tuesday and you then agreed in principle. I think, however, that something written is necessary to overcome the resistance of the personnel branches of the services. Would you mind signing the rather mildly worded directive attached? In accordance with my information on the needs and number of personnel in the services, I am suggesting that the Army accept further resignations beginning in October and the Navy in January. (67)

Roosevelt was pummeled by Currie about the "China problem" and obviously overwhelmed on a daily basis with all aspects dealing with the United States. Yet the President issued a memorandum on 30 September to the Secretary of War Stimson stating:

> *I have been informed that the Chinese Government has hired 100 pilots and 181 ground personnel to man and service 100 P-40's. In the next few months we are delivering to China 269 pursuit planes and 66 bombers. The Chinese pilot training program here will not turn out well-trained pilots until next summer. In the interim, therefore, I think we should facilitate the hiring by the Chinese Government of further volunteer pilots here. I suggest, therefore, that beginning in January, you should accept the resignations of additional pilots and ground personnel as care to accept employment in China, up to a limit of 100 pilots and a proportional number of ground personnel. I am directing Mr. Lauchlin Currie to see that representatives of China carry out the hiring program with the minimum of inconvenience to the Army and also to see that no more are hired than necessary.* (68)

President Roosevelt reinforced the use of mercenaries overseas but did not take note that Currie specifically asked that Army pilot recruitment for China begin in October and not January 1942. This may have been a simple oversight on Roosevelt's part. Currie made note of this and sent another memorandum to Roosevelt on the 3 October saying, "In order to have these additional pilots ready for combat at the beginning of the year it would be necessary to authorize hiring immediately. May I reopen this subject with Secretary Stimson and ask that he reconsider what was doubtless his recommendation to you?" Roosevelt sent a note to Hopkins and Currie about this and noted "Yes."

Currie also notified Madame Chiang Kai-shek on 16 October that "Authority has been granted for you to hire 200 more pilots here." Yet Currie knew the limit on pilots was 100 with a proportional amount of ground support crewmen. (69)

Chennault, far away from the shenanigans in Washington, D.C. made the assumption that the bombers and their pilots destined for China were on their way and this couldn't be further from the truth. One wonders what his reaction would have been had he realized the situation unfolding out of sight before him. Not knowing the facts at the time, he dispatched this telegram to Soong on the 21 September from Rangoon, Burma:

Dear Dr. Soong:

I have studied the tables of organization and estimates of personnel required for the organization and operation of the new bombardment groups as prepared by Gen. T.C. Shen and Capt. R. Aldworth. This matter has also been discussed in detail with H.E. Madame Chiang Kai-shek and with the senior officers of the Commission of Aeronautical Affairs.

As a result of these discussions, a decision has been reached to assign the Hudson bombers to a volunteer group and the Douglas DB-7's [sic] to a Chinese group. I concur fully in this decision since I believe there are sufficient trained Chinese bombardment personnel to operate the Douglas bomber group.

The organization of the Hudson bomber group may be arranged on either of two plans. If cost is not considered I would choose to have all trained personnel employed in America. Under this plan, all of the pilots, co-pilots, mechanics, radio, armament, clerical and administrative personnel would be volunteers from the U.S. services. Guards, mess attendants and laborers only would be furnished by the Chinese. Under this plan, the group organization would follow the plan proposed by Capt. Aldworth rather closely. Inclosed herewith and marked Exhibit "A" is the estimate of the volunteer personnel required under this plan.

Under the second plan, only key personnel are volunteers and most of the members of the group are to be furnished by the Chinese – an organization similar to that of the First American Volunteer Group (Pursuit). The Commission on Aeronautical Affairs assures me that well-trained Chinese personnel are available for assignment to this group in order to complete the full required strength. This organization will be far more economical than the other and should be almost as effective in operation provided that friction between various factions of Chinese personnel can be eliminated. Inclosed as Exhibit "B" is my estimate of the number of volunteer personnel required under this plan.

If it is desired that I exercise general supervision and command of the new bombardment group as well as the First American Volunteer Group (Pursuit), it will be necessary to organize a staff for a composite Wing. This will require the employment of a small number of additional personnel. Some of the personnel who will serve on the Wing staff are already employed on the First A.V.G. staff.

In order to operate a bombardment group, it will be necessary to furnish the group a considerable amount of special equipment. An approximate estimate of needed equipment is inclosed and marked Exhibit "C".

It is impossible for me to draw definite plans for the organization of the bombardment group (or groups) until I receive your instructions regarding the plan be followed and information regarding availability of volunteer personnel and the required equipment.

*With my highest regards and best wishes, I am
Most sincerely,
(signed)
C.L. Chennault* [70]

Obviously, there was a breakdown of communication between all parties involved because Chennault informed Soong that the Chinese Air Force would increase by 300 to 500 aircraft by the 31 October. This was simply not the case although he formulated his future objectives based on that date.

Knowing that the acquisition of B-17s was probably a lost cause, Chennault focused on the assets that he could expect, namely the Lockheed Hudson and Douglas DB-7 bombers. Although they would be utilized against Japanese positions fighting within China, he still intended them to bomb the Japanese homeland. In his letter to Soong, Chennault included the following table with approximate distances in statute miles to possible targets in Japan.

	Chuchow	Hengchow	Kanchow	Kian	Manila
Nagasaki	730	1150	1060	1020	1460
Kobe	1060	1485	1410	1360	-
Osaka	1085	1510	1435	1385	1780
Tokyo	1355	1780	1690	1645	2010 [71]

While a large swath of individuals both inside and outside the United States government were involved in the ongoing lend-lease pact with China it appears that the American ambassador to China, Clarence E. Gauss was left out of the loop on much of the secret air operation and to what was transpiring over several months in 1941. Gauss telegrammed Hull from Chungking on 23 September (received two days later) about an American civilian who could play a valuable role and stated in part:

> *Currie may be interested in the following: William Douglas Pawley, an American citizen who built and operates the aircraft factory at Loiwing on the Yunnan-Burma border and who also built and operates an extensive aircraft plant at Bangalore for the Government of India, visited Chungking last week briefly and told me that he has at Loiwing over 1000 experienced Chinese mechanics and skilled workmen of various classes together with a technical staff of 250 including a substantial number of graduates from American technical colleges and 12 Americans of whom 9 have had 6 to 7 years experience [in?] China and with Chinese workmen; that this force could readily be used in whole or in part as the framework for a maintenance and operations organization for the Burma Road; that if requested by the Chinese Government he would be prepared to undertake such a project if given full authority in his field of operations; but that he does not wish to take the initiative in this matter, believing that it should come from the Chinese side.* [72]

Pawley was involved in China for several years promoting American aviation interests, received a commission on the P-40s, and his company, CAMCO, is actively recruiting American pilots. How Gauss only became aware of him at this late date is not only interesting but distressing. The following week after the Gauss correspondence, Roosevelt sent a memorandum placing Currie in a position that more or less had him assume responsibility for the secret air operation that was still in a legal limbo.

While everyone within the United States government pretended to keep the bombing plan against Japan secret, on 31 October, the news weekly magazine *United States News* (that would become the *U.S. News & World Report* in 1948) published a piece a potential bombing targets in Japan and where the potential sites that these aircraft could depart from and shown in a two-page illustration. Then again on 18 November, *New York*

Times correspondent and Pulitzer Prize recipient, Arthur Bernard Krock, penned a piece where American bombers could depart the Philippines and then bomb Japan, finally landing in Vladivostok, Russia. There they could refuel, take on a new payload of ordnance and whack the Japanese again on the return trip. Krock postulates these bombing missions would free up both the United States and British fleets and produce a naval force outnumbering the Japanese. In conclusion Krock finishes with a haunting paragraph stating:

> *Before Mr. Kurusu [Japanese ambassador] leaves Washington he may have been officially acquainted with these new circumstances of war making in the far Pacific area for official transmission to his Government. The information will probably have an important effect on the progress of the American-Japanese discussions.* (73)

With General Magruder in town on his military mission, Chiang Kai-Shek informed him of the of a potential Japanese attack on the Yunnan Province in November and what the ramifications were. The Gimo tells him that the only way to fend off an attack on Yunnan was the introduction of the Royal Air Force in Singapore and further support of the A.V.G. Magruder agreed, and with lend-lease aid arriving at a snail's pace that the RAF should intercede or "…perhaps organized units from the Philippines." (74)

On 28 October, Magruder sent a lengthy cable to General Marshall and Secretary Stimson about his meeting with Chiang Kai-shek. In part he stated:

> *One point he picked out the first thing was aviation and stated this item was the principal item at this time. He was very strong and exceedingly fluent in a request that he would like to have our Mission take over and have complete control of his aviation. Then, to take complete charge of the general development of the aviation section. He disregarded the forces of his own—that is the Chinese—and stressed particularly the American Volunteer Force under Chennault. He acted and seemed to think the American Volunteer Force was the only one that counted.* (75)

The Gimo had all but given up on his CAF as an effective fighting entity and that he could only count on Chennault and his meager force of 99 Tomahawks to blunt the Japanese onslaught. He continued his narrative that if Kunming falls the war is over and Magruder seems to agree on this point. The Gimo also added that the British should assist the A.V.G. in any way possible.

Even before meeting with Chiang Kai-shek, Magruder assessed the potential attack on Kunming and within the same cablegram stated, "There is but slight doubt that if this attack is made and is a success the resistance of the Chinese would stop. Without effective air support it is true without doubt that the enemy's decisive effort might be successful." [76]

Magruder followed up in the same cable on the status of the Chinese Air Force and stated in part:

> *The 30th of October I had a talk with the Generalissimo, who frankly stated that his Chinese force that is the Air Corps has become a complete washout. That he was afraid of its combat efficiency. He then urgently asked that our mission assume this organization, take it over, and reorganize same; also, reorganize its training. He asked about our sending an Air Corps officer of high rank to take over and command his force. He insisted to the fact that full and absolute authority, free from any and all Air Corps interference or politics.* [77]

This information filtered to Currie and was then redirected to Secretary of State Hull and for unknown reasons, was relayed in a cablegram to the Consul General of Rangoon, Austin C. Brady, to be forwarded to Chennault. Brady was never in the A.V.G. loop but was involved in lend-lease to China. He once complained about goods being stockpiled in Rangoon such as 200,000 gas masks that the Chinese never requested and were taking up warehouse space, His only aviation connection is that he once hosted at his home for a single night, Fred Noonan, the navigator on the ill-fated trans-Pacific flight of Amelia Earnhardt. Hull (and Currie) sent the following cable to Brady on 13 November:

> "It has been suggested that we supply personnel for the reorganization and operation of the whole Chinese air force including the A. V. G. It is felt that this is impractical. As an alternative we suggest the following on which we should like your action. We understand that the Chinese have some first-class pilots. Our thought is that you might organize one

or possibly two all-Chinese groups with officers and pilots selected by you and under your tactical command. We would undertake to secure more Americans to assist you as staff officers in your larger duties. We believe this preferable either to turning planes over to Chinese air force or to assuming any responsibility for operation of Chinese air force. If this experiment is successful you could organize still another Chinese group as American equipment becomes available along with the organization of further American groups. We are uncertain as to whether any of the Chinese planes are suitable for your combat purposes. Are facilities available and adequate for the training of both American and Chinese groups in Burma? Whenever couriers are available, I should appreciate more detail on your progress and problems. Your cable to CDS [China Defense Supplies] just received. Will try to meet your requests."

The contents of this telegram should be regarded as strictly confidential for the Consul General and Chennault only.

Hull [78]

What is interesting in this dispatch is that Hull (and/or Currie) opened with "It has been suggested that we supply personnel for the reorganization and operation of the whole Chinese air force including the A. V. G." Yet the Generalissimo had informed Magruder that he was completely satisfied with Chennault and the A.V.G. and was interested in the United States assuming control of the CAF. So, was this just a miscommunication of the times or did Hull and/or Currie provide this disinformation to Chennault for a yet another undetermined reason?

Just a day earlier Chennault cabled Currie directly and stated:

Competent Chinese pilots estimated at 200 bombardment and 150 pursuit. For operation of American planes all of these would require some transition and unit training. If these pilots were completely relieved from commission aeronautical affairs and placed same status as American volunteer units except in matter of pay, I believe I could organize, train and operate effective groups. Pay of these pilots should not be equal to that of Americans but should be raised. As an experiment I am willing to undertake one group imme-

diately, P-48 planes to be used as they arrive. Thirty American staff officers at least would be urgently required for this group together with some administrative and technical personnel. The transition and the unit training facilities are available and adequate in Burma. The number of combat machines the Chinese have is so small as to be negligible and suitable bombers number only about 20. (79)

Currie was caught off guard and had no idea of the current state of the Chinese Air Force. He replied to Chennault on 22 November this time directly and stated:

Your cable of November 12 came to us as a bombshell. None of us had any idea of the status of your equipment until that time. Nothing at all had come in from the Magruder mission except a cable on solenoids and bomb racks, and one containing certain proposals that the Army deemed impractical [the United States assuming control of the CAF. I am hopeful that one result of all this will that a supply officer will be sent out to strengthen the air arm of the mission. (80)

Pawley had some success during November recruiting personnel for the second A.V.G. (the bomber wing) and forty-nine ground personnel departed for China on the 21 November. This initial spearhead of American volunteers became stranded in Australia with the outbreak of war. One thing is evident is that Pawley did make an incredible effort with volunteers then on their way overseas while the United States government floundered and did not have a single bomber in route to China. That being said, Chennault was interested in only qualified personnel while Pawley simply wanted to fill the established quotas.

It was during November 1941 that Pawley contacted the British Air Ministry with the idea of their country providing volunteers for service in China, presumably as employees of CAMCO. This is uncharacteristic of Pawley, being a "money-man" unless there was something in the deal to profit him. This would need to be with CAMCO contracts dealing with the pilots and ground personnel as he had no apparent financial interest in British supplied aircraft.

This is also confirmed with a Magruder cablegram to the War Department on 3 December. Magruder was visiting with the British in Chungking at the time and touched on several issues including a tentative proposition to provide the Chinese with a squadron of Buffalos and a squadron of Blenheim bombers. He also mentioned additional British support for Chennault and the possibility of constituting an "international volunteer group." Magruder's cablegram was sent the same day when the Japanese naval task force was about at their halfway mark to their intended target since departing Hitokappu Bay on the 26 November,

The idea of the British providing Brewster F2A Buffalos was certainly no gift for the Chinese but possibly a good idea by them to unload the heavy and unstable monoplane fighter. Built by the Brewster Aeronautical Corporation, the company operated three manufacturing facilities, in Long Island City, New York, Newark, New Jersey, and, in 1941, in Warminster Township, Pennsylvania. The Brewster F2A Buffalo was no match for the Japanese Mitsubishi A6M2 Zero. The British and Dutch had severe losses early in the war and tried to improve its performance by halving the fuel and ammunition on board on fighter missions, but it made little difference – the bird was a dodo. An interesting side note is that Finland had great success against the Soviets in their war against the communists. The Finns purchased and flew the Model 239 variant against the Soviets – ironically another United States lend-lease partner.

Japan Strikes First

As the United States secret preemptive strike plan (the Chinese version) continued to flounder, Japanese attack plan(s) sailed along smoothly. Initiated just a few months earlier, in February, they were about to bear fruit. In the waning days of November, the War Department was considering direct bombardment of Japan from bases in the Philippines using Boeing B-17 and Consolidated B-24 bombers.

These plans, as noted earlier, would have the bombers depart the Philippines, strike Japan and land and refuel at Vladivostok, Russia. Although a lend-lease partner (presumably for fighting the Germans on the western front) Russia had signed a nonaggression pact with Japan back on 13 April. Did American planners really believe that Russia would abrogate their agreement with Japan over this operation which to borrow a phrase from Secretary Stimson was a "half-backed idea?"

As Marshall, Macarthur, Arnold, Stimson, et al, hashed out various options for bombing Japan from the Philippines, no mention is made of Chennault and utilizing airfields in eastern China that were significantly closer than Vladivostok. Author Alan Armstrong, in his book Preemptive Strike, believes it was the relationship between Chennault and Chiang

Kai-shek. Armstrong states:

> *"Perhaps American military planners distrusted Chennault and Chiang Kai-shek. After all, Chiang Kai-shek's Kuomintang-led Nationalist government suffered from corruption. Chennault, with his abrasive personality and his theories on fighter tactics running counter to Air Corps dogma, had offended and angered a number of his colleagues."* (81)

Armstrong is spot on, but perhaps the American planners also believed Chennault was corrupt as an employee of the Gimo and someone who was making pretty good money compared to his American counterparts. Armstrong also points out that our military strategists considered that fuel supplies may have been better in Vladivostok than the fields in eastern China. Yet getting fuel to China would be no more insurmountable than delivering fuel to Russia. Consider also that that Hap Arnold did not inform Chennault of the Doolittle raid when it took place in 1942 and potentially using his assets in China in recovering the pilots, citing security issues. You either trust someone or you don't. And the American military obviously did not trust Chennault.

All of this was a moot point as the Japanese concluded their preemptive strike operations against the United States and Great Britain. On 6 December an Australian pilot radioed the position of a Japanese naval task force off the coast of British Malaya (a set of states on the Malay Peninsula and the island of Singapore under British control) before being shot down. In a touch of irony, the Aussie was flying an American built Lockheed Hudson.

On the 7 December, Pearl Harbor was attacked. The following day the Philippines were assaulted and historians would wonder why Macarthur was not relieved of his command at that time with his ineptitude. The Japanese had accomplished what the United States could not – a preemptive strike with incredible and satisfactory results. The only saving grace was that the American carriers, the *Lexington* and *Enterprise* were not at Pearl Harbor, but delivering fighter aircraft to Midway and Wake Island, and the *Saratoga* was making headway to California. The battleships at Pearl Harbor were just anachronisms of the past. Admiral Harry Yarnell was proven right – unfortunately it took 2,335 lives lost at Pearl Harbor to prove it. And at the same time, the secret plan to bomb Japan from bases in China with American pilots and aircraft, died with those men.

1. Alsop entered the US Navy and used his political connections to be assigned as Staff Historian to Claire Lee Chennault's Flying Tigers. On 7 December 1941, while in Hong Kong he was interred by the Japanese. Six months later he was repatriated through a prisoner exchange as a journalist, even though he was a combatant. He returned on the neutral ocean liner Gripsholm and returned to China as a civilian Lend-lease administrator in the fall of 1942 and eventually rejoined Chennault in Kunming and served with him for the remaining months of the war.

2. Mowrer later served in the United States government in the United States Office of War Information from 1942 to 1943.

3. Foreign Relations of the United States Diplomatic Papers, 1940, The Far East, Volume I 893.248/186.

4. Foreign Relations of the United States Diplomatic Papers, 1940, The Far East, Volume IV 893.248/188.

5. Morgenthau diaries.

6. Xu, Guangqiu, War Wings, Pg. 154.

7. Morgenthau diaries.

8. Ibid.

9. Foreign Relations of the United States Diplomatic Papers, 1940, The Far East, Volume IV, 893.248/190, The President of the Chinese Executive Yuan (Chiang) to the Secretary of the Treasury (Morgenthau).

10. Morgenthau diaries.

11. Ibid.

12. Ibid.

13. Ibid.

14. Ibid.

15. Ford, Daniel, Flying Tigers, Kindle version, Location 501.

16. Morgenthau diaries.

17. Langer, W. L., & Gleason, S. E. (1953). The Undeclared War, 1940-1941: The World Crisis and American Foreign Policy, Pg. 715.

18. By-Line: Ernest Hemingway. New York, NY: Charles Scribner's Sons (1967), Pg. 335-339.

19. Ibid.

20. Ibid.

21. Chennault, Claire Lee, Way of the Fighter, Pg. 101.

22. Forrest C. Pogue, George C. Marshall: Ordeal and Hope New York: Viking: (1966), Pg. 353.

23. Young, Arthur N., China and the Helping Hand:1937-1945, Cambridge, MA, Harvard University: (1963), Pg. 149.

24. Carrozza, William D. Pawley, Pg. 80.

25. Ibid. Pg. 81.

26. Malcolm, Rosholt, Days of the Chiang Poa: A Photographic Record of the Flying Tigers-14th Air Force in China in World War II, Amherst WI: Palmer Publications, (1978), Pg. 24.

27. Carrozza, William D. Pawley, Pg. 85.

28. Freis, Herbert, The Road to Pearl Harbor, Princeton NJ: Princeton University Press, (1950), Pg. 187.

29. Cole 1974, Pg. 39-40, Wikipedia reference 146.

30. Duffy, James P. Lindbergh vs. Roosevelt: The Rivalry That Divided America Washington, D.C., Regnery Publishing, (2010), Pg.181.

31. Foreign Relations of the United States Diplomatic Papers,1941, The Far East, Volume IV, Mr. Lauchlin Currie to President Roosevelt, March 15, 1941

32. Pakula, Hannah, The Last Empress: Madame Chiang Kai-Shek and the Birth of Modern China. AU: Orion Publishing Group, Limited: (2011) Pg. 555. According to Pakula, in J. Edgar Hoover's extensive FBI files, someone characterized the doctor as "a Polish Jew [who] should be watched."

33. Pakula, The Last Empress, Pg. 362.

34. The Papers of George Catlett Marshall, Vol. 2, "We Cannot Delay, July 1, 1939-December 6, 1941" Baltimore and London: The Johns Hopkins University Press: (1986), Pg. 458-459

35. National Archives, Record Group 59.

36. Joint Board 355 Papers.

37. National Archives Record Group 59.

38. Joint Board 355 papers.

39. Ibid.

40. Foreign Relations of the United States Diplomatic Papers,1941, The Far East, Volume, 893.24/1121½: Telegram. Madame Chiang Kai-shek to Mr. Lauchlin Currie, Administrative Assistant to President Roosevelt, Chungking, July 22, 1941.

41. Foreign Relations of the United States Diplomatic Papers, 1941, The Far East, Volume V, Mr. Lauchlin Currie to President Roosevelt, Washington, July 19, 1941.

42. Foreign Relations of the United States Diplomatic Papers, 1941, The Far East, Volume V, 893.51/7281: Telegram, Mr. Owen Lattimore, American Political Adviser to Generalissimo Chiang Kai-shek, to Mr. Lauchlin Currie, Administrative Assistant to President Roosevelt.

43. National Archives, Paraphrase of a coded radiogram received at the War Department at 7:24 August 9, 1941.

44. Foreign Relations of the United States Diplomatic Papers, 1941, The Far East, Volume V, 893.248/226, The Ambassador in China (Gauss) to the Secretary of State, No. 24.

45. James M. McHugh Papers, 1930-1965, Collection Number: 2770, Division of Rare and Manuscript Collections, Cornell University Library.

46. Joint Board Papers 355, Serial 691.

47. It appears Scobey made full Colonel and was involved in the internment of Japanese-Americans to internment camps.

48. *Foreign Relations of the United States Diplomatic Papers, 1941, The Far East, Volume IV.*

49. Donovan was an American soldier, lawyer, intelligence officer and diplomat. A decorated veteran of World War I, he is the only person to have received all four of the United States' highest awards: The Medal of Honor, the Distinguished Service Cross, the Distinguished Service Medal, and the National Security Medal. A registered Republican, many historians believe he may have been President if he was a member of the Democratic party.

50. *Foreign Relations of the United States Diplomatic Papers, 1941, The Far East, Volume V,* 893.248/232.

51. Ibid.

52. Ibid.

53. Ibid.

54. Ibid.

55. Hoover Institution Archives, Claire Chennault Records, Box 2.

56. *Foreign Relations of the United States Diplomatic Papers, 1941, The Far East, Volume V,* 893.24/1111a: Telegram.

57. Armstrong, Alan, Preemptive Strike: The Secret Plan That Would Have Prevented The Attack On Pearl Harbor, Guilford, CT: Lyons Press: (2006), Pg. 168.

58. Ibid.

59. *Foreign Relations of the United States Diplomatic Papers, 1941, The Far East, Volume V,* 793.94/16992¼: Telegram.

60. Samson, Jack, The Flying Tiger, Pg. 110-111.

61. Armstrong, Alan, Preemptive Strike, Pg. 103.

62. Chennault, Claire, Way of A Fighter, Pg. 117.

63. *Foreign Relations of the United States Diplomatic Papers, 1941, The Far East, Volume V,* 893.248/231a: Telegram.

64. *Foreign Relations of the United States Diplomatic Papers, 1941, The Far East, Volume V,* 893.248/233: Telegram.

65. National Archives, Chennault letter, posted September 29, 1941, P.O. Box 2000, Rangoon, Burma.

66. Ibid.

67. *Foreign Relations of the United States Diplomatic Papers, 1941, The Far East, Volume V,* 893.154/386: Telegram.

68. Franklin D. Roosevelt, Presidential Library and Museum, digital collection.

69. *Foreign Relations of the United States Diplomatic Papers, 1941, The Far East, Volume V,* 893.24/1190: Telegram.

70. National Archives, Record Group 59.

71. Ibid.

72. *Foreign Relations of the United States Diplomatic Papers, 1941, The Far East, Volume V,*

893.154/386: Telegram.

73. The New York Times, November 18, 1941, Pg. 10.

74. Foreign Relations of the United States Diplomatic Papers, 1941, The Far East, VOLUME V, 793.94/16992¾: Telegram.

75 Ibid.

76. Ibid.

77. Ibid.

78. Foreign Relations of the United States Diplomatic Papers, 1941, The Far East, Volume V, 893.248/252a: Telegram.

79. National Archives, Record group 59.

80. Hoover Institute Archives, Claire Chennault collection, Box number 2.

81. Armstrong, Alan, Preemptive Strike, Pg. 195.

Michael Lemish

Afterword

*"For all sad words of tongue and pen, the saddest are these,
'It might have been."*

John Greenleaf Whittier

IN RETROSPECT, THE FIRST major question to be asked is, if Chennault had been able to obtain long range B-17 bombers or even medium range bombers and attack the Japanese homeland, could this have prevented the Japanese from launching a sneak attack on Pearl Harbor? If implemented in a timely fashion under Joint Board 355, Chennault and the Chinese would have acquired 150 bombers and 350 fighter aircraft well before the attack on Pearl Harbor.

Yet even with 150 bombers Chennault was in no position to bring Japan to her knees or drive her from China. One only has to look at the massive raids launched by the United States with B-29 Super Fortresses starting in the later part of 1944 to see that was nonsensical. Eventually it took two atomic bombs to have Japan capitulate.

It is critical to keep things in perspective. Both the B-17 Flying Fortress and the B-29 Super Fortress had about the same service ceiling, yet the B-29 could carry 5,000 pounds of bombs for 1,600 miles while the B-17 would muster 4,500 pounds of bombs for half the distance. This would have meant that Chennault's B-17s, had he acquired them, would have carried a minimal bombload to Japan. Also consider what the Japanese endured later in the war. During just the first incendiary raid on March 9, 1945, 346 B-29s departed the Marianas to attack Tokyo. Over 1,600 tons of bombs were dropped destroying about 16 square miles of the city and killing more than 80,000 people. And this was just one of many incendiary and conventional bombing attacks against Japan.

This is not to say that a Chennault aerial attack on Japan may have caused her to make a change in its military plans going forward. Just consider the effect of the simple leaflet dropping on the homeland several years earlier. In his book, *Preemptive Strike*, author Alan Armstrong believes so and stated:

> It does appear that the timely execution of the Joint Board Plan offered America and the Associated Powers the means to force Japan to expend further resources in China, and may well have prevented the Japanese attack on Pearl Harbor. [1]

The United States clearly understood that war with Japan was in the cards within the immediate future. Military planners wanted Japan bogged down in its war with China as much as possible. The sanctions against Japan both in forms of financial terms and squeezing her for raw materials (e.g. petroleum and metals) meant that the Japanese needed to look to military acquisitions to replace these losses. Clearly both Secretary of War Stimson and Chief of Staff Marshall knew this. Yet they considered China not just second banana, but third banana to Great Britain and the Soviet Union. This was even more evident after the start of World War II.
On the flip side is that Roosevelt's "secret" plan to bomb Japan may have accelerated her plans and their desire to attack Pearl Harbor. All along the Japanese were aware of what the United States was trying to do and that a potential bombing of their homeland was anything but a clandestine operation. They didn't need any spies, but just read the newspapers and magazines to see what was going on. What the Japanese military did not realize at the time was the incompetence of American politicians and military strategists to implement an anticipatory strike against a potential enemy.

Secretary of War Henry Stimson once considered Claire Chennault's plan to bomb Japan as "half-baked." Chief of Staff General George Marshall questioned whether Chinese pilots were capable of flying four-engine high-performance aircraft and was concerned about the loss of these valuable aircraft - Although Chennault originally intended that these bombers be piloted by Americans.

The few B-17s available in the Pacific at the time were entrusted to General Douglas MacArthur at Clark Field in the Philippines. On the 8 December, twenty-six Mitsubishi G3M bombers and twenty-seven Mitsubishi G4M bombers dropped 636 bombs over Clark Field destroying twelve B-17 planes and damaging four. Thirty-four P-40s were destroyed on the ground or in aerial combat. The B-17s were under the direct command of Major General Lewis H. Brereton, and General Hap Arnold would later call Brereton asking "how the hell" he was caught by surprise nine hours after receiving news of the Pearl Harbor attack. General MacArthur would emerge unscathed from this Japanese attack. General George C. Marshall would later remark to a reporter, "I just don't know how MacArthur happened to let his planes get caught on the ground."

Claire Chennault was no Svengali and he did make many missteps in his life. He is accurate though, along with President Roosevelt, that a preemptive strike against Japan may have had profound and positive results. The United States was just unable to respond in a timely fashion and what occurred at Pearl Harbor and the Pacific War that followed is forever cemented in history.

Other points in history can clearly be used as a comparison during the undeclared war between China and Japan assuming that direct and irrevocable intervention took place. It also depends if the United States was truly allied with China. The United States vacillated on this point given the dribs and drabs that were afforded the Chinese through lend-lease and its Europe first policy. The isolationist movement in America had a strong effect over the government and the military that reverberated across the world stage.

Of all the incidents over the years between the United States and Japan leading up to Pearl Harbor, there is one event that should have galvanized our country to bypass the Neutrality Act and embrace China as a strong ally. This would be the sinking of the USS *Panay* (PR-5) gunboat in the Yangtze River by Japanese forces in 1937. But unlike the U.S. Navy ship that blew up in Havana Harbor in 1898, it was not a "Remember the Maine" moment.

The United States emerged from the *Panay* incident with as much resolve as a canvas sack full of wet mice. The presence of American flags (also painted on the deck), which would have been visible from the air suggests the attack had not been a mistake, but perhaps a type of unauthorized action known by the classical Japanese name Gekokujō. Gekokujō is a Japanese term for "overthrowing or surpassing one's superiors." The *Panay* was pounded by two aerial bombardment runs and then shelled by shore batteries.

The United States State Department accepted the "incident" as an error from the Japanese and accepted a monetary stipend for the inconvenience. As Barbara Tuchman stated in *Sand Against the Wind*, "Public reaction in so far as it was represented by Congress was not to roar but to shrink." [2]

Some people believe that the attack on the *Panay* wasn't meant to destroy a military asset but to see how the United States would respond. If this was the case, then the Japanese military got the answer they were looking for. In the end this was 1937 and the United States took no action against the Japanese - Just another link in a chain of events culminating with World War II. Had the United States taken more decisive action and provided Chennault and China with the tools to bomb Japan, would this have changed history and perhaps prevented the attack on Pearl Harbor?

1. Armstrong, Alan, Preemptive Strike, Pg. 200.
2. Tuchman, Barbara, Sand Against the Wind, Pg. 228.

Post Script: The Key Players

JOSEPH ALSOP joined the U.S. Navy and was staff historian for the A.V.G. On December 7, 1941 he was in Hong Kong and captured by the Japanese. Able to convince his captors that he was a foreign correspondent he was released six months later in a prisoner exchange. He returned to China in late 1942 as a lend-lease administrator. After the war he worked covertly for the CIA for a short time. Although a closeted homosexual, in 1961 he married American socialite and writer Susan Mary Jay Patten. The couple divorced in 1978 and Alsop passed way in Georgetown, Washington D.C. in 1989.

HAP ARNOLD was one of the principal architects of heavy long-range bombing in Europe and against Japan. The stress of the job took its toll and Arnold had four heart attacks between 1943 and 1945. In 1945 he directed the founding of Project RAND (which later became the RAND Corporation, a nonprofit global policy think tank). In 1949 Arnold's final rank and grade changed to that of General of the Air Force, and he remains the only person to have held the rank. He died at the age of 63 in Sonoma, California.

CLAIRE CHENNAULT, after the dissolution of the Flying Tigers in 1942, became Lieutenant General of the Fourteenth Air Force. He divorced his wife, Nell Thompson in 1946 and married Chen Xiangmei (Anna Chennault) and fathered two children with her. He then founded CAT (Civil Air Transport) in 1946 along with Whiting Willauer. The firm used surplus aircraft such as the C-47 Dakota and the C-46 Commando. CAT would later be purchased by the CIA and morphed into Air America and operated during the Vietnam War.

TOMMY CORCORAN, after the war became what most inside the beltway would say was the first modern lobbyist. He was instrumental in the takeover of a New York City radio station by a friend of his which led to investigations by Congress and the FCC. Corcoran's phones were wire tapped between 1945 and 1947 by the FBI and it was alleged that he tried to improperly influence Supreme Court decisions.

LAUCHLIN CURRIE was just one of many blamed for the loss of China to the Communists after the war. Implicated with many others as Soviet spies, Currie appeared before the House Committee on Un-American Activities in August 1948 to refute the charges. In 1949 he was appointed to head the first of the World Bank's comprehensive country surveys in Colombia. In December 1952, Currie returned to New York to testify at a grand jury investigating Owen Lattimore's role in the publication of secret State Department documents in Amerasia magazine. In 1954 when he tried to renew his United States passport he was denied and spent his remaining years in Columbia. He died on December 23, 1993 of a heart attack in Bogota.

JIMMY DOOLITTLE and his sixteen B-25 crews took off from the USS *Hornet* (CV-8) aircraft carrier on April 18, 1942 and carried out the famous raid on Japan. In 1943 Doolittle changed the policy requiring escorting fighters to remain with their bombers at all times and that was a major influence on the European air as the fighters flew ahead and spearheaded the bombers. In 1946, Doolittle headed a commission on the relationships between officers and enlisted men in the U.S. Army. Columnist Hanson Baldwin, shortly after the Korean War, said the board "caused severe damage to service effectiveness by recommendations intended to 'democratize' the Army—a concept that is self-contradictory."

EARNEST HEMINGWAY never returned to China. Many historians suspect he was a NKVD agent (precursor to the KGB) with the codename Argo. In 1954 Hemingway was awarded the Nobel Prize in Literature for the "Old Man and the Sea." On July 2, 1961 Hemingway killed himself in Ketchum, Idaho with a 12-gauge shotgun. His fourth wife, Mary Welsh stated at the time that he was just cleaning the weapon. Recently researchers believe that Hemingway may have suffered from CTE (Chronic Traumatic Encephalopathy) from numerous concussions received on the battlefronts he visited and during numerous boxing exhibitions that he participated in.

CORDELL HULL was the longest serving Secretary of State but no favorite of President Roosevelt who often deferred many key matters to the Undersecretary Sumner Welles. Hull was instrumental in forming the United Nations and was recognized for this by receiving the Nobel peace prize in 1945. Yet Hull will ultimately be remembered for his actions in 1939 by recommending to the President that the German ocean liner, the SS *St. Louis*, with 936 Jewish refugees on board, not be permitted to land. That decision sent the SS *St Louis* back to Germany on the eve of the Nazi Holocaust.

CHIANG KAI-SHEK, after the Japanese were vanquished resumed his civil war with the Communists. After Canton fell the Gimo retreated and set up his KMT government in Chungking while he and his son directed military operations from Chengtu. On 10 December 1949, when Chengtu was laid siege by the Communists, the Gimo and his son escaped aboard a plane named May-ling, and were delivered to Taiwan, never to return to the Chinese mainland during their lifespan.

MADAME CHIANG KAI-SHEK made several trips to the United States during the war and spoke at events supporting the Nationalist movement that would draw crowds of 30,000 people. A favorite of publisher Henry Luce, she would appear on the cover of *Time* magazine three times. She was diagnosed with breast cancer in 1975 and would undergo two mastectomies in Taiwan. The feisty lady would endure this and die in her sleep at her Manhattan apartment on October 23, 2003, at the age of 105.

OWEN LATTIMORE was publicly charged as a Soviet agent in 1948 but during the McCarthy hearings he was accused as a Communist but not a Soviet agent. In 1952, Lattimore was indicted for perjury on seven counts, but all were overturned three years later. He died May 31, 1989, in Providence, Rhode Island.

CHARLES LINDBERGH sought to be recommissioned in the USAAF after Pearl Harbor but was denied this request by Stimson. Lindbergh was involved with several aviation companies during the war in research and development. Beginning in 1957 he had sexual encounters with three European women while still married to Anne Morrow and fathered several children. In later years he became involved with several environmental causes. Lindbergh spent his last years on the Hawaiian island of Maui, where he died of lymphoma on August 26, 1974, at the age of 72.

GENERAL GEORGE MARSHALL became Secretary of State from 1947 to 1949 and advocated rebuilding Europe in what was called Marshall Plan. He was awarded the 1953 Nobel Peace Prize for this effort. He died in 1959 and was buried with full military honors at Arlington National Cemetery.

HENRY MORGENTHAU and Cordell Hull often sparred over the disposition of Jewish war refugees. No doubt there was no love lost between these two powerful men. In 1944 Morgenthau began drafting a plan the would strip postwar Germany of her heavy industries favoring a more agrarian economy. In 1945, when Harry S. Truman became President upon Roosevelt's death, Morgenthau insisted on accompanying the President to Potsdam and if not he threatened to quit. Truman accepted his resignation immediately. The remainder of his life was devoted to Jewish philanthropies and he died in Poughkeepsie, New York, in 1967.

MAO BANGCHU was entangled in an embezzlement scandal in the early 'fifties, following accusations that he misappropriated $19,440,000 USD from the Taiwanese government. To avoid prosecution in Taiwan, he fled to Mexico by bus via Nogales, Arizona. He then assumed the name Carlos Gomez Lee Wong. In 1955 a Mexican Court barred the extradition of General Mao, and he was freed from prison. He died in 1987 at the age of 83.

WILLIAM PAWLEY moved from airplane salesman to politician after the war and was appointed to Ambassador of Peru in 1945 by President Truman and later Ambassador to Brazil in 1948. How he made the slide from commercial aviation to politics is not quite clear. Pawley played a role in Operation PBSUCCESS, a CIA plot to overthrow the Guatemalan government of Jacobo Arbenz in 1954 after Arbenz introduced reforms affecting the United Fruit Company. Pawley is thought to have served CIA interests in Peru, Brazil, Panama, Guatemala, Cuba and Nicaragua between 1945 and 1960. Officially he committed suicide in January 1977 in Miami, Florida because he suffered from the depilating and painful disease shingles. Although some people suspect he was executed for his nefarious actions in his past.

T.V. SOONG like many influential Chinese nationals after the defeat of the Nationalists in the Chinese Civil War, moved to New York City and lived there until his death while on a business trip to San Francisco at the age of 79.

JOSEPH STILWELL was a Republican and Roosevelt hater. On October 19, 1944, he was recalled from his command by Roosevelt because of the high casualties in Burma and difficulties encountered with Chinese and British commanders. He was met by just two Army generals upon his return and was told not to answer any media questions about China whatsoever.

Henry Stimson initially opposed the Japanese-American internment program but caved in under pressure. Stimson took direct personal control of the entire atomic bomb project. with direct supervision over General Leslie Groves, head of the Manhattan Project. President Harry S. Truman followed Stimson's advice on every aspect of the bomb. A month after his 83rd birthday (October 20, 1950), he died from complications from a second heart attack.

Sumner Welles was forced out of the government after the FBI revealed he had solicited two men for sex. He was a target of the House Un-American Activities Committee but never formally sanctioned. He died in New Jersey in 1961, survived by his third wife and several children.

Whiting Willauer joined forces with Chennault after the war to form Civil Air Transport (CAT). He even had a C-47 modified with an enclosed air-conditioned office. He served as ambassador to Honduras from 1954 to 1958 and to Costa Rica from 1958 until his retirement in 1961. He assisted the CIA team in neighboring Guatemala with the overthrow of President Jacobo Arbenz Guzman.

Index

02U-12 Corsair biplane, 41
0C-2 Falcon biplane, 37,38
02MC biplane, 44

A

A-20 Havoc bomber, 120, 173
A5M-9 "Claude" fighter, 92
A6M2 fighter, 115, 210
Adair, Captain C.B., 157, 159
Adams, Walter, 35, 41
Advanced Aircraft Aviation, 34
AFC. *see* America First Committee
Air America, 221
Aldworth, Richard, 157, 203
Alsop, Joseph, 125, 126, 212, 221
America First Committee, 161
American Military Mission, 195, 196
American Volunteer Group, 126, 139, 151, 153, 159, 160, 173, 183, 188, 196-198, 203, 204, 206- 209, 221
AMMISCA, *see* American Military Mission
Andrews, Maj. Gen. Frank, 70
Arnold, Gen. Henry H. "Hap," 104, 141, 142,158, 167-172, 174, 180, 188, 200, 210, 211, 218, 221
A.V.G. *see* American Volunteer Group
Aviation Exploration Corp., 36, 39, 51

B

B-10 bomber, 67, 103, 104
B-17 bomber, 70, 134, 140, 144, 146, 150, 151, 185, 204, 210, 217, 218
B-18 Bolo bomber, 69
B-24, bomber, 171, 210
B-25, bomber, 78, 105, 186, 194, 222
Baird, Lt. Stuart, 62
Baskey, Earl, 34, 35,39,41
Bellanca. 93
Blackburn-Lincock fighter, 52
Boeing, 26, 46, 62, 67, 70
Boeing 218 fighter, 47, 48
Boeing Model 299 bomber, 67-70
Boeing, William, 52
Boone, Maj. Rodney, 114
Boxer Rebellion, 13, 63, 83
Brewster Buffalo fighter, 210
BT-2 trainer, 44, 81, 82
Burma Road, 116, 117, 138, 146, 177, 183, 205
Butler, Neville, 143

C

CAF *see* Chinese Air Force
CAMCO. *see* Central Aircraft Manufacturing Company

Canton Aviation Bureau, 33, 35
Canton Aviation School, 62
Castle, Jr., William, 56
CDS *see* China Defense Supplies
Central Aircraft Manufacturing Company, 91, 100, 105, 154, 155, 157, 158, 164, 165, 200, 205, 209
Central Aviation School. 67, 87
Challenger Robin, 37, 38
Chance-Vought Corp., 41
Chance-Vought Corsair biplane, 39, 40, 42, 43
Chengtu, 126, 150, 151. 156, 163, 185, 223
Chennault, Claire, 67, 166, 174, 184, 219, 220, 221
  aircraft procurement, 183, 192, 194, 195, 197, 199, 202, 209, 210, 217
  American support, 94, 96, 98, 111
  A.V.G. activities, 151, 152, 154, 157-159, 164, 182, 183, 188, 196, 198, 204, 206-208
  conducting Japanese attacks, 89-92, 104, 121, 177, 204
  Fourteenth International Squadron, 99-101
  Japan visit, 78
  conducting Japanese attacks, 89-92
  contracting with China, 79-87
  relationship with Morgenthau, 139, 144, 154
  relationship with Pawley, 105, 108-110, 114, 115, 153, 155
  U.S. departure, 75-77
  U.S. military relations, 126, 127, 131, 138, 140, 141, 156, 171, 173, 175, 181, 182, 188, 196, 211, 218
Chiang Ka-Shek, 26, 27, 30, 38, 55-57,62, 63, 65, 67, 71, 73, 79-82, 85. 90, 99, 104, 116, 117, 132-134, 136, 141, 144, 159, 160, 166, 177, 180-184, 196, 199, 200, 206, 207, 211, 223
Chiang Kai-shek, Madame, 53, 77, 79, 81, 85, 86, 88, 90, 92, 99, 133, 148, 156, 177, 181, 184, 185, 193-196, 202, 203, 223
Chinese Air Force, 7, 23, 43,52, 54, 55, 57, 65, 67,73, 79, 81-83, 85, 88, 90, 100, 102-104, 107, 114, 116, 132, 160, 167, 170, 171, 183-185, 196, 197, 204, 206-209
China Aircraft Company, 39
China Defense Supplies, 161, 164-167, 190, 208
China National Aviation Corp., 35, 52, 57, 99, 192, 193

Index

China Weekly Review, 36
Chungking, 155
CIA, 21, 189
Clagett, Gen. Henry, 167, 183-185
Clairborne, Capt. John, 62
Collier's, 146, 147
CNAC *see* China National Aviation Corp.
Commerce Department, 32,54, 55
Connecticut, USS, 13
Coolidge, President Calvin, 69
Corbin, Lee, 46
Corcoran, Tommy, 157, 165, 166, 221, 222
Craig, Gen. Malin, 68. 69
Cunningham, Edwin, 41
Currie, Dr. Lauchlin, 144-146, 150, 160, 163, 164, 166, 167, 169-172, 176-178, 180, 181, 183, 185, 186, 188, 193-202, 205, 207-2209, 213, 222
Curtiss BF2C-1 biplane, 81
Curtiss H75-M-Special fighter, 90, 91
Curtiss Hawk fighter, 60, 62, 64
Curtiss Hawk II fighter, 72
Curtiss Hawk III fighter, 91, 92
Curtiss P-1 Hawk fighter, 59
Curtiss-Wright, 26,35,39, 51, 52, 57, 60, 61

D
DB-7 bomber, 171-173, 179, 186, 193, 195, 203, 204
De Havilland Aircraft Company, 30
Deeds, Capt. Edward, 62
Domei, 88
Donald, William, 79, 80, 87
Donovan, William, "Wild Bill," 189, 190, 192, 214
Doolittle, James H. "Jimmy," 57-61
Douglas Aircraft, 26, 43, 44
Douglas BT-2 trainer, 81
Drysdale, Col. Walter, 54

E
Eastern Airlines, 35
embargo:
    China, 27, 29-32, 27-39, 41, 93-96, 106
    Japan, 93-96, 106, 118, 140, 156, 187
Enterprise, USS, 17
EP-1 fighter, 107, 109
Ethell, Jeff, 70

F
FBI, 78
Fiat B.R.3 bombers, 63
Fiat CR.32 fighter, 64, 65

Fleet Problem 13, 15,17

Flying Fortress, 67, 69, 74, 134, 138, 139, 150, 151, 163, 164, 171, 173, 217
Flying Tigers, 10, 46, 57, 75, 122, 139, 141, 151, 212, 213, 221
Fourteenth Volunteer Squadron, 99, 100, 101, 103, 104
Ford, Gerald, 161
France, 27, 27, 28, 30, 40, 115, 160, 162, 173, 186

G
Gauss, Clarence, 71, 92, 122, 184, 183, 194, 205, 213
Gayle, Lloyd E., 31, 32, 34, 39
Gee-Bee R-1 racer, 60
Gellhorn, Martha, 146-149
Germany, 8, 17, 20, 22, 23, 39, 113, 117, 121, 125, 131, 140, 160, 161, 223,224
Great Britain, 22. 23 27,28, 39, 41, 117, 130, 140, 143,144, 153, 161, 162, 165, 167, 176, 178, 179, 182, 187, 192, 196, 199, 200, 211, 218
Green, Joseph, 106, 123, 127, 129
Grew, Joseph, 88, 97
Gypsy Moth trainer, 30

H
Hall, Weston, 39, 40, 46
Hamilton, Minard, 52
Hankou, 32, 33
Harding, President Warren, 27, 28, 31, 42
Hawaii, 25, 18, 118, 132, 135, 159, 171
Hawks, Col. Frank, 60
Hayward, R.O., 35
Hearn, Russell, 88, 89
Hemingway, Earnest, 11, 146-151, 184, 212, 222
Hill, Peter, 68
Hiroshima, 22
Hitler, Adolph, 22, 78, 121, 131, 140, 160-162, 195
Holbrook, Roy, 79, 80, 84
Hornet radial engine, 44
Hornet, USS, 78
Hoover, J. Edgar, 78, 148, 213
Hoover, President Herbert, 42
Hopkins, Harry, 165, 168, 180, 189-192, 195, 199, 200, 202
Hornbeck, Stanley, 109, 117, 130, 131
Houston, USS, 171
Howard, Edward, 62
Hu Shih, 127
Hudson bomber, 138-140, 171-174, 179, 182, 183, 192, 193, 195, 199, 203, 204, 211
Hughes, Charles, 30

Index

Hull, Cordell, 20, 66, 71, 72, 88, 89, 93, 94, 96, 109, 110, 117, 118, 130, 132, 133, 135, 137-140, 142, 144, 147, 184, 205, 207, 208, 222, 223, 224
Hurley, Patrick, 42, 73
Hurricane, fighter, 194, 195

I
Ingersoll, Ralph, 146, 147, 149, 150
isolationism, 8, 23, 93, 95, 115, 118, 119, 121, 140, 161, 162, 165, 170, 172, 219
Izumo, 89, 90, 122

J
J.B. No. 355, 175, 176, 180, 181, 187, 188, 190, 192, 213, 217
J.N.4 "Jenny," 28, 29
Jagersfontein, MS, 159
Jenkins, Douglas, 33, 35

Jouett, Col. John, 54-56, 60, 61, 65, 66, 71, 82
Junker, 26, 195

K
Kellogg, Frank, 31, 38
Kennedy, John F., 161
Kennedy, Joseph, 121, 200
Keys, Curtiss Melville, 35, 38, 51
Klotz, Henrietta Stein
Knox, Frank, 115-117, 125, 129, 135-140, 156, 171, 172, 175, 177, 180, 188
Kobe, 77, 78, 138
Kung, Dr. H.H., 57, 63, 64, 66, 82, 86, 98, 99, 107-110

L
Lampert, Florian, 69
Lattimore, Owen, 159, 173, 177, 178, 180, 181, 201, 213, 222, 223
lend-lease, 22, 161, 162, 164, 168, 170, 172, 174, 176, 182, 186, 195, 196, 200, 205, 206, 210, 212, 221
Lexington, USS, 15
Lindbergh, Charles, 32, 33, 73, 118-121, 161, 162, 213, 223
Lockheed, 67, 138, 140, 171-174, 179, 182, 183, 195, 204, 211
Lord Lothian, 130
Lordi, Colonel Roberto, 63, 64
Los Angeles Times, 82, 122
Lovett, Robert, 172, 174, 188
Luce, Claire, 80, 81
Luce, Henry, 81

M
MacArthur, Gen. Douglas, 56, 58, 70
MacMorland, Edwin, 170
MacMurray, John, 31, 38

Magruder, Brigadier General John L.
Mahoney-Ryan, 32
Mao Bangchu, Gen., 84, 85, 116, 125, 129, 138, 139, 144, 155, 224
Marco Polo Bridge, 83, 101, 158
Margetts, Lt. Col. Nelson, 45
Marshall, Gen. George, 139-142, 144, 155, 167-170, 176, 180, 185, 188, 190, 195, 196, 206, 210, 218, 219, 223
Martin B-10 bomber, 67
Marysville Journal-Tribune, 61
Mayer, Lt. Col. William, 181
McDonald, William, 78, 81, 84
McHugh, Maj. James, 156, 185, 201
McQuillen, Maj. Francis, 184, 185, 213
Mitsubishi A5M fighter, 92
Model 299 bomber, 67-70
Model B Ryan, 37
Morgan, Robert, 37, 38
Morgenthau Jr., Henry, 71, 72, 98, 110, 114, 117, 127, 129-132, 134-140, 142, 144, 147-149, 151-154, 161, 164, 170, 190, 224
Mao Pang Tzu, Gen. *see* Mao
Mowrer, Ansel, 125, 197, 212
Mukden Incident, 47
Mussolini, Benito, 63, 64

N
Nagasaki, 22
Nakajima A1N2 fighter, 47, 48
Nanjing, 31, 33, 35-41, 43, 44, 46-48, 55, 65, 90, 96
Nanking, 30, 39, 44, 45, 51, 54, 81, 85, 91, 92, 98, 99, 106
Nationalist Air Force, 47, 48, 55
Nate (Type 97) fighter, 126
Neutrality Pact, 160, 161
Newman, Floyd, 43
New York Herald Tribune, 125
New York Times, 17, 160, 171, 215
Northrop, 89

O
Oahu, 15, 17, 18, 89
Operation Zet, 94
Osaka, 78, 134, 138
OX-5 engine, 28, 34, 35, 37

P
P-36 Mohawk fighter, 91

Index

P-40 Tomahawk fighter, 91, 129, 137, 138, 144, 151-155, 164, 175, 182, 188, 190, 195, 195, 197, 202, 205, 207, 218
P-43 Lancer fighter, 174, 175, 179
P-66 Vanguard fighter, 174, 175
Pan-Am, 26
Panay, USS, 96-98, 106, 219
Patterson, Robert, 175, 177
Patterson, Allen, 105, 106, 108-110
Pawley, William, 56, 57, 60, 61, 72, 73, 84, 90, 94, 98, 99
Pearl Harbor, 13, 17, 21, 67, 78
attack, 22, 23
Peking, 26, 29, 33, 39, 51
Philippines, 99, 133, 135, 139, 142, 171, 184, 187, 188, 206, 210, 211, 218
Ployer, Major, 68
PM, 146, 149
Polikarpov I-15 fighter, 101, 116
Polikarpov I-16 fighter, 92, 102, 166
Polin, Max, 52
Pratt and Whitney Wasp engine, 41, 60, 107, 108, 172
President Coolidge, SS, 96
President Garfield, SS, 75-79
President Hoover, SS, 56, 90
President Pierce, SS, 158
President Taft, SS, 56
Price, Earnest, 39

Q
Qingyu Zhang, Col., 37

R
Rajchman, Ludwig, 164
Rankin, Jeanette, 20
Republic P-43 fighter, 174, 175, 179
Robertson, Major William, 35, 37, 39
Robertson Aircraft Company, 17, 21
Rogers, Leighton, 62
Roosevelt, Elenore, 147
Roosevelt, James. 24, 190, 191
Roosevelt, President Franklin D., 10, 11, 17, 65, 66, 72, 97, 110, 11, 113, 115, 119, 121, 125, 127, 133, 142, 148, 151, 160-162, 169-172, 190, 192, 195, 199-202, 205, 219, 222, 224
Chiang Kai-shek relations, 133, 134, 144-146
Currie relations, 145, 146, 160, 163, 164, 166, 169, 176-178, 180, 188, 193, 200, 201, 202, 205
covert operations, 21, 114, 155, 157, 163-166, 173, 176, 200, 218
embargo, 93-96, 118, 140, 187
infamy speech, 18, 20, 24, 135

Roper, Daniel, 93
Russia, 27, 37, 65, 81, 84, 92, 94, 110, 161, 166, 185, 190-192, 196, 201, 206, 210, 211
Ryan Brougham, 31, 33

S
Saratoga, USS, 13, 16
Savoia-Marchetti S.72, 64
SB-2 bomber, 102, 104
Scaroni, Colonel Silvio, 64, 65
Schurman, Jacob, 30
Scobey, Lt. Col. W.P., 176, 177, 187, 188, 213
Seattle Times, 67

Seversky, 105, 107, 109, 110, 174
Shanghai, 29. 31. 33, 35-37, 39, 44, 46-48, 50 - 53, 56, 60-63, 65, 79-81, 86, 89, 90, 92, 97, 99, 106, 109
Short, Robert McCawley, 45-51, 61
Shumaker, Floyd, 43-45
Sinclair, Sir Archibald, 199, 200
Slevin, James, 28-30
Sloniger, E.L., 38
Smith Sebie Biggs, 81
Soong, Charlie, 79
Soong, T.V., 38, 47, 48, 52-54, 57, 63, 71, 72, 77, 81, 98
Soviet Union, 11, 21, 27, 61, 73, 94, 96, 101-103, 115-117, 145, 147, 148, 151, 152, 156, 160-162, 164, 181, 190, 195, 196, 198, 210, 218, 222, 223
Stalin, Joseph, 101, 160, 161, 164
Stark, Adm. Harold, 111, 113, 114, 116, 123, 139, 157, 177, 188
Stilwell, Gen. Joseph, 141, 195, 224
Stimson, Henry, 38
Sun Fo, 35, 37-39
Sun Yet-San, 26, 35, 38, 39

T
T-32 Condor, 60
Tatum, Sterling, 79
Teal flying boat, 37
Terrill, Lt. Clarence, 62
The New Yorker, 146
Time, 146
Tokyo, 17, 22, 78, 122, 125, 130, 131-133, 138, 186, 217
Tower, Leslie, 67, 68
Trippe, Juan, 73, 74, 98
Tsui, Twen-ling, 111, 123

U
United States News, 205

V

V-116 bomber, 100
Vladivostok, 61, 206, 210, 211
Vultee, 98, 100, 101, 174, 179, 197
Vultee P-48 fighter, 174, 209

W

Waco-10 biplane, 34
Waco 240A fighter, 52
Wang, Pei-chun, 51, 52
War Department, 42, 44, 55, 56, 126, 127, 139, 170, 177, 180, 181, 186, 187, 209, 210, 213

Welles, Sumner, 66, 143, 155, 179, 180, 192, 195, 222, 225
Westervelt, George, 52, 54, 57, 74
White, Harry Dexter, 145, 147, 148
Wichita, SS, 93
Willauer, Whiting, 166, 167, 221, 225
Williams, Richard, 67
Williamson, Luke, 78, 79, 84
Wright Cyclone engine, 60, 91, 100, 173
Wright J-5 Whirlwind engine, 33, 34
Wuhan Civil Aviation Company, 32

Y

Yamamoto, Adm. Isoroku, 13
Yarnell, Adm.l Harry, 13 15, 17, 23, 116, 211
YB-17 bomber, 69, 70
Yen, Col. Eddie, 79
Young, Dr. Arthur, 47, 128, 212
Young, Clarence, 55
Young, Phillip, 127-129, 135, 136, 138, 144, 153, 155

Z

Zero fighter, 115, 125, 126, 185, 210
Zhang Weizhang, Gen., 32, 33, 34, 36, 38, 62
Zhengting, Wang, 95, 96

The Author

Photo: Jill Hayward

Michael Lemish is the author of *War Dogs – A History of Loyalty and Heroism* and *Forever Forward – K-9 Operations in Vietnam*. He has contributed to military documentaries produced by the BBC, Discovery, The History Channel, PBS and *The Robert Hartsock Story* produced by New Shepherd Films. He has written for such publications as *The American Legion Magazine, Aviation History, The Atlantic Flyer – General Aviation News* and the scouting magazine *Boy's Life*.

He resides in Massachusetts along with his retired military working dog Lucy (N430).

 Lightning Source UK Ltd.
Milton Keynes UK
UKHW020622011219
354483UK00002B/22/P